The Foreign Policy of
New States

By the same author

The Mexican Revolution, 1910–1914;
  the Diplomacy of Anglo-American Conflict

Latin America: Internal Conflict and International Peace

Revolution (Key Concepts in Political Science)

A Study of Revolution

Mexico

The Mexicans: How they Live and Work

Emiliano Zapata

The Concept of Class

The Falklands Crisis: the Rights and the Wrongs

Politics, Power and Revolution:
  An Introduction to Comparative Politics

Boundary Disputes in Latin America

Revolution and International Politics

Guatemalan Insurgency and American Security

Guatemala, a Nation in Turmoil

The Foreign Policy of New States

Peter Calvert
Professor of Comparative and International Politics
University of Southampton

WHEATSHEAF BOOKS

First published in Great Britain in 1986 by
WHEATSHEAF BOOKS LIMITED
A MEMBER OF THE HARVESTER PRESS PUBLISHING GROUP
Publisher: John Spiers
Director of Publications: Edward Edgar
16 Ship Steet, Brighton, Sussex

British Library Cataloguing in Publication Data
Calvert, Peter
  The foreign policy of new states.
  1. International relations
  I. Title
  327   JX1395
  ISBN 0-7450-0079-9
  ISBN 0-7450-0245-5 Pbk

Typeset in 11/12pt. Times British by Gilbert Composing Services
Printed in Great Britain by Mackays of Chatham Ltd, Kent

THE HARVESTER PRESS PUBLISHING GROUP
The Harvester Group comprises Harvester Press Ltd (chiefly
publishing literature, fiction, philosophy, psychology, and science
and trade books); Harvester Press Microform Publications Ltd
(publishing in microform previously unpublished archives, scarce
printed sources, and indexes to these collections); Wheatsheaf Books
Ltd (chiefly publishing in economics, international politics, sociology, women's studies and related social sciences); Certain Records
Ltd, and John Spiers Music Ltd (music publishing).

Contents

Preface

For at least the past 400 years, foreign policy-making has been regarded not only as a major function of the state apparatus but also as its leading—perhaps only—activity. To this day the senior position in most countries is that of the minister of foreign affairs. To conduct foreign policy, in effect, is to prove oneself to be in charge of a state—a sovereign state capable of making its own decisions without reference to any outside or higher authority.

Yet in practice, for the citizens of most states, foreign policy seems to have very little direct relevance to their own lives. When they read about it in the papers, or hear about it on the radio or the television, it is as if they were watching the doings of little green men from Mars. Certainly they do not expect to have any influence over it. Then, when they are plunged into war, or called up to fight for their country, they follow instructions in the belief that in some way it is right; yet they played little or no part in the way it was arrived at. At the same time, whether they know it or not, many decisions of other countries or of international organizations do in smaller or larger ways affect them very much. The growing awareness of the role in international affairs of non-governmental organizations (NGOs) of various kinds has also been reflected in recent years in both great-power rhetoric and the demands of Third World states for a New International Economic Order (NIEO).

Previously, smaller and newer states accepted the assumptions of the international system as they found it. Finding that it reflected the manners and customs of the great powers, they aspired themselves to become great powers and to shape the international system. They often did not closely analyse their own motives, their own policy-making process; still did they less consider whether or not it was a fit instrument for the purposes to which they wanted to put it. They simply assumed that it was like that of the great powers in miniature, while the great powers themselves often failed to realize that smaller ones had a policy process at all.

It is the contention of this book that, in a world composed largely of new states, it is necessary to examine these processes more closely. This in turn leads us to look at the problems of foreign policy with a new perspective. In turn this will lead us to reassess the roles of the great powers of the past, present and future—including the so-called superpowers of our own time. Foreign policy-making, as seen here, is the occupation primarily of a very small élite dominated above all by considerations of their own political (and often personal) survival. Foreign policy therefore is ancillary to domestic policy and serves its needs. Indeed, at times it is hardly seen as 'real'. Instead it forms an arena in which the policy-makers can perform for the critical eye of the internal political élite in a dramatic performance designed to bring credit upon themselves. It is this dramatic imperative as well as the short life of Third World governments, subject alike to the hazards of domestic political turmoil and military intervention, the limited power resources on which they can call and the intervention of greater powers in their affairs, that account for the frequency with which great powers misjudge the intentions of small ones. Such misjudgements are compounded by the 'need' for the great powers to be seen to be exercising their weight in world affairs, which though traditionally ascribed to them, and in practice tacitly accepted, rests in fact on very insecure foundations.

Research for this book was carried out at the University of Southampton as part of a research programme on 'North/ South Security Relations' funded by the Ford Foundation. I should like to thank my colleagues John Simpson and Caroline Thomas for reading and commenting on the typescript, the publisher's reader for helpful criticism, and Angela Williams for transcribing and typing the text.

Broadstone, Dorset
6 February 1986

1 The Illusion of Foreign Policy

There is probably no subject in which it is so important to distinguish between myth and reality as foreign policy. By *policy* we mean a continuous process of decisions and their implementation taking place within the organizational structure of a state. Policies are not simply any decisions; they consist of only those that structure detailed actions and form a framework for decisions taken lower down an organizational hierarchy. They involve an exchange of information both within state agencies and also between those agencies and also a variety of external interest groups, and are directed at ensuring a higher probability of a desired set of outcomes in the future. It is the future direction of policy decisions, their strategic quality, which distinguishes them from routine decisions designed to implement existing policy. By *foreign policy* we mean, in the words of Joseph Frankel, 'decisions and actions which involve to some appreciable extent relations between one state and others'.[1] We include in this relations between the state and external non-governmental organizations (NGOs).

Like internal policy decisions, decisions in foreign policy are taken in the name of the public interest, and it is the fact that they are which legitimates them in the eyes of the citizens. This does not mean that individual decisions may not be taken partly, or even primarily, to benefit specific interest-groups; only that, characteristically, they are justified in public as being in the wider interest of society.

We begin with one simple model of policy-making. For systems analysts it can be seen as a three-stage process. The policy-maker is confronted, on the one hand, with a series of demands for action and, on the other, with a known inventory

1

and later socialization a feeling of national identity. This national identity, however, is no easy thing to define. In it are mixed up historical and geographical, ethnographic and sociological considerations; and the product of stories told to the child by its parents, by its relations and friends and both in and out of school. Out of this it sorts an overall 'reality' which may be very far indeed from the truth. Yet, when in due course it comes to vote, or to discuss the doings of the day over a pint of beer, it will draw upon this stock of information, or disinformation, and the resultant product, based on the myth it has formed, and which makes its life meaningful, will inform its political discussion and its political action, for better or for worse.

We can be sure that makers of foreign policy themselves share much of this background. They should be much better informed of the facts, since they have access to sources of information not available to the ordinary citizen, and should have undertaken a serious study of the capabilities, limitations and possibility of the situation in which they find themselves, including an in-depth analysis of the true nature of the world. But have they? And what is that nature? The world is a large place. Can any one individual really hope to comprehend what it is, still less seek to guide the destinies of even a single one of the states into which it is divided? How many of the convenient simplifications—or to use the more technical term, models—which we use to try to make it intelligible are really useful, and which of them, if any, do more to confuse than to enlighten? And when many people get together to make policy, do they strengthen each others' knowledge or only their prejudices?

Today, for example, it has become quite customary to talk about 'the Third World' or 'the South' when discussing modern new states. This reflects some real difficulties in finding a really accurate general term. By 'new states', we should logically mean those areas, formerly part of colonial empires, which have only recently gained or regained the status of independent countries. But in practice, as we shall here, we also cover states which have never been effectively colonized, like Thailand and Ethiopia, as well as countries that have been independent for more than a century, like Brazil and Mexico, since their experience has a great deal to tell us about the problem of asserting one's position in a world already dominated by established powers. By the term 'the Third World' we mean something rather different: the bulk of the land area and the overwhelming majority of the population of a world which is otherwide divided—polarised—between East and West. The 'western', the sophisticated, developed and industrialised world of the United States, Western Europe and Japan, is the First World. The industrialising, future orientated countries around the Soviet Union which accept its leadership, constitute the Second. But there is no similar unifying factor holding together the Third. It consists, simply, of all those states in the world which are not easily classified under the first of second headings, which form the subjects rather than the actors of the international system, and which otherwise have very little in common.

Just what do they have in common? First, as we have just noted, almost all have experienced colonial rule in one form or another. Their experience both of colonization, and of the struggle for decolonization, has played a major role in making them what they are and giving their leaders a psychological outlook towards the rest of the world. But the similarities must not be exaggerated. Subjects of different colonial empires, in different parts of the world, had very different experiences of colonial rule, learnt different languages and customs, and were orientated differently towards the outside world. To this day there is surprisingly little coming and going between the inhabitants of British, Dutch and French-speaking Caribbean islands, even though they are so close together, and might be expected to feel much the same about a past of slavery and open racial discrimination. The division of Indonesia and Malaysia by the colonial powers in 1824 still keeps apart areas that in the days of Mahajpahit were under a common ruler, speak virtually the same language and practise Islam. Decolonization has not driven them together. Instead they have moved further apart, as the rulers of each sought to assert their individual quality and independence of all outside influences.

Second, therefore, the Third World states have in common the desire to build a strong state. The more elusive this goal seems to be, the harder it is pursued. They assert their own national symbols, fly their own flags, speak their own languages, raise their own armies, and work physically to occupy and to control their own territory. This is so important that a major part of this book will be devoted to the strengths and weaknesses of such states, since it is as a by-product of their zeal, or lack of it, in pursuing these objectives that the foreign policy issues of closer links, defensive lines, geopolitical ambitions, and boundary disputes arise. Most Third World states are so weak that it is at their boundaries that their most significant problems arise, but for this to happen they must first reach the boundaries and so come into conflict. South America's relative freedom from large scale international wars historically owes much to its vast size and the formidable natural obstacles between its component states.

Third, the states of the Third World are poor. But they are not uniformly poor. Can we distinguish between them? Not easily. States such as Tanzania, Somalia and Mozambique are very poor indeed, among the poorest in the world. But here as elsewhere perception is more important than reality. Tanzania is proud of its autonomous development and holds it up a model to others. Mozambique has had to seek help wherever it can. Brazil is generally seen as being of the Third World, but if used of their own country the term would be indignantly rejected by most Argentines, who see their culture as a European one, and despise poverty-stricken and cocaine-ridden Bolivia, also a neighbour, as an 'Indian' country. Moreover the most startling economic growth of the last decade has taken place in 'Third World' countries such as South Korea, Taiwan and Singapore.

Lastly the majority of the Third World states wish to remain non-aligned in relation to the confrontation between East and West. Hence for their leaders the three world categorization is in some ways an attractive one, since it acts at least to redress the concentration of much that has been written since 1945 on the confrontation between the East and West. For this, too, we must at least be grateful. It places on the agenda the question of economic development, which is in itself something of an item of confrontation between East and West, but which clearly has a much more immediate reality to many of the countries of the

Third World. Yet, like all models, it is only a partial approximation to the truth. It has, moveover, the disadvantage that it introduces a new and spurious element of confusion by suggesting a greater degree of coherence in foreign policy between Third World states than really exists.

This is scarcely surprising, since the very notion of the Third World itself, after an early partial conceptualization under Perón in Argentina, who spoke of a 'Third Position', was realised for the first time at the Bandung conference of 1955. The leaders—in particular Nehru of India, Chou En-lai of China, Sukarno of Indonesia, Nasir of Egypt and Tito of Yugoslavia—who came together at Bandung deliberately set out to establish a new view of the world, in which states need not ally themselves with one or other of the two power blocks that had coalesced between 1945 and 1947, but could instead remain 'non-aligned'. But the political posture of non-alignment, and the related policy of neutralism, has existed much longer and is not confined to the countries of the present Third World. It rejects power politics, and yet for those who believe in power politics it cannot be taken seriously, for, as Martin Wight argues, in power-politics terms the idea of balancing two superpowers with a coalition between small ones is a 'false triangle', a balance that simply cannot work.[4]

Non-alignment and development are two very different concepts. The fact that they co-exist in an imperfectly realised image of the Third World, and of the states that make it up, is in itself significant. We are concerned, in short, not solely with the reality of foreign affairs, whatever that may be, but with images of how those relations ought to be conducted. Partly for this reason many people have come to favour the term 'the South' for those countries for which economic development is the overriding consideration. With the wealth of the world in the hands of the aligned, it was hardly likely that they would fail to use it as a bargaining counter against the non-aligned. Those who were particularly favoured by geography to play off East against West persevered, and some were successful, at least for a time. The states concerned, even then, varied very considerably, and later attempts to align the non-aligned have not uniformly been successful. The formation of the Organisation for the Solidarity of the Peoples of Africa, Asia and Latin

American (OSPAAAL) at the second Tricontinental Conference at Havanna in 1966 was afterwards to be followed by Fidel Castro's insistence that the non-aligned states ought to be the 'reserve' and 'natural allies' of the Soviet Union; effectively a contradiction in terms.[5]

MODELS OF DECISION-MAKING

The traditional view of foreign policy making is that it is a rational activity pursued by skilled men and women fully aware of all the relevant facts and enjoying the time to scrutinize all possible options before selecting the correct one. In other words, the view of policy-making outlined above as a model of the process, is taken to be not merely the way things ought to be but an accurate representation of reality. This view, which Allison has termed the 'rational actor model', has gone virtually unchallenged since at least the mid-eighteenth century.[6] Like so many of our modern political ideas it is at least in part a creation of the Age of the Enlightenment. To the men of the Enlightenment human affairs, like the natural world, were, and ought rightfully to be, the subject of study and analysis according to the scientific criteria of rational argument and inference from established data. Understanding of the relations between human beings, they believed, ought to be subject to the same kind of treatment as these other natural phenomena. In the hands of Auguste Comte this belief was elaborated into the concept of a science of society which he termed 'sociology', which would advance upon and form the logical culmination of the scientific discoveries of his own and the previous age.[7]

But it is important not to confuse a scientific approach to the study of international relations with a rational basis for its practice. Clearly we must study foreign policy rationally. But to do so does not guarantee that we will be able to understand it. The motivation of specific actions and decisions may not be rational in our terms. As Allison points out, two further models of policy-making which he advances are each in their own terms rational in the sense of seeking to maximize the probability of achieving policy objectives—the problem is that the outcomes are not. That is to say, within them the efforts of the actors concerned to obtain their goals and their interaction with one another does not necessarily provide the 'best' answer to the problem in hand nor can it be regarded as purposeful action.[8]

Of these two alternative views, the first, termed by Allison 'the organizational process model', is based on the notion that government is not a totality but the sum of a number of different organisations each with its own goals and its own procedures.[9] The goals are in each case the maintenance of the organization, its budget and its staff. Such organizations develop over a long period of time and adopt standard operating procedures, by which individual problems are dealt with, and routines, by which various chains of events are analysed and dealt with piecemeal. The aim of the exercise is to process the input of material in the most efficient possible manner, consonant with the overall objectives of the organization, but it does not follow that the achievement of these objectives is necessarily consistent with the best interests of the society as a whole, or even of organizations within the society other than those actually making the decisions. Thus, for example, a war ministry may well press for military action, which it regards as being the rational response to the particular set of military problems with which it is presented, oblivious of the fact that the economic structure of the country is not capable of sustaining a long war. So it involves the society as a whole in a conflict which it is bound to lose. The achievement of the narrow objectives, the response by the war ministry, is thus achieved at the expense of the greater good of the society at large, and may well result in the collapse of its government.

The second alternative to the rational actor model Allison terms the 'governmental politics model', though most now know it instead as the 'bureaucratic politics model'.[10] In this the fundamental unit of analysis is not the organization but the individual. Each individual is seen as holding a job for which there are certain responsibilities and certain possibilities. Each individual, therefore, has the objective of maximizing his own job satisfaction and sense of achievement, and he does this by competition with other individuals within the organization of which he forms a part. The outcome of the game which each member of the organization plays is the set of decisions which, though rationalized in terms of the objectives of the organization, or even of the society as a whole, are nevertheless in part a product of the interplay of individual interests and desires. Where they represent organizations they define the national interest as the organizational interest, and decisions are taken as the outcome of competition between these individuals. The outcome does not maximize any single objective and so can be considered purposeless. It cannot be considered as rational in terms of being the best possible solution to the problems of the society as a whole, though it may well be the best solution from the viewpoint of how key individuals see the interests of the organization they represent.

Rosenau believes that these models had already been incorporated in what he earlier termed 'pre-theories' of foreign policy-making, and that only trivial points of difference remain to be settled. His own attempt at pre-theory is based on five sets of explanatory variables. Idiosyncratic variables are those relating to the policy-maker himself, 'his values, talents and prior experiences, that distinguish his foreign policy choices or behavior from those of other decision makers'. Role variables are those which relate to the position he holds, and would be likely to recur regardless of his personal background and predispositions. Governmental variables are those aspects of the governmental system which affect the foreign policy process positively or negatively, while societal variables are those 'non-governmental aspects of a society which influence its external behavior'. Finally, systemic variables are those relating to 'the external environment or any actions occurring abroad that condition or otherwise influence the choices made by its officials'. He then argues that the relative importance of each of these groups of independent variables will vary according to standard criteria of classification of the state and its political and social system.[11]

Rosenau's pre-theory, however, is essentially a complex determinist model with little room for any concept of 'rationality' in the sense of choice or purposefulness. Its emphasis is on the visible and measurable, and little distinction seems in practice to be made between the making of decisions and the making of policy. In his *Linkage Politics* (1976)

Rosenau recognized the great complexity of national systems, and rightly emphasized the need for the student of national politics and the student of foreign policy to work together despite a tendency towards mutual ignorance and incomprehension.[12] But at the same time, Michael Brecher was developing a rival model of foreign policy-making which went far further into the realms of the unknowable and the unmeasurable.

Brecher's model was based in the first instance on the distinction made by Harold and Margaret Sprout between the operational environment—the domain of the rational—and the psychological environment.[13] The emphasis here, however, confirmed by empirical research in the form of the massive study of Israeli foreign policy to which it gave rise, is on the psychological environment, divided into two main categories: the 'attitudinal prism' of the decision-makers as individuals, and 'images of the élite' (i.e. the distance between the perceptions the élite have of the world and its reality). 'Decision makers', Brecher argues, 'act in accordance with their perception of reality, not in response to reality itself.'[14]

Though as Korany points out, the evident deficiencies of the rational actor models to explain Third World policy decisions have left the field free for the 'psychological-perceptual school', who seem to have won virtually in a walkover, problems still remain. The most obvious are that it has encouraged a tendency to ignore operational variables, and 'by basing its advance on detailed answers to complex psychological questions related to the decision-maker's perceptions, stress, and coping, the approach has complicated rather than eased the problem of data accessibility in Third World foreign policy analysis'. Specific empirical research projects have found that key participants are, not surprisingly, unable to say exactly how they reasoned or even to recall how they felt at key moments of a crisis situation, even when they have apparently been willing to do so.[15]

The student of foreign policy must therefore stand back from the process of policy-making and seek to understand it in his own terms. He may use each and all of the models outlined above and, indeed, from each of them he will gain some insight. Allison himself uses his own three models to analyze the Cuban

Missile Crisis of 1962 from various angles, producing as a result a much clearer understanding of the complexity of the crisis and in detail showing how certain aspects of the events of the period, otherwise inexplicable, are capable of being understood in terms of one or more of the models employed.[16]

The problems for the student of foreign policy in Third World countries is that a sufficient amount of information is not always available. The United States is an unusual country in which it is assumed that the people have a right to be informed about the actions of their government and a mechanism exists, the press, radio and television, by which information is made available while decisions are actually in the making, and decisions justified in order to gain support so that they can be implemented. That is not the case in almost any other country in the world. Furthermore, there was very little attempt to restrict this flow of information about the Cuban Missile Crisis, as such as was later to be attempted by the Nixon administration and more recently by President Reagan.[17] The death of the principal actor on the American side and the replacement of the principal on the Soviet side within only a couple of years of the events concerned also meant that information was released much more freely and much sooner than it might otherwise have been. Against this it can be argued that in Third World countries with less formidable responsibilities than those of initiating global nuclear catastrophe there is not the same reason for secrecy and that information may in some circumstances be more easily discovered by individuals. This is undoubtedly true; what is not true however is that there is a more efficient institutionalized pattern for disseminating this information, and this necessarily acts as a severe limitation on the capabilities of the social scientist to obtain this information.

Historically, foreign policy has been seen as being the preserve of a specialist educated élite, and the Brecher model recognizes this. Its practice has been regarded as one of the highest functions of government, and as such jealously guarded by the few. History books, with their emphasis on the role of single important individuals, tend to emphasise the élite character of policy-making.[18] The problem is that their emphasis on the role of great powers, of wars and of historic failures of judgement may well be misplaced. For most of the time, most of the countries of the world actually interact with each other very little. Much routine practice of foreign policy is in effect a simple passing of paper work to and fro, dealing with routine questions relating to trade, the issuing of visas and other rather minor matters. It is only in times of crisis that foreign policy becomes more important to a government than many aspects of its domestic affairs. In addition foreign policy lends itself to exploitation by politicians anxious to glorify their own domestic political position.

Even in relatively weak governments, a great importance is attached to the freedom from internal political constraints which foreign policy offers. American political analysts have long noted the relative freedom with which the President of the United States operates in the foreign policy field, despite the network of constitutional and customary constraints with which he is nominally surrounded.[19] As a result, much of the action with which we are familiar in the foreign policy field is relatively little concerned with real actions and real outcomes. It can best be interpreted in terms of a fourth model, that I am going to term the 'dramatic actor' model.[20]

The dramatic actor model sees policy-making above all in terms of a public performance. Once again the basic unit of analysis is the individual. The purpose of the individual is to present the best possible performance of the role to which society has assigned him. He finds, as he assumes this role, that there is already in existence a *stage*, namely the country concerned and its neighbours, the United Nations and its regional organizations and NGOs; a *script*, namely the historic documents of the past and the speeches of his predecessors; a *cast*, namely his political supporters and opponents; and *props* such as guns, ships and tanks, which may be made use of in the course of the drama which is to follow. Nevertheless, the purpose of the drama is to be representational. Decisions are not primarily to be seen as important for what they actually achieve, but rather for how they are seen contributing to the action and hence to the standing of the actors involved. And the audience, too, is part of the action, though given the complexity of the audience and the distinction between various groups and levels within it, it is far from easy at times to determine what any given action means in terms of a particular sector of that audience.

An important recent example of the dramatic element in world politics has been afforded by the American invasion of Grenada in October 1983. The use of a substantial military taskforce, numbering more than 15,000 people, and equipped with ships, missiles, aircraft and helicopters, as well as a substantial landing force, would seem at first sight to be somewhat excessive for the occupation of a 133-square-mile island, whose population was, at least in theory, longing to be liberated.[21] But the point of the Grenadan invasion, of course, was not simply to carry out the effective occupation of Grenada, it was to serve notice on other powers in the region that the United States, was, if necessary, prepared to use force in support of what it considered to be its vital interests. The invasion of Grenada, therefore, was not directed primarily, still less solely at the Grenadans themselves, but was intended as a warning and as an object lesson to the Nicaraguans, and behind them the Cubans and the policy-makers in the Soviet Union who were believed to support them.[22] The importance of demonstrating overwhelming military force was simply to point out the lesson of what could be done in Grenada could be done elsewhere, and the importance of the action in dramatic terms was highlighted both by the dramatic language with which President Reagan spoke of it ('we got there just in time') and by the way in which the real difficulties of the occupation were minimized, the many casualties among Grenadans were ignored, and the fact that the resistance was presented by Grenadans rather than Cubans was consistently misrepresented.[23] To liberate Grenada from a sinister Cuban invading force was one thing, to occupy a small island against the resistance of its own forces would have been quite another, and a much less attractive lesson to the outside world. Accordingly, that aspect was concealed as far as possible.

Second, though it is tempting to think that the United States invaded Grenada for the well-being of the Grenadans, to 'liberate' them from an oppressive, socialist military government, there seems no doubt that the primary objective was to serve the interests of American domestic politics, and so is next best interpreted in terms of Allison's bureaucratic politics model. These interests included the standing of the president himself and of certain of his advisers within the White House, to say nothing of that of the Republican Party in the Senate and the country. Now, the idea that foreign policy should serve the interests of domestic politics is in no way new. States have always acted in foreign policy on occasions primarily for domestic reasons. What makes the interpretation of these reasons so much more complicated in the last quarter of the twentieth century, however, is the fact that the separation of domestic and foreign politics has been breaking down. It is now a truism of international relations that states no longer form isolated sovereign entities.[24] Not only do they interact with each other much more freely than ever before, but they are interpenetrated by organizational, trade and other linkages to an extent which makes it extremely difficult to distinguish in some respects between the foreign and domestic spheres. Such a traditional matter of domestic policy as the maintenance of a stable currency—the earliest, and in some respects still the most crucial distinguishing mark of the nation-state—has become something which is a matter for concern to international banking, trade, finance and many other organizations. The well-being of the national currency is affected by events as diverse as the discovery of new oil resources, the striking of new bargains in international trade or even an ill considered speech by a leading politician which casts doubt on the security of the country's creditworthiness.

The sphere of foreign policy is often used to solve problems in internal politics. This necessarily implies that the realm of foreign policy is seen as secondary to the sphere of domestic politics, and the international consequences of the actions that a government takes are seen as of less direct importance to itself than those consequences that most nearly touch its citizens. If this is the case of the superpowers, though, it is even more true of smaller countries, and particularly of the new states where the élites which have found themselves on the international stage for the first time have taken full advantage of it to act in a way which to them seems to conform to the standards set by the greater powers. The game of foreign politics is therefore something which they have entered into with great enthusiasm, and yet their relatively small size, their poverty and the lack of resources open to them in foreign politics do not enable them in practice to act in the fashion of the larger states. This avidity with which they have assumed the foreign policy role has probably done much in some cases to stabilize their internal politics. But it has been achieved at a cost of locking their countries into an international system of political bargaining and reciprocal obligation, which, despite the arguments of the dependency theorists, would probably not have influenced them to anything like the same extent had they not made it a prime object of policy that it should do so.

It is therefore vital to an understanding of the comparative making of foreign policy that we have an adequate understanding of the nature of comparative politics itself. This requires first of all a proper understanding of the problems involved and the methods that have to be employed.[25] It is simply of no value at all to assume that the foreign policy of another state will resemble that of one's own, or even serve as a mirror image to it. Yet people do. It is often assumed, for example, that a shortage of economic resources will deter a state from an adventurous foreign policy. Yet there have been many examples, of which the Gulf War (1980–   ) between Iraq and Iran is only the most recent, of states with very inadequate resources being precipitated into major conflicts by politicians like President Saddam Hussein, who believed, apparently, that the extraordinarily heavy costs were well worth it in terms of their policy objectives.[26] In other words, the idea that a policy will not be adopted if the costs are too high does not tell us anything about how high is too high. The assessment of what constitutes a cost sufficient to deter a given line of behaviour is something which in the first instance depends entirely on an understanding of the internal political dynamic of the state concerned. The student of international relations therefore requires an exceptional understanding of comparative politics. The political systems of the modern world are numerous and very diverse; a great deal of attention has had therefore to be devoted to attempting to sort and classify information relating to them, and establishing a vocabulary suitable for understanding the politics of different countries.[27]

In the past the ethnocentric nature of the study of foreign

policy meant that other countries tended to be interpreted in terms of the institutions and structures of one's own. In the nineteenth century, European scholars assumed that a newly discovered society would have a chief who would act in some way as a European monarch. It was assumed, too, that there might well be some kind of assembly of the notables of the country, and that that might be regarded as very similar to a European parliament. Yet even in the independent states of the nineteenth century it is apparent that the existence of assemblies did not in any way imply the existence of a parliamentary system of government. In fact, by the early nineteenth century a quite distinct system, embodied in the relationship between the American presidency and the Congress of the United States, was already receiving extensive imitation in the Western hemisphere. It did not do so unmodified, however, and the reason why it did not, lay precisely in the overwhelming significance of internal politics in determining the nature of political structures and the political balance. Had it simply been a case of imitating institutions which had proved successful in other states, and had it been possible to transplant those institutions across national lines, this would undoubtedly have been done, just as in the twentieth century we see the would-be Marxist states adopting ruling parties with central committees and leadership structures similar to those which they believe have served the Soviet Union well and will therefore serve them equally well.

In Grenada, for example, such a structure was one of the creations of the Bishop administration and the New Jewel Movement (NJM) under his leadership. The records of their proceedings which have been released since the American conquest of Grenada demonstrate all too clearly that despite adopting these forms, they lacked the coherence and structure which we attribute to the Soviet Union itself, and that the institutions thus taken over functioned in a way very different to those of the East European states, which they loosely imitated.[28] They demonstrate, too, how far the foreign policy of even the smallest states is conditioned primarily by domestic considerations. For Grenada to seek to emulate the Cuban or even the Soviet example in internal politics was one thing. For it then to behave in a way which suggested that it *was* a

Cuba—let alone a Soviet Union—was quite another matter. Thus when Bishop publicly stated that in the event of his fellow socialist countries in the Caribbean being attacked, Grenada would lend them fraternal support was a statement which if taken literally was frankly absurd, however endearing it might be.[29] If it were to be taken seriously at all, it could do no other than call upon his tiny country the critical attention of a much greater force, namely that of the United States itself. Hence by such ill-advised statements—however well intentioned—the NJM brought upon itself the nemesis which finally befell it in 1983.

The gap between the power of states in the twentieth century has actually been widening. Power is a complex concept, and in politics, unlike engineering, it cannot be measured in absolute terms. Newly emerged states are not in a position effectively to act on the same level as better-established ones, and the gap between even the most powerful of second-rank nations, such as Britain or France, and the superpowers is continuing to widen. In fact, the whole spectrum of power is being stretched, so that at the one end the smallest and weakest states are able to influence world affairs hardly at all, and at the other end the largest ones have the capacity to annihilate the whole of life on the planet many times over.[30]

The politics of Third World states have to be understood therefore not just in their own terms but within the context of the framework which enables us to distinguish aspects of different political systems. This brings us to the question, indeed the problem, of the nation-state. For the purposes of international relations the modern world is divided into a set of territorial units, commonly called 'nation-states' although this term is in fact a misnomer. By 'state' we refer to a community organised for political purposes which is in legal terms independent of any higher authority. By a 'nation' we refer to a group of people united by a common sentiment of ethnic solidarity, religion or culture. There are therefore nations without states, states without nations, nations with more than one state and states with more than one nation.[31] However the term 'nation-state' is commonly used in international relations to designate all formally organized and recognized states of whatever constitution, and it will have to serve, provided that we can distinguish clearly between nation and state in more specific usage.

NEW STATES

By 'new states' we refer to those states that have relatively recently obtained their independence. This term has its own problems. It is not, as we have already seen, synonymous with that difficult concept 'the Third World', which is one of the reasons why it is used here. Though since 1945 the vast majority of new states have been created by the process of decolonization in the Third World, some non-Third-World states (e.g. Norway, Ireland, Iceland, Israel) are new. Assuredly there are specific problems of newness common to all states taking up their role in the international system for the first time. But the experience of states that have by now had a much longer period of independence, in particular the Latin American countries, repeatedly proves not only to be relevant to those of their neighbours that have become independent more recently (Cuba and Panama in the early twentieth century, Belize, Trinidad & Tobago, Barbados, Jamaica etc. after 1945), but also to the experience of new states in other parts of the Third World.[32] There also seems to be good grounds for saying that in this context newness lasts a long time. Ireland, for example, which became independent in 1921, pioneered the way for the later decolonization of the overseas British colonial empire. Like the other successor states, it has had specific policy problems relating to the consolidation of state power, the need for national development, the desire for neutralism and non alignment, a trade war, financial penetration, to name but a few. It has therefore both paved the way for later new states and, it seems, retained a distinctive degree of sympathy for them and so for the problems of what we now call the Third World, as witnessed by the open disavowal there of the Reagan policy of intervention in Central America.

In Europe there are also several other new states whose experience should be studied: Norway (1905), Albania (1912), Finland (1917), Czechoslovakia, Yugoslavia, Poland and

Hungary (1918) and Iceland (1941). The largest group of these owe their independence to the dissolution of empires following the First World War, as do Outer Mongolia (1921), Egypt (1922) and Iraq (1936). The Second World War hastened the independence not only of Iceland but also of Syria (1941/46) and Lebanon (1941/46), Jordan and the Philippines (1946), India and Pakistan (1947), Ceylon (Sri Lanka), Burma and Israel (1948), Indonesia (1949), Libya (1951), Laos (1953), Cambodia and the two Vietnams (1954), Morocco, Tunisia and the Sudan (1956) and Malaya (1957, enlarged as Malaysia, 1963). By the time the last state to have been shaken loose by the Second World War, Somalia (1960), had become independent, the general move for decolonization had already begun with the independence of Ghana in 1957 and Guinea in 1958, and in 1960 most of the remaining French possessions in Africa and Madagascar became independent. By the end of the 1960s Britain's decolonization was nearly complete, though the former autonomous colony of Southern Rhodesia had proclaimed in 1965 a unilateral independence under white settler rule which was not recognized by the rest of the world. In the mid-1970s the Portuguese empire abruptly fell apart following the revolution of 1974 in Portugal itself, while its neighbour, Spain, quietly divested itself of some of the world's most unattractive properties. Of the great empires of the period before 1914, today only that of Russia survives as a single administrative unit.[33]

When a state becomes independent, it becomes legally a full and equal member of the modern international system. Its properties as a state are therefore determined externally and to an extent also internally by the nature of that system, and it will be helpful to recall here what Wight regards as the six main properties of that system.[34] It is, first, a system composed of sovereign states. Each state, once independent, has a right to determine its own internal affairs, a right recognized specifically by the Charter of the United Nations, though frequently breached in practice. Second, as a number of recent cases show, membership is by mutual recognition. But for a new state this means recognition by other existing states Rhodesia achieved no recognition by existing states; as Zimbabwe it was accepted. When general recognition of the

seen a subsystems of the political system. The political system itself—that is to say, the organization of state power as a political entity influenced by the demands made upon it and resulting in outcomes in the form of decisions—also consists of a network interrelating subsystems concerned with various aspects of policy or separate areas of administration. The difference is that its decisions are authoritative, they compel obedience.

The use of systems-analysis concepts to try to understand better the way in which different states function has been challenged in recent years from those who feel that has produced too mechanistic and deterministic a picture, and it may well be that we have to remind ourselves from time to time that there are many countries in the world whose governments pay very little attention to influence in the form of demands, and who use a considerable measure of force both to repress their population and to extract the maximum out of them in terms of economic resources.[35] But in fact such qualifications do not in any way invalidate the overall concept; they merely lead us to lay the emphasis on rather different areas of the system's behaviour to those which might have been fashionable in the first euphoria of the age of decolonization.

The notion of the system, too, takes us firmly and decisively away from the immense variety of institutions that have been created in different states. Parliaments, for example, differ very considerably, even in Western Europe. The parliament of Sweden (the fourth oldest parliament in the world) developed independently, and under quite different conditions from the parliament of the United Kingdom (the third oldest), and its practice has continued to diverge from that of the latter.[36] Its Speaker is much more important, the role of the government is different, the voting procedure varies and the process by which it is elected as immeasurably more fair. Even within the Nordic countries there are considerable variations in parliamentary practice. Their electoral systems differ somewhat one from another, the way in which business is handled varies and so too do the powers of the various elements of the paliamentary system. It is precisely these kinds of practical differences that the establishment of a distinct social-scientific terminology of political systems is designed to clarify; for example, just as in

medicine to say that you have a pain in the stomach, though a
normal enough complaint, is not capable of leading to an
accurate diagnosis unles the doctor understands in his own
terminology precisely what is meant by it in terms of the human
being as a system and what systemic malfunction this symptom
indicates.

In the rest of this work, therefore, I propose first of all to
examine the way in which states differ, and in particular the
way in which Third World states are organised. Having taken
account of the nature of the political structure, and its relations
with the social and economic systems, we can then see how the
machinery of foreign policy making fits into these structures
and what its purpose is. This in turn leads to us to
consideration of the rules of the game established for
international politics. The ability to act within the international system depends on one's understanding of what that
system actually is. This done, I propose to turn my attention to
the capabilities of the various countries concerned. The variety
of ways in which countries gain the ability to influence others
will be discussed, followed by the limitations on their freedom
of action, both internal and external.

For the fact that foreign policy is seen here as being
dominated almost exclusively by internal considerations does
not detract from the right of the international system to be
considered as a distinct entity, even if I would not concede it the
paramount importance that the international systems theorists
do.[37] State boundaries certainly in some ways have become
more meaningless in recent years. Aircraft fly over them, radio
waves ignore them and diseases are hardly checked by them.
The important thing, however, is that they have not ceased to
exist. Indeed, they show great reluctance to disappear: the
Rhine, for example, is no less important as a boundary between
France and Germany today than the English Channel is
between Britain and France, and in practice it is much easier to
cross. Yet this does not mean in any way that the differences
between France and Germany have been eliminated, nor that
free movement across the border implies the disappearance of
that border. The border, as this example shows all too clearly,
is symbolic in its importance. Though the Rhine constitutes the
boundary between France and Germany at one point, north of

the River Mosel it ceases to do so and flows entirely through German territory. So it is nothing in the nature of the river as a geographical entity that determines its role as a boundary, it is merely the importance attached to it by political decisions. That is what I mean when I talk about the symbolic importance of boundaries, and indeed of most other actions and entities in foreign policy.

The existence of international organizations is clearly significant, but we must not forget that they are the creation of national governments, each of which have given up to them only so much power as they have been willing to relinquish, or have been forced to by others to concede.[38] This process is still very partial. When we come then to discuss the way in which foreign policy is actually conducted, we shall find that the decisions of national governments continue very much to reflect local political concerns and that, conversely, the benign force often ascribed by optimists and well-wishers to the international political system is again almost entirely symbolic. This can be seen most clearly in the behaviour of so-called 'revolutionary' states, namely those states who for ideological reasons believe that they have permission to change the international system in accordance with fundamental principles of their own choice. So marked a feature of major revolutions has this been, that it can indeed be regarded as almost the distinguishing feature of such movements.[39] Yet the interesting thing is that despite the pressures that are brought to bear on it, the development of the international system has proceeded extremely slowly, by evolution rather than by revolution, the incremental increase of its structure taking such a long time that it has become highly doubtful whether it can adapt fast enough to the situation of the late twentieth century to save the world from nuclear catastrophe. It is obvious that the major risks in this situation lie less in the symmetrical relationship between the superpowers than in the asymmetrical relations presented by the different relationships of each of the superpowers with individual Third World states. Accordingly, the understanding of the way in which Third World countries themselves formulate, conceive and implement their foreign policy is of greater urgency than ever if we are to understand the hazards to navigation they present for the superpowers.

ETHICS AND NEW STATES

The most difficult of all questions in foreign policy, moreover, are ones of ethics. Modern social science has tended to try to avoid questions of ethics by relegating all such matters to the supplemental category of 'value judgements'. But writers on foreign policy have found it necessary to take into account perceptions of values and there is good reason why this should be the case.[40]

All human action is governed by values. It is impossible to imagine any choice being made that does not involve evaluating one possible outcome against another. A value in fact is the worth that a decision-maker puts on something. Hence all political decisions are taken within a framework of values, within which the rational actor may be expected to have established a hierarchy. In most political societies this involves concepts of the general will and of the general good or the national interest. Decisions are taken in the name of the general will and for the sake of the general good, the welfare and even the life of the individual citizen being regarded as secondary in the scale of values to the overriding interest of society. And this is the case whether or not any mechanism exists for ascertaining or approximating to the general will, and in dictatorial societies as well as in democratic ones; the only difference is that in the case of a dictatorial society it is the dictator alone who takes it upon himself to declare what constitutes the general will or the national interest.

In the constitutional order of a single political system it can be argued, as Locke argued, that there exists a contractual obligation both on the subjects to obey and on the rulers to rule wisely. As with the framers of the American Constitution, this contract can actually be put into written form and used as the basis for a future government. In this sense the writing of a Constitution is a contractual step, and, not surprisingly, such documents generally—though not always—embody a bill of rights or set of constitutional guarantees ensuring the rights of the individual before the state.

Contractually, however, outside the bounds of the state the Hobbesian state of nature prevails.[41] Not only does the individual have no guarantees, except insofar as they are given to him by his membership of a given state, but his state has no guarantee of any kind against other states, except insofar as specific contractual obligations exist to which that state has been a party. Such agreements include treaties made by two or more states, general conventions such as the Geneva Conventions that specifically bind signatories but are held by the international community to have a wider application, and the Charter of the United Nations itself. The problem is that none of these documents have any effective sanction except that of reciprocal observance; that is to say, if they are broken by one signatory, others may break them in dealings with that signatory. There is certainly no international police force independent of states that can act to secure compliance with the wishes of the international community. More seriously, while the ethic of the nation state is, as we have seen, generally a collectivist one, calling on the individual to sacrifice his or her personal interests for the good of the community as a whole, that of the international community is an individualist one, in which each state is seen as having the right and indeed the duty to pursue its national interest as far as it feels called upon to do so, regardless of the effect on others. To this extent, therefore, the chaos and danger of the international system is a dreadful warning to all of us as to what our countries would look like if the advocates of unlimited individualism were ever to be allowed to have their way.

Now an individualist ethic need not necessarily be a selfish one, and to act in one's own self interest— whether as a nation or as an individual—does not necessarily mean harm or suffering for others. But this can only be the case provided that they too have the freedom and the capacity to act in their own self interest also. And here we have to take into account of the very wide disparity in capacity between states, a disparity which, moreover, is in no way compensated for by institutional advantages such as can be ensured by the domestic legislation for individuals or groups of citizens.

The question is, therefore, how far do new states in entering into the international community, take up the duties as well as the rights of statehood? Has the international community as a whole the duty to enforce certain minimal standards of behaviour on individual states, even if this infringes their theoretically absolute right of sovereignty? On this the present position is, unhappily, at best ambiguous. At times debates in the United Nations and elsewhere have seemed to show that new states wish very much to control the actions of old ones, but they do not wish to be subject to the same control themselves.

Some of their decision makers, indeed, have argued that they do not wish to be bound by the outmoded ethical values of the existing international order. They have their own values. Obviously it is possible to envisage a working international system in which tolerance is given to different systems of ethical values operated by different states. But it is not possible to envisage a working system where any group, large or small, enforces its values to the exclusion of all others. Decision makers may well then have to tolerate in the international arena many ideas and actions that they would consider unethical in their own countries, which presents them with something of a dilemma.

Worse still, the right or duty to act on behalf of a state's national interest may well, as in the case of a declaration of war, involve a decision maker in actions which within his own state he would rightly consider unethical. It is a most serious question whether for example the killing of a baby can ever be justified purely because it has occurred as the result of the explosion of a bomb dropped by a man in uniform from a military aircraft which is the property of a national government in the course of a declared war between states. Can something that is so patently unethical in an ordinary context simply be excused because we choose to look at the area of the world outside the bounds of the territorial state as being subject to a different and less well regulated form of political order? If so, what ethical considerations exist to restrain even the most appalling atrocities, such as those made the subject of international opprobium by the Nuremberg Trials at the end of the Second World War, and how many of today's statesmen might find themselves before a new Nuremberg tribunal if the international community had the power for a moment to call them to account?

2 The Rules of the Game

International relations can be viewed as a game with an arena, actors, roles and even a script. The object of the game, insofar as one exists appears to be for individuals to secure wealth, power and status. To do so they must control a state, or operate within a game in the capacity of a non-state actor in such a way as to be accepted by states as a legitimate participant. It is, however, states that have dominated the modern world system, and it is on these that we must first concentrate. The game has no formal beginning, but we can view it as being a game played in rounds punctuated by major wars, after which, as in 1648, 1815 and 1919, the actors readjust the world order to take account of changing realities.

The arena itself consists of the world organized for political purposes. It comprises therefore not just the physical world but also that intangible entity we call the international system. The international system consists of the sum total of the interactions between the various states into which the world is geographically divided. Within it there exist also regional subsystems, and other lesser groupings of states, to say nothing of a wide range of non-state actors that seek to gain advantages by influencing states in their policies. The international system has a continuing existence, so that it is not possible for a state to opt out of it completely. However, a state does retain the option to play actively or passively within the game of international politics. That is to say it may seek actively to influence others, to secure its objectives, to extend its boundaries and so forth, or it may seek merely to resist pressures that are brought to bear upon it and to accommodate to them as little as may be appropriate.

The principal actors are states. The problem with the word

'state' is that it has a wide range of meanings. A state is essentially the community organized for political purposes, and to a student of internal politics this tends to conjure up the image of a community in which people participate actively in the making of policy.[1] The United Nations in its charter envisages a world of democratic states, such as has indeed begun to emerge during the twentieth century. But the world of international politics is not concerned with the internal structure or functioning of states. It is sufficient that a state government exists and is evidently in control of the foreign-policy-making process for it to be recognized as such by other states, and the problem with the foreign-policy process is that it comprises a rather specialized branch of state activity which is generally in the hands of a very small élite.

States are antecedent to the existence of the international order, and hence they are attributed by the rules and customs of that order with qualities which they do not possess in practice. Their principal attribute is said to be that of sovereignty—the ability to determine all matters within their national boundaries without reference to outside help.[2] In practice, the concept of sovereignty has never been an accurate description of the behaviour of states. It is a legal concept which enables a rational picture of international action to be built up, but this is not to say that this rational picture is in fact a true one, and in fact in the latter part of the twentieth century it appears to have been becoming less and less accurate.

What constitutes a state for the purposes of international behaviour is recognition by other states. Traditionally this was a bilateral process, and between states of roughly equal capacity it did not much matter whether they were recognized or not or whether any diplomatic interaction took place between them, if they were not neighbours. The growth of great powers which sought to influence lesser states altered this picture during the nineteenth century. It became very difficult for a state to continue to operate if it were not recognized by the great powers, and the importance of recognition was the greater the nearer the state was to a major state capable of exercising influence over it. Since 1945, however, the existence of the United Nations has somewhat transformed the picture. This organization presumes the existence of a given number of state entities. When there is a dispute within one or other of these entities it is assumed that the seats attached to that state had a legitimate holder; it is not assumed that the state thereby ceases to exist. Thus, although Bangladesh seceded from Pakistan, its separate existence was recognised and its admission to the United Nations sponsored by India, which had acted as its midwife; in the case of Biafra and Katanga the United Nations membership took the view that these were not proper legitimate separate entities and that they would continue to recognize only the states of Nigeria and the Congo (Zaire), respectively. The inconsistency of this position, in which disputes of this kind are resolved principally with reference to the balance of voting within the international community and the interests of the greater powers, is obvious. It is compounded by serious disputes as to what constitutes a legitimate state. Not only have these disputes created a range of 'pariah states', which include not only those, such as South Africa and Israel, which are disapproved of by a large number of members of the United Nations, but also Taiwan, which has owing to its disputed past a reasonable claim to independence but is excluded from that organization absolutely. Within the United Nations the use of criteria to differentiate between states does in fact run contrary to the traditions of international politics, but it is certainly not contrary to the intentions of the authors of the charter. The United Nations, unlike previous organizations, was intended to comprise only states in good standing who could be counted upon to maintain their obligations and who would observe certain standards of civilized behaviour. The United Nations, in short, is not a world government, nor is it intended to be; it is not in fact even an assembly of all the nations in the world.[3]

A state is in some senses, as far as internal politics is concerned, merely a non-state actor that has succeeded in gaining recognition as a state. The confused picture we have of the modern state stems from the clash between appearance and reality which lies at its heart. In theory, as mentioned above, a state is a political community organized for political purposes. It should, therefore, seek the common good and seek to involve its citizens as far as possible in the making of decisions. In practice the legitimacy accorded to the state, and the respect accorded to its institutions, in the belief that only in the maintenance of a common political order can the welfare of all be secured, is made use of by small groups of people to claim political power and to use it against their political opponents. To gain control of the structure of the state is to have a licence to print money and to settle old scores, and many political organizations and individuals use their power to control states in precisely this sense.[4] Although it is undoubtedly true that the majority of member states of the United Nations purport to be some kind of democracy, in many of them political participation is very limited, and that the great majority of them are under some kind of authoritarian rule, often that of their own armed forces.[5]

Despite this, the institutions of the state continue to be accorded a respect which is not accorded to non-state actors. More significantly, a state is protected against the consequences of its misuse of power by the assumptions of international society, and with it are protected those individuals who at any one time control it. In many states a kind of tacit agreement operates between government and major opposition forces by which the government is able to survive as long as it obeys certain minimal standards, and conversely the 'trade union of rulers' ensures that only the worst villains who succeed in escaping alive on the fall of their governments face possible prosecution let alone punishment. Few of the Latin American dictators who have inflicted so much misery on their fellow-citizens have ever been successfully extradited; an exception being Marcos Pérez Jimenez of Venezuela. Some have returned to try to regain power and been unsuccessful; like General Banzer of Bolivia and General Rojas Pinilla of Colombia, they have usually come to no harm. A spectacular exception was Anastasio Somoza Debayle of Nicaragua. Despite on his fall being the largest landowner in Costa Rica and having no less than five homes in the United States, he was unable to make use of any of them, and, within a few months of taking advantage of the hospitality of his fellow-ruler General Stroessner in Paraguay, Argentine terrorists successfully killed him in the main street of Asunción by blowing his armour-plated car open with a bazooka and then spraying its occupants with machine-gun fire.[6] He was not successfully pursued by any government. It can well be said that if all property is theft, state property is the most successful form of theft.

For international-relations purposes we should distinguish sharply between two forms of non-state actors. First of all, there are international organizations to which states belong.[7] Though not states themselves, and lacking in a geographical base which guarantees the primacy of existing states, such organizations have a recognized diplomatic role. They are therefore accorded the right to talk to states, to press courses of action upon state governments and to communicate information. They act, therefore, as channels of what may be termed, provided the term is taken extremely loosely, 'international public opinion'. They enable, that is to say, a state's foreign-policy apparatus to determine how it is viewed by the outside world, but they do not in fact necessarily exercise any marked degree of power to change its actions.

Non-state actors of this kind include the United Nations itself, its related agencies, such as UNESCO, the World Health Organization, the International Labour Organization, and so forth, and a number of organizations set up by states for common functional reasons, the oldest of which is the Universal Postal Union, which exists to enable the transmission of mail between states on common terms.[8] Sometimes these can become directly engaged in issues of urgent international policy. Civil aviation is an example of such a field, as is broadcasting. Both are nominally within the control of national governments still believing themselves to be acting under an overarching 'grant' of sovereignty. In practice, many technical requirements make it necessary for governments to operate closely within a set of rules and a regime in each case established under the auspices of international organizations set up for specific purposes. A major air crash, therefore, or a battle of wills over the use of a certain wavelength, become international issues of concern not only to the national governments involved but to the entire community.[9] Within the debate which such an incident or event provokes, the international organization necessarily exercises an influence out of all proportion to its actual physical strength, given that its staff are the major repositories of information relating to the operation of the system as a whole and are therefore in a position to guide the decisions of those many members who are not most directly involved. Whether they make use of this power is, of course, a different matter.

Some theorists have gone further and argue that the logic of increasing technological sophistication and the need to co-operate in specific functional fields form a powerful force for the unification of the present nation states.[10] Belief in this argument formed a major part of the justification for the creation of the European Economic Community (EEC), which from the beginning was intended to evolve into a supranational governnment.[11] In practice, it has not done so—at least not yet. Gaullism in the early 1960s arrested its expansion, and the Luxembourg Compromise of 1965—by which any state that wished to could exercise a veto in any matter deemed to affect its national interests—effectively brought the period of constitutional evolution to a halt. Even the institution of direct elections to the European Parliament—the world's only freely elected transnational parliament—was unable to restore the lost momentum, given that the existing institutional arrangements limited the powers of that parliament to such an extent that it proved unable to assert an effective role against the entrenched interests of the individual nation states.[12] The EEC, therefore, remains an international organization, though one of a kind much further advanced towards unification than other international organizations.

International organizations of this kind must surely be sharply differentiated from other forms of non-state actors, which we will for convenience group in a second category. Of these, the oldest, and still in many ways the most significant, are transnational corporations. The so-called multinational corporations (MNCs) of today, more properly thought of as transnational corporations (TNCs), are giant combines operating across dozens or even hundreds of countries. Many control enormous financial and economic resources, and have on many occasions been seen to use that power to obtain decisions they want from national governments on which they are prepared to exercise their influence.[13] Thus high officials of International Telephone and Telegraph (ITT) sought the help of the United States government in 1970 to overthrow the government of President Allende in Chile, though it appears that (at least at the time) that help was not given. United Brands of Boston was implicated in bribing the then president of Honduras to fail to enforce a rise in the country's banana export tax, and so broke the front by which the Union of Banana Exporting Countries were attempting to negotiate a general rise. When the facts were revealed, through the suicide of the president of the company, the military of Honduras intervened to force the president's deposition.[14] Such activities, and would-be activities, are often seen as a wholly modern phenomenon. It is doubtful if this is really the case. Like their predecessors, the joint-stock companies of the seventeenth and eighteenth centuries, or the chartered companies of the larger imperial powers, such as the British and Dutch East India companies, these modern corporations operate from a territorial base.[15] They are, therefore, ultimately under the control of a single state. That state government can, if it wishes, decide to intervene at any time to modify the conditions under which they operate, or even to dissolve them. On the other hand, if it feels that the activities of the company are in general in the national interest, or if it lacks the political power-base to curb its activities, it may not do so, even if the company appears to be acting in an improper manner by the standards of domestic trade.

What has given the transnational corporations so much importance in discussions of the recent world order has been the fact that they are not, on the other hand, so easily controlled by the governments of the smaller states in which they operate. Transnational corporations are, it is true, not always based in great powers or superpowers. Royal Dutch-Shell is an example of a corporation based in a relatively small country, the Netherlands, which nevertheless operates on a worldwide basis and is widely believed to have considerable political influence. However, most of the world's largest multinational corporations are now centred upon the United States, and it has long been a principle of United States foreign policy to back the overseas activities of their corporations as part of the policy of spreading the influence of their political and economic order. In an extreme form, this policy under President Taft (1909–13) was termed 'dollar diplomacy', and though the term has fallen into disrepute, the United States still tends to pursue the policy. In recent years the British and French governments have openly competed for large overseas contracts for nationally based firms, and President Reagan has used the prospect of placing large contracts with European countries as an inducement to get their governments to support his Strategic Defence Initiative (SDI), popularly known as the 'Star Wars' proposal. The transnational corporations are therefore seen as surrogates for their metropolitan powers, as non-state actors operating in state interests. Tempting though this view is it has to be treated with some caution. The complex political structure of a country like the United States makes it difficult to draw any direct relationship between the interests of corporations and the interests of the country as a whole. The widely quoted dictum of one of President Eisenhower's cabinet officers 'what's good for General Motors is good for the United States' is not only a misquotation of the original but is in any case neither economic nor political sense, given the nature of American politics, in which the interests of corporations are divided unequally between the political parties.[16]

On the other hand, as will be seen in Chapter 6, the operation of transnational corporations within a small country does limit the number of options open to the government of that country, and poses considerable problems to it in the exercise of its own national economic programme. At best this means that it is unable to generate resources for its own use that have already been allocated for other purposes; at worst it means that a powerful financial interest operating without too many scruples is able to outbuy any other internal interest within the state, and so to secure its own narrow political objectives. The only consolation of this last scenario is that the objectives are in fact generally so narrow. Hence, unless a government has through its public statements locked itself into a position of confrontation from which it cannot retreat, it usually finds it possible to work with existing foreign corporations, regardless of its ideological attitudes. Transnational corporations may appear on occasions to operate like state governments, and indeed many of them have budgets far in excess of those of the smaller members of the United Nations. Moreover, they do, in some cases, influence governments to the extent of trying to induce changes in governments or at least in political office-holders. Yet they do not seek to supplant the governments which they influence or control.

The same cannot be said for terrorist groups and other organizations. 'Terrorism' is a loaded term, and one man's terrorist is another man's freedom fighter, but there is no other generic term covering the entire gamut of forcible ways of seeking political power in face of entrenched political opposition.[17] The distinctive characteristic of such groups is that they do not seek simply to influence state governments, but to set themselves up in their place as potential alternative governments. For this task they can and do seek to gain strength through the resources of the international political system. It has for many years been recognized that for such organizations the international system constitutes an almost ideal environment in which by the skilful use of dramatic incident and theatrical presentation they can hope to gain support and strength which they would not be able to do within the purely domestic environment.[18] It is seldom, however, realized that in so doing they are in fact merely making use of the international system in the way that national governments do; that their use of the international system was pioneered by state governments, and that state governments operate also on a dramatic basis. It is for this reason that the actual behaviour of states differs so much from their theoretical behaviour.

In theory states are sovereign entities isolated from one another, each entitled to their own integrity and to non-interference in their internal affairs. In practice, states seek to modify the behaviour of other states by a range of inducements and threats, the orchestration of which, indeed, forms a large part of the major activity of diplomatic organization. Not only do they seek to influence each other's behaviour, they also seek permanently to change it by inducing structural changes in governments they perceive as hostile in order to make them more friendly, and by supporting governments they perceive to be friendly in a way that incurs a sense of mutual obligation. This conflict between the rules and norms of the international system can only be clarified by distinguishing clearly between these two forms of agreement.

Unlike a national system, the international system does not enjoy a single unified system of law enforceable by courts according to a standard tariff of punishments. International law partakes of the nature of domestic law insofar as it is recognized by states as being law and capable in theory of enforcement. But the structures to enforce it are incomplete, and states enjoy a freedom of action, therefore, which an individual does not enjoy in the domestic context.

International lawyers distinguish between the field of private international law—namely, the system of rules which regulates the behaviour of individuals of different states towards one another within the international state context—and public international law, which regulates the behaviour of states towards one another. We are here mainly concerned with the latter, but in practice states have not only been called upon to defend their nationals abroad, they also reserve the right to do so on their behalf whether requested or not. Hence private individuals and their grievances may on occasion, and in fact frequently do, become a subject of international disputes between states.[19]

The problem with the notion of public international law stems from the fact that there is no single legislator. Initially, this was not seen as a disadvantage, since the early theorists of international law assumed the prior existence of a universal divine law of which all human law was only an expression. The legislature, therefore, was divinity itself, the law, once ascertained, was fixed and unchanging, and there was no need for an earthly legislature. But this view of law was already out of date before it was fully formulated. The rise of secular states in Europe was accompanied by the development into law of customary rights and duties, in England the origins of the Common Law. To this in time were assimilated both the scholars' codification of the divine law, and, on the international level, the actual bargains made between individual states. These, which we would now term 'bilateral agreements', were made between pairs of states over a period time in such a way as to bring a degree of consistency into the relations between states generally. In the process, however, the original foundation of international law, namely the ideal of universal divine law, was gradually eroded, a process accelerated by the Reformation and Counter-reformation in Europe, and by the extension of the European system to a wider world of non-Christian states.[20] Once the notion of a universal law, to which human law was merely declaratory, was abandoned, it became necessary to seek some other foundation for the system as a whole, but for many years this was not practicable insofar as there was no consensus that such a basis was needed.

It is for this reason that the emergence of the modern state system is generally dated to 1648, when, at the conclusion of the Thirty Years War, the powers of Europe made a series of agreements by which modern diplomacy was established.[21] The multilateral agreements made on this occasion, and on the conclusions of later European and international wars, in themselves constituted the next set of structures in international law, backed towards the end of the nineteenth century by a growing series of multilateral agreements of a limited functional nature. By this time the basic principle on which quasi-legislation was based, namely that treaties should be observed, was well established. The observance of treaties in practice, on the other hand, was not, and it has rightly been said that the series of major European treaties of the eighteenth and nineteenth centuries stand as a monument to the speed with which rulers forget their promises. In an effort to reconcile appearance with reality the First Hague Conference in 1899 made a first step in securing agreement on certain common rules of conduct: this line of development has codified to some extent the laws of war and has been extended by agreements to limit certain categories of weapons, notably chemical weapons. A Second Hague Conference followed in 1907, which in retrospect was to act as a forerunner of the League of Nations—first proposed by the British scholar Goldsworthy Lowes Dickinson, urged by Woodrow Wilson of the United States and agreed by the representatives of the powers at Versailles in 1919.[22] The League was an attempt to establish the basis of a world government capable of co-ordinating and consolidating the existing system of law, Tennyson's 'Parliament of Man', a legislature for the entire world. Significantly this was to become the first international organization to be based on the juridical equality of states rather than the old notion of a hierarchy of states ranging from the great powers downwards.[23] These principles were revived

both the institution and the structure of international law into disrepute.[27] The framers of the League believed that states which engaged in persistent wrong-doing could be called to account by the international community as a whole, and anxious as they were to avoid war, actually proposed a mechanism by which this should be done, namely the international application of economic sanctions on the offending government. Sanctions fell into disrepute during the 1930s largely because, as again against Zimbabwe in the 1960s and South Africa since, they have never really been applied, and in the post-war world of the United Nations it was decided instead to strengthen the powers of the Security Council so that they could bring the power of the great powers to bear upon wrong-doers in a more direct fashion. The concurrent holding of the Nuremburg war trials, held by the victorious Allies, not under international law but under the law of Germany as it had existed prior to 1934, was intended as a demonstration both of the fact that there were universal principles of behaviour that civilized nations were expected to uphold and that wrong would face prosecution.

Unfortunately, however, the growing disunity between the great powers in 1946 and 1947 meant that the further development of a system of acceptable standards was cut short, though in recent years the development of the concept of human rights, the establishment of links between the United Nations and regional and private human rights organizations, and the insistence of the United Nations General Assembly of discussing flagrant breaches of human rights in selected states, have all resumed the process of development interrupted by the onset of the Cold War.[28] It can, therefore, be said that today there are certain things which a reasonable state is unlikely to do, though probably for reasons of policy rather than for reasons of law. But the right of sovereignty and the notion of non-intervention in the internal affairs of a country still protects a great many states from retribution. The use of torture is an example, since technically it is a matter of internal jurisdiction though contrary to the principles of the charter of the United Nations to which its member states have all subscribed. In 1973 Amnesty International reported substantial allegations of the use of torture in fifty-two countries, covering every region of the world except Oceania, from Brazil to Burundi, Haiti to India, South Africa to Spain—and including both the United Kingdom and the USSR.[29]

As far as international disputes are concerned, the principle that treaties (even if made prior to 1945) are to be observed continues to be held. Unfortunately, again national self-interest has overriden the principle of inviolability of treaties. In the case of new states in particular, the feeling that treaties have been made without their participation, or on their behalf by colonial powers has led to a desire to wipe the slate clean and start afresh. The so-called 'unequal treaties' which conceded the right to be tried by their own officials (extraterritorial jurisdiction) to nationals of the European powers in various parts of the Ottoman Empire and the Far East, were renegotiated in Siam/Thailand as early as the 1930s.[30] This was followed after 1949 by the rejection by the People's Republic of China of the territorial concessions made by the imperial governments of the past, which included not simply the cession of Hong Kong in 1842 and the later lease of the New Territories of Hong Kong to Britain, but more dubiously the concession of trading rights at Macao to Portugal, which, given the unequal strength of the two powers, it is hard to argue that Portugal forced on China.[31] Even in the case of some old-established powers, the belief that a treaty was unequal because made with a former great power, has given rise to a claim that it should be rejected. By this argument its government supports Venezuela's claim for one-third of the territory of the independent state of Guyana, formerly British Guiana, which became independent in 1966. And this argument has spread even to the former great powers.[32] Spain, for example, formerly one of the world's most successful colonial states, now claims the return of Gibraltar from Great Britain (captured in 1708 but formally transferred to Britain by the Treaty of Utrecht in 1713) on the grounds that it is a colonial survival. It does not, however, accept the right of Morocco to demand the return of its own enclaves in Ceuta and Melilla, nor does it challenge the other aspects of the treaty by which Gibraltar was ceded which gave Spain the effective monopoly of trade with the Americas and made its government and a few of its citizens extremely rich.[33]

Fortunately for the peace of the world, states are to some extent restrained from pursuing these and similar bizarre lines of self-aggrandisement by the restraints of international custom which establishes norms of international behaviour which in some ways are more compelling than the formal structures of international law. It is in this structure of norms that we can locate those dramatic rules by which the international system actually functions.

Norms have no legislator. They are established by custom and habit, over a long period of time. The norms of the international system help preserve the existing order, including a complex structure of diplomacy by which it operates, and the natural inconsistencies between norms established in different periods and different places go a long way to account for the anomalies between the appearance and reality of the international order. One of these norms, as we have already noted, is that at any moment in the evolution of the modern state system some powers have always been recognized to be stronger than others. The operation of norms and custom has been most dramatically shown at those moments in world history in which revolutionary states have sought to change the existing order by violent and hence dramatic means.[34] The United States in its day was such a state, as the USSR was after 1917. More recently, Cuba, Libya and Iran have each in their different ways sought to alter the structure of the existing international order and to establish new norms of international behaviour. By setting up the Tricontinental (i.e. OSPAAL), Cuba sought to create a norm of revolutionary action.[35] Libya sought to scrap the existing structure of diplomacy and established the so-called People's Bureaux, staffed by students and spies, in place of the existing embassies staffed with officially accredited diplomats; these were accepted by other powers as having the same status and so assimilated to the international system.[36] Iran, more negatively, has breached one of the major norms of international behaviour by holding a group of American diplomats hostage for 444 days, and using this as a counter-pressure upon the United States to what it perceived as its overwhelming influence in their own country.[37] What has been striking about each of these initiatives is not that they have been momentarily successful, but that they have not in fact varied the norms of the international system. It is still generally the case that states do not overthrow other states by revolutionary means, that they conduct their diplomacy with one another through the structures that have existed in one form or another since before 1648, and that they do not use individual citizens of another country in order to try and enforce political objectives on that country's state government. The strength of these norms is not disproved in any of these instances, or even in similar instances involving action by other states, simply because in the vast majority of cases the norms have continued to be observed.

The behaviour of revolutionary states varies considerably. Not all revolutionary states, defined as those undergoing a major social revolution, feel it necessary to attempt to modify the international system. On the other hand, the international implications of a major social revolution in a strategically significant state are considerable. In short, the policies of a revolutionary state are distrusted by other states, even friendly ones, because in the case of a leading actor they may give rise to a reversal of alliances, and as with Frederick II of Prussia's celebrated reversal of alliances in 1756, such a major disturbance of the existing balance of the world order could mean war. Meanwhile, the existence of a revolutionary state does make all too clear the inefficacy of international law to deal with individual cases. Breaking the rules of the international system in such circumstances constitutes such good internal politics that its disadvantages in the international arena are not only overlooked, they can be turned to positive advantage. Fidel Castro's defiance of the United States, his refusal to accept the implications of the financial pressures brought to bear upon him by the Eisenhower administration, enabled him to appear in the role of a hero before his fellow Third World states in the United Nations. Iran, by breaking the rules of the international system that you do not harm the person of other countries' diplomats as well as the norm that you do not use the bodies of private individuals to exert pressure on other countries, did not incur any punishment from the international community as a whole. The fact that the victims concerned came from the United States, a superpower, was considered by many members of the United

Nations to indicate that they had only got what they deserved. This is an unfortunate precedent insofar as the opportunities for a small power to obtain redress for injustice to its citizens or for breaches of the international order are clearly much less than those available to great ones. To this extent, even if it were true that the modern international order were the creation of the great powers, it would be in the interests of the smaller powers to maintain it and not to seek to supersede it. Although the formal rhetoric is often in conflict, it does seem that in general the smaller members of the United Nations have accepted the value of the organization and indeed have moved beyond this stage to seeking to use it for their own purposes as a collective expression of opinion. Although this is unacceptable to each of the superpowers on many occasions, each has found it expedient when disregarding the decisions of the United Nations to dress up their actions in the cloak of legality. Such *ex post facto* justifications then receive the support of other member states according to the existing alignment of the system of alliances developed on each side.

TREATIES AND ALLIANCES

The modern alliance structure is the product of the latest phase of development of the system of international treaties which began in Europe in the Middle Ages. Treaties are of course much older, and have been recorded in stone or impressed on clay since ancient times. A treaty is simply an agreement between two or more sovereign states made in the most formal manner possible to indicate their joint intention that it should endure either in perpetuity or for such a lesser period as may be specified in the treaty. Treaties, to be valid, therefore, must be made by duly appointed agents of their respective governments with full powers to negotiate on their behalf. They must be recorded in a form that is acceptable to both parties, generally in the form of parallel texts in the several languages of the negotiation, each of which, or one of which, is declared to be the definitive text. The agreement then must be ratified, a formal process of legislative action confirming in the most solemn fashion possible the commitment of that government to the maintenance of that treaty. Problems can arise at each of these stages.[38]

There are various sorts of treaties, and not all of them carry a great deal of political significance. Treaties not only deal with matters such as military alliances, they also deal with commercial matters, such as the regulation of trade, with the establishment of communications by land, water or electronic means, with cultural matters, such as the circulation of books, the protection of copyright, and so forth, and indeed with any matter which may be of mutual concern to two governments. Many such treaties are therefore relatively uncontroversial and the negotiation of them involves no special problems other than that of perseverance and goodwill on both sides. For a treaty of any kind to be effective, however, it is normally the case that it must involve some kind of reciprocal obligation. A one-sided treaty which imposes obligations only on one party is unlikely to be kept, because as soon as that party feels that it has nothing to gain from the treaty, it will be in a position to denounce it as invalid. However, treaties seldom have this overtly one-sided characteristic; a more common situation is a treaty between a great power and a small power which, though imposing reciprocal obligations on both powers concerned, is nevertheless likely to be much more advantageous to the great power rather than to a small one. Canadians, for example, criticized the reciprocity treaties of the Taft administration on the grounds that they gave the United States effectively unilateral entry to Canadian markets; a foolish speech by the then Speaker of the House in the United States persuaded them that this was but the forerunner of a political takeover.[39] In recent years the unequal nature of trade treaties between great powers and lesser ones has been recognised by a variety of devices, including provisions that any trade under the agreement must involve the actual transfer of technological knowledge or expertise from the great power concerned to the lesser one in such a way as to enhance its long-term economic position. Reciprocal advantages need not of course be of the same kind: a commercial advantage can be counterposed by a military one for example.

When a country wishes to denounce a treaty, the easiest way for it to do so is to allege that the terms of the treaty have not been kept by the other party, in other words, that the terms of the bargain have not been carried out. Guatemala, for example, claims that the Boundary Treaty of 1859 regulating its frontiers with Belize (formerly British Honduras) has been invalidated because the British government has not, it claims, used its best endeavours to create communication by land or water between the two countries. The British government claims that the terms were observed, and that adequate communications links have in fact since been constructed.[40]

Attention to the precise form of the wording of the treaty is therefore of crucial importance and this gains significance where the text of the treaty is recorded, as is generally the case, in more than one language. Attention to technical detail of this kind accounts for the very long period that even the simplest treaties tend to take to negotiate. The state concerned may also allege that the other party has not only ignored or overlooked but has actually broken the terms of the treaty through some specific action, but this, quite naturally, governments tend to avoid unless they are actually looking for a pretext for conflict or war. On occasions they feel they cannot overlook a flagrant breach of a treaty, as in the case of Germany's invasion of Belgium in August 1914 in breach of the Treaty of Guarantees of 1839.[41] A specially interesting case is presented by the United Nations (formerly League of Nations) mandated territory of Namibia/South West Africa, where the United Nations has held South Africa's mandate to have been terminated by its failure to observe the terms of subsequent United Nations resolutions, but lacks the power to enforce its wishes against the evident desire of some of the larger powers not to be drawn in.[42]

Ratification presents another area of complication. The European state system originally envisaged that treaties negotiated on behalf of sovereign rulers would be ratified by those rulers. The development of democratic government, however, has introduced a new level of complication. A major difficulty has been encountered by all other powers that have sought to negotiate treaties with the United States, whose constitution provides that treaties must be ratified with the advice and consent of the Senate. Not only has the Senate refused consent to many treaties, notably the Treaty of Versailles of 1919 setting up the League of Nations, but it has also sought in many other cases to attach a series of conditions to its ratification which seek to override the negotiations of the original treaty.[43] It was precisely to avoid this kind of complication that the sovereigns of early modern Europe developed the system of full powers under which treaties are negotiated, since they reasoned that it added nothing to the respect for a treaty or for a government to spend a long time negotiating a treaty which was not going to be ratified. Negotiating a treaty involves an investment of political capital for any government. Failure to ratify it involves a loss of political credibility. Negotiation of a unsuccessful treaty, which creates serious internal problems, is for reasons of internal politics to be feared, and the worst of all possible states of affairs would be to negotiate an unsatisfactory treaty, and for it then to fail because the satisfactory aspects of it were rejected by the other side.

A successfully negotiated treaty can fail at ratification for many reasons. A change of government is perhaps the most common, but there are others. A government may have second thoughts when it has had time to study the terms of the treaty which its agents negotiated in good faith. Other information may come to light which suggests that they are not getting as good a bargain as they thought they were. Whatever the reason, the government concerned then exercises its right not to ratify the treaty. An excellent example is the Treaty of Tlatelolco, which Argentina has signed but not ratified, while in consequence Brazil and Chile have refused to waive Article 28 of the Treaty so that is can come into effect immediately as far as they are concerned.[44] The need for ratification can in itself, therefore, become a diplomatic card for a government to play in its attempt to persuade another government to accommodate itself to its wishes.

The most important treaties have historically been those setting up a military or defence alliance. There is no need for a state to enter into alliances if it does not wish to, an example being Switzerland which maintains a strict system of neutrality, and has done so since it was declared a neutral state by the powers at Vienna in 1815. Contrary to a widespread belief, Finland and Austria are not precluded from entering into alliances by the treaties granting them their independence, though Austria's assertion of neutrality has been accepted by many other countries.[45] In the Third World, the colonial powers generally have tried to retain at least the friendly co-operation of their former colonies. South and South-East Asia illustrates the range of possibilities: Vietnam, Laos and Cambodia have been since 1975 aligned with the Soviet Union; Pakistan and the Philippines are aligned with the United States; Burma and India have opted for full neutrality. Nor does this exhaust the possibilities, for Malaysia, avoiding more formal links, has entered into a regional association, the Association of South-East Asian Nations (ASEAN), with Singapore, Thailand, Indonesia and the Philippines, designed to show simultaneously their common solidarity and their dealignment from outside influences.[46]

However, historically other states have found themselves drawn into alliances, often by way of treaties of non-aggression, which purport to bind the two parties concerned to settle all disputes between them in a wholly peaceful manner. Treaties of non-aggression can be, and have been abused, as in the case of the treaty between Hitler's Germany and Stalin's Soviet Union in 1939 (the Molotov/Ribbentrop Pact), which was broken unilaterally by Hitler in 1941 when he launched his surprise attack on the Soviet Union. In consequence, although they have been—for some inexplicable reason—favoured by Soviet diplomacy in the post-war period,[47] they have not been so highly regarded in Western Europe. Instead, the system of defensive alliances has been constructed centred upon the United States. The earliest of these in order of historical development was the Inter-American Treaty of Reciprocal Assistance (the Rio Pact) of 1947,[48] followed by the ANZUS Treaty between Australia, New Zealand and the United States[49] and the setting up of the North Atlantic Treaty Organisation (NATO) in 1949.[50] These treaties are multilateral, involving a number of states, but in fact historically alliances have frequently been concluded on a bilateral basis, and indeed on a basis which cross-cut and conflicted with existing systems of alliance with which they purported to be in harmony. In short, alliances can be concluded on a bilateral basis which go beyond the structure of a multilateral alliance and indeed seem in some ways to be in conflict with it.

Military alliances of this kind bind their participants to take military action in certain specified circumstances, usually in the event of attack from a specified power or powers. The multilateral alliances envisage a wider range of contingencies, and indeed, as in the case of the Rio Pact, may envisage different sorts and degrees of military action in different circumstances. Thus that pact does not require the same kind of response from states to war within the Western hemisphere as it does to an attack from the outside.[51] This reflects the fact, that whilst there is seldom much doubt that a state of military conflict exists, there can frequently be much doubt as to how it exactly began. It is normal in such circumstances for each side to blame the other and, indeed, it is frequently the case that the nature of the military dispositions of the two countries concerned are such that each can be said in some way to have contributed to the outbreak of war. Nevertheless, it has been a working assumption of the international system since the Treaty of Versailles in 1919 that in all cases wars can be regarded as having specific causes, and that therefore blame can be attached to specific powers. The power that first resorts to military force, if it can be identified, which is not always the case, is therefore the one that is usually held to blame for the ensuing state of hostilities. A celebrated example was Paraguay, blamed by the League for the outbreak of the Chaco War in 1932, though the initial moves towards war had in fact been made by Bolivia.[52]

However, since 1919 opinions about the outbreak of war in 1914, on which the Treaty of Versailles was predicted, have changed considerably. Many historians now believe that a major cause of the outbreak of the First World War was in fact the existence of the alliance structure itself. By this structure a conflict between two powers within the respective alliance systems was automatically translated into a European conflagration.[53] Some go further and argue that the existing structure of alliances in East and West make a war of the future of this kind not merely probable but indeed inevitable; that, in short, alliances do not safeguard the peace, they make war inevitable.[54] While there is a great deal in this argument, it also has to be said that the wording of most existing treaties is such that it leaves a great deal of discretion open to the states concerned as to whether they regard a state of war as existing or not. It is possible for a state unilaterally to reject the notion of a state of war, and indeed to put a conclusion to hostilities by unilaterally declaring them to be at an end, as in the case of the United States and Germany at the end of the First World War. The problem with modern alliances is that the alliance structure is backed by a considerable permanent structure by which military force is co-ordinated and controlled, and to the extent to which this military structure goes further than mere consultation and involves an immediate response being delegated to military officers, the situation has passed correspondingly out of the control of the diplomats and of the statesmen. In the case of the lesser powers the problem is particularly acute, since it is in the highest degree improbable that the quick response time of modern military systems would in fact allow time for them to be consulted. In practice, therefore, such an alliance is predicated on confidence by the lesser powers on the decision-making ability of the alliance leaders to whom, effectively, they are subordinated, whether they know or acknowledge this or not.[55]

The existence of this complex structure of alliances owes much to the circumstances in which the Second World War actually broke out, and specifically to the surprise attack in Pearl Harbor in the Pacific by the Japanese in December 1941. The trauma provoked by this event was such that it led the United States dramatically to reverse its policy of avoiding military alliances with other states, which was embodied in Washington's so-called Farewell Address (1797) and had remained a basic principle of US foreign policy until the conclusion of the Rio Pact.[56]

Although the fear of surprise attack has always existed, and goes far to explain the existence of alliances in history as well as at the present, the development of an integrated command structure and military force is new. Although in the past military forces have been lent or even sold from one state to another, and no clear distinction was drawn between national armies and those who today would be termed mercenaries, in the past hundred years it has become increasingly an assumption of the international community that force is something which is properly waged only by one's own citizens and, furthermore, that all of them are liable to some form of military service. The importance of universal military service is notably greatest where the threat to national independence is greatest, and this, particularly, is especially the case with neutral states such as Switzerland, Sweden—more recently—Austria. As a result, in the modern system of alliances, governments have locked entire populations into a balance of threat and counter-threat which is without parallel in early modern times. Technological developments such as the nuclear-tipped ballistic missile, the cruise missile and the submarine launcher have strengthened the dependence of these alliances on highly complex technological infrastructure, capable of devastating response in a very short space of time. In consequence, many of the assumptions of the traditional international system—that there would be time for negotiation before a conflict begins, that war should not be undertaken until it has been formally declared, that women and children should be as far as possible protected from the consequences—have been tacitly abandoned in the new military planning. There are understandable fears that the whole machine may be out of control, driven by the relentless demands of industries to produce more weapons systems and to sell them to their respective governments. President Eisenhower's warning against the dangers of 'the military–industrial complex' is frequently quoted, but apparently not heeded.[57]

The inhabitants of the Third World states are generally only very imperfectly aware of the strength and power of these military alliances, but many of their governments wisely choose to fight shy of the horrifying consequences that a miscalculation poses for a member of such an alliance. Whatever their political sympathies, therefore, they have, as we have seen, avoided entering into such alliances, and an attempt to establish the East/West alliance structure in the Middle East, as in South-East Asia, has consistently proved unsuccessful,[58] though this is not to say that East/West conflict does not exist in these areas, as it manifestly does. What this does mean is that as far as the greater part of the world is concerned, the decision whether or not to go to war still appears to lie in the hands of the Third World governments concerned. Although in general they have not chosen to involve themselves in the East/West conflict, they have continued to reserve the right to involve themselves in conflicts with their neighbours, and such conflicts are evidently not yet regarded as being unacceptable by the international community in general. Indeed, insofar as the consensus of the General Assembly of the United Nations now lies with Third World countries which remember the Second World War, if at all, only as an occasion on which they were called upon to contribute to a conflict which they had in no way provoked, they do not necessarily see the provisions of the charter of the United Nations seeking to end war altogether as being applicable to themselves. What their governments do not realise is that it was the horrific consequences, not of nuclear warfare which had not yet been experienced, but of conventional warfare as it was practiced between 1937 and 1945, which gave rise to the United Nations itself. Since technology in conventional warfare has progressed so far in the interim, even what might have seemed to be a relatively limited conflict is now likely to result in severe damage even in Third World states, and even given their relatively slight capacity to injure one another.[58]

Furthermore, it is apparent from the example of most modern wars that the one lesson that has been learnt most effectively has been the wrong one, and that the involvement of the civilian population in general conflict is now the first step, and not the last step, in the outbreak of a war of any kind. War, in short, is no longer something which the consensus of the international community can be counted upon to oppose, however ineffectively. It has become instead an instrument of policy by Third World states among themselves in their effort to emulate the departed colonial powers of former times and to establish their own place in the world. It is a measure of the durability of the norms of the international system that despite many flagrant breaches of the intention of its formal rules, in general the tendency has been, quite unofficially, to maintain the spirit of the rules of war in armed conflicts between states, though not, unfortunately, in conflicts within one state.

Such rules are in part the product of formal agreements between states but, significantly, not necessarily between those states that actually observe them. The world has changed a great deal in the last fifty years, but the use of chemical warfare pioneered in World War One has since then been to a considerable extent controlled. If it has been controlled, however, it has been controlled more by tacit agreement that some kinds of weapons are too frightful, or are too dangerous to the user to contemplate, than by any clear statement of this fact. And it may well seem, therefore, that in the operation of the rules of the game it is the unwritten, unspoken rules that in the end are the more powerful.

3 The Domestic Environment

What is a typical country? That is one of the most difficult questions in the world to answer. Typical in what respect? In population, in area, in military potential, in economic resources, or what? There is no easy answer to a question such as this. The fact that there is not, points up the enormous difficulties of generalisation and emphasises, if emphasis is needed, how important it is to distinguish precisely between different types of country.

It is customary, when studying individual countries, to look first at their geographical position and historical background. Again, this is clearly very important. However, it is no less important not to surrender to the notion that every country is unique, and that therefore there is no point in trying to compare it with any other. The Third World may be a diffuse enough concept, but it would not have gained the popularity it has had it not meant something in the minds of those who use it. What the countries with which we are principally interested here have in common, therefore, is the fact that they are all subordinate actors in the world drama. We may not be able to determine what is a typical country, but the one thing we can be certain of is that the United States and the Soviet Union are not typical.[1]

This is important, since it has long been customary in the English-language literature from the United States to assume that the world's political systems will necessarily tend to evolve towards that of the United States. This viewpoint, adopted at or around independence in 1776, has become so much part of the basic assumptions of all American writers that they often do not realize the extent to which their writing carries the covert message. Their Soviet opposite numbers, on the other hand, are all too plainly aware of the importance of the message that they wish to convey, which is that the world is in inevitably going to tend towards the system used in the Soviet Union. Both cannot be right, and there is reason to believe that neither is right.[2] We must attempt to keep at bay such assumptions, as far as possible, in looking at the nature of political systems in the present day world.

As the majority of Third World states have undergone a period of colonial rule, a most important influence on each of them is their particular experience of this rule. Empires create their own legitimating myths, and most people probably accept at face value the idea that great empires are created by military conquests. The myth of glory is, after all, part of the self-image not only of the colonial power but also of those who have succeeded in freeing themselves from its rule. But in the formation of the great European land-based empires expansion into sparsely populated territory (e.g. Russia and Siberia), marriage of dynastic heirs and heiresses (e.g. Austria–Hungary, the union of England and Scotland) and diplomacy (e.g. partition of Navarre between France and Spain, or Poland between Russia, Prussia and Austria) all played an equally significant part. And indeed often, especially in the remoter areas, as in the seaborne empires of Spain, Portugal, Britain and France, the subject peoples conquered one another; Cortés using the Tlaxcalans to defeat the Aztecs, Britain using Indian troops in Burma and Indonesia, and so on. In fact, from the mid eighteenth century onwards it was India that supplied the manpower for the dramatic expansion of the British Empire while Britain supplied the ships that enabled its land forces to be deployed, as France was later to do with the aid of the famous Foreign Legion and the troops of North Africa.

Empires, however, differ considerably in the extent to which they have given their people's room for self-government, and the later empires have done this more successfully than the earlier ones. We may, therefore, distinguish three main types. First there are presidential states such as the Latin American countries, who have had a common experience of Spanish colonial rule, became independent in the main at the beginning of the nineteenth century and adopted a presidential system of government with the major powers of government concentrated in the hands of a single chief executive. A second type are those states with the experience of rule by Britain, France or the Netherlands, in each of which independence came in the middle of the twentieth century, under a parliamentary-style system in which power is not concentrated but shared among a number of co-equals for whom the prime minister (or in France and Finland a presidential figure) serves as a co-ordinator and leader rather than a director and decision-maker. A third set of countries are those who have had the experience of rule by authoritarian systems: the Baltic states and in particular Poland, the Balkans including Rumania, Bulgaria, Yugoslavia and Albania, and Korea, Vietnam, Laos and Cambodia in South-East Asia, whose experience of authoritarian rule is much longer and deeper than that of the relatively brief period of colonial subordination. The largest group of such states, however, includes all those countries who were formally part of the Turkish Empire, stretching from Morocco in the west to Iraq in the east, including those states already mentioned that have also had influences from Central Europe. In general, these states have adopted a system of government with an authoritarian leader, a single ruling party and a strong sense of ideological control, whether this is of a traditional sort, as in the case of Islam, or a modernizing sort, as in the case of Marxism-Leninism in Eastern Europe. Communist states, however, differ from the others mentioned in this category in the distinctive way that the single ruling party expounds the official ideology and the extent to which the official ideology determines every aspect of policy-making.[3]

Attempts to classify states by their political structure, however, run into the repeated difficulty that modifications occur from time to time which substantially alter the expectations which we can have of them. Since independence, not only have a large number of African states modified their political systems to give a dominant role to an executive president, but many of these changes have been accompanied by military intervention, which has had the effect of establishing an authoritarian system.[4] Any generalization based on the assumption that political systems are going to remain constant will accordingly be fallacious. A spurious

individual, and his ability to appoint ambassadors in turn to other countries is an important part of his prerogative. Furthermore, if, as is often the case, he is also commander-in-chief of the armed forces, the formal role which he plays in the military system means that important defence functions are also handled by him personally, and inevitably this co-ordination of civilian and military requirements of policy-making is one which, if he exercises efficiently, can be very valuable.

In parliamentary systems, on the other hand, ambassadors' accreditation to the head of state is of little practical importance since the head of state's functions are severely circumscribed. The diplomatic representative has to deal, as for day-to-day purposes it is intended that he should, with the foreign minister, often known as the minister of foreign affairs.[7] The foreign minister, however, is only one member of a cabinet, appointed by the prime minister, who may or may not have formal constitutional responsibilities in the field of foreign policy. In Britain, for example, the prime minister does not, technically, have such responsibilities. The prime minister is first lord of the Treasury and therefore has direct constitutional responsibility for that department. By convention in the twentieth century the prime minister's power has been extended to cover the major policy aspects of a wide range of other activities, in particular foreign policy, the oversight of which has, upon occasions, been combined with the prime ministerial office, as under Ramsay MacDonald in 1924.[8] Prime ministers vary considerable in the extent to which they dominate their cabinets. But it remains a fundamental principle of cabinet government that the ministers responsible for each department participate collectively in the policy-making process, and however strong the leadership which a prime minister gives, it is still subject to this control by colleagues.[9] In one sense, prime ministers are more powerful than presidents in that the nature of the parliamentary system enables them to pass legislation required by their party. But on the other, they are weaker, because as leaders of political parties they are not given the safeguard of a fixed term of office, and are subject to the day-to-day will of the parliamentary body to which they are responsible. In most of the world's parliamentary systems, which are the product of coalition government, this means that the government is highly responsive to public opinion, unlike the situation in Britain.

Although to some extent foreign policy represents a special case, in that it is regarded as being to some extent a closed sphere of activity for the élite policy-makers, at the same time within a parliamentary system it is always capable of being challenged by the Opposition, which has indeed a duty to do so and has the opportunity to call for parliamentary debate on questions in this area as in all others. Furthermore, a prime minister, although he/she appoints the minister of foreign affairs, does not necessarily have the power to dismiss him/her. If the individual concerned, as is often the case, is a future claimant to political power, then the probability is that the or she represents a substantial, and indeed crucial interest group within the party. By contrast, the presidential secretary responsible for foreign policy is very much the presidential creation; he or she can be dismissed as easily as appointed, and indeed much more easily, since appointment is subject to confirmation by the legislature (the Senate alone in the United States and some other states).[10]

In both systems, political parties are of considerable importance in determining, on the one hand, who is likely to be recruited to the key position of minister of foreign affairs, and on the other, what the ideological constraints would be upon that official in the conduct of his office. I have already referred to the fact that in most of the world's parliamentary systems the majority which forms a government is the product of a coalition, arrived at after the election of the legislature in response to a process of bargaining between the interested parties. Not only does this process of bargaining involve ideological considerations, but it usually has its outcome in a very specific allocation of posts. In newly emergent states, where political parties are a much more recent formation, there is a very wide range of possible behaviour which may be expected. Considerable enthusiasm has been shown in southern Africa, in for example, Tanzania, Malawi and, more recently, Zimbabwe, for the idea of a one-party state. This appears to be because, quite erroneously, it is believed that a one-party state eliminates the irritation of having to deal with opposition within the system and frees a government to carry out a comprehensive programme of social and economic reform. Naturally, such is not the case, since the abolition of alternative political groupings merely leads to the factional-izing of the ruling party, and its ultimate disintegration. Without effective competition its cohesion is lost, and it succumbs, more often than not, to challenges from outside the system, and in particular from the challenge presented by the military.

Even if this is not yet the case, the party will tend to become subordinated to the particular interests of the group in power. The desire of new states to create a focus for national unity by building up the charismatic personality of its leader leads to the personalisation of political parties.[11] The parties concerned become simply the vehicles for the election of leaders, and to some extent their personal property, and so they fail to develop the important role of feeding political opinion into the ruling circle. The result is a weak party structure, characterized by shifting political coalitions which come into existence only for the winning of elections and disintegrate between times, the exact reverse of the process of coalition formation which is characteristic of the mature parliamentary system.[12] These 'one off' political parties form an inadequate basis for the long-term conduct of any policy, still less the very lengthy diplomatic negotiations that normally accompany any sub-stantive change in foreign policy.

It is of the greatest importance to distinguish between factional or temporary political parties of this kind and interest groups. Interest groups exist in all societies, but they may well remain latent and not emerge into active political competition unless their own particular interests appear in some way to be transgressed. The most fundamental of these groupings are termed by Almond 'non-associational groups' since they are in broad social categories such as race, class and caste, into which the individual is born and does not opt to become a member.[13] Such groups are normally latent, and it is only in certain unusual circumstances that they form active interests in their own right; they constitute , on the other hand, categories which enable political parties to organise their appeal more effectively. Among institutional groups, groups to which one belongs by virtue of having to earn one's living, we find again a wide range of possibilities: the armed services; professional groupings such as teachers, lawyers and doctors; religious bodies—all form institutional groups. Yet as the examples given will show, their interests as groups are not necessarily the same as the organizations which purport to represent them. Lawyers as a grouping, for example, have interests which are not necessarily accurately represented by the professional bodies which speak in their name. Beyond this, a third category, that of associational groups, is formed by all other organizations having a permanent existence, to which the individual belongs to choice. Among this large third category are to be found those bodies specifically designed for enforcing demands on governments, which are most frequently referred to popularly as 'pressure groups'. Pressure groups are, in effect, simply associational interest groups organized for the purposes of bringing about specific political results. Like all the other interest groups they are distinguishable from political parties by the fact that they do not seek political power in their own right.[14]

In all countries, non-associational groups form the basic structure of latent interest articulation. Though in India considerable attempts have been made to dismantle the caste system, and in China attacks were made under Mao Zedong on the fundamental structures of the family and clan, neither can be said to have been at all successful.[15] Hence, though some of the older works in comparative politics suggest that these structures are relatively unimportant in more developed societies, there is reason to believe that this is not in fact the case; that their operation is merely disguised by the multiplicity of alternative avenues of interest articulation. In any case, their importance in the Third World context is undoubted, and it is a fundamental need of any analysis of foreign policy in a Third World state to have as detailed a knowledge as possible of the family relationships, origins and other basic personal details of the ruling élite. What must also be understood is that the considerations based upon the policy-makers by these relationships are to them of transcendental importance. They take precedence over all other possibilities and avenues of approach, and in the last analysis the loyalties which they establish form fundamental bases of any form of political action.

THE ARMED FORCES

Among institutional groups, the most important are those which have direct connection with the government itself. Among these, one stands out both for the fact that it is central to the operation of Third World government, and that it has an unusual ability to enforce its will through its control of the means of force. The importance of the armed forces is all the greater since their maintenance is one of the principal symbols that a new state exists at all. Armed forces are of various kinds, but navies and air forces are basically, as far as most countries are concerned, derivatives of the army, which remains the premier force. This is inevitable because the army, being ground based, controls directly or indirectly the centres of political power, and is of the most significance in the maintenance of internal security. It is hence the only one of the armed forces which has the capacity in most circumstances to act independently in political matters.

Armies have well-defined structures which involve characteristics which make them particularly effective as political organizations. They are hierarchically organized. The directing body, the officer corps, is relatively small, compact and educated. Its members are bound together by their training, their service and structure of family and other ties which has grown up around it. They enjoy the privilege of being part of the government and enjoying the relative wealth and privilege open to leading members of the élite. And by virtue of the fact that most Third World countries have relatively little use for the armed forces for the traditional occupation of fighting neighbouring countries, the military are compelled to develop a political role in order to justify their existence. This pattern can be seen in its most developed form in countries of Latin America, where it has taken more than a century and a half to grow up.[16] It can also, however, be seen in more recently independent countries, such as Indonesia or Pakistan, where the relative sophistication and high level of education of the population means that we cannot attribute military intervention to the poor development of political awareness.[17] This explanation has always been popular in the West (and for that matter in the East), and seemed to get added impetus from the circumstances that after the rapid decolonization of the French African states in 1960 there occurred a remarkably large number of military coups in that continent within a relatively short space of time—Togo, Congo (Brazzaville), Dahomey in 1963; Zanzibar, Gabon, Sudan in 1964; Burundi, Algeria, Congo (Leopoldville), Dahomey (twice) in 1965; Central African Republic, Upper Volta, Nigeria, Uganda, Ghana, Burundi, Nigeria and Burundi (again) in 1966. The consequences of some of these are with us to this day in the shape of new military governments and prolonged political instability.[18]

Attempts to suggest that military governments is the sign of a lack of legitimacy among civilian office holders, however, have several objections. First of all, in the circumstances of the new states there is not always a clear distinction between military and civilian members of society. The huge apparatus of tradition, of formalization of military academies and so forth has not yet had time to become well established. There have been, moreover, few glorious victories against the colonial powers to parallel those of the period of North American or Latin American independence. The majority of the states that have reached independence since the Second World War have done so peacefully, and by negotiation. In the circumstances, therefore, it is hard to see how superior legitimacy could have accrued to the military establishment. However, second, we must not overlook the important symbolic value of maintaining one's own military forces. As mentioned previously, the existence of military forces is in fact one of the principal signs of an independent nation's state, capable of acting on its own in relation to other states. Third, we must not underestimate either the extent to which military training contributed to the total stock of education in modern statecraft available to newly independent states in and after the 1960s. Owing to the rivalry between the superpowers, which merely builds on and extends the rivalry between the great powers which was a feature of nineteenth- and early twentieth-century politics, there has always been competition to extend military education to officers from allied states. Such officers, naturally, will not only gain experience in the military arts but will also return to their countries, taking with them a liking for the country in which they studied, and a willingness to associate themselves with its policies. Although this may to some be sinister, it is scarcely new or surprising.[19] But it does have the implication that the officers concerned have been educated at an impressionable age within the structures of a modernizing society, and take these ideas back to their own country.

Fourth, then, this implies that these modernizing military officers have more in common with a small, foreign-educated élite within the civilian part of their own countries than they have with the mass of the population at large. The existence of these structures of education, therefore, creates additional reinforcement, a sense of separateness of this élite, and in turn engenders, as military intervention has spread, an imitative tendency for educated intellectuals to turn to the armed forces for support for their own political notions. Military intervention, when it came, was accordingly not simply a matter of the military acting on their own, but of an alliance between military and civilians for specific political purposes, in which the civilians took much of the initiative, and the military contributed the force.[20] The pattern of military intervention thus set has continued, and will continue, and it has very important consequences for decision-making.

Any country which has armed forces is necessarily going to have to take account of the military interest in the making of foreign policy. Such an interest is not necessarily to wage war, but it is to ensure that war, if waged, will be waged on terms satisfactory to the military, and the armed forces therefore have an obligation as well as an opportunity to express their views on the conduct of foreign policy in relation to their own particular sphere of interest. The problem is defining what this sphere of influence is. At its narrowest it might appear to be concerned simply with the physical defence of the national territory. At its widest it can include the maintenance of the existing form of government, of the social structure and of the national way of life itself. The military easily associate themselves with the guardianship of the constitution, and there are frequently politicians who agree with them. We can indeed distinguish a number of different responsibilities which the military assumed. First of all, there is the defence of the national territory. Second, there is the maintenance of national integrity and the institutions which represent it. Third, there is the training of youth, its inculcation in the military way of life as the highest expression of national goals. Fourth, it supplies military personnel to take part in, and on occasions to head, the government. Fifth, and lastly, the military may assume a role of interpreting the national will, believing that the choice of civilian politicians, by votes or by elections, does not accurately represent the true will of the nation.

What makes these different capacities the more important, is the unique position of the military in being both within government and enjoying a special relationship to it. The fact that the armed forces are funded by the state means that they enjoy a stability and continuity which no other interest group within the society enjoys, with the possible exception of the religious establishment. The nature of their association with government, however, gives them a direct involvement in the process of decision-making, which, as already pointed out, extends to advice on defensive postures, the procurement of weapons, the size and disposition of the military establishment, and a wide range of matters related to each of these points. The military are the largest spending department of government, too, up to the point at which the modernization of the economic structure enables the government to dispose of free economic resources in education and social security, the two areas which in modern developed states outstrip even the military establishment. This is, however, not uniformly true of all developed states, and it is clear that the military expenditure of the superpowers is in fact very considerable indeed in proportion to their expenditure on any one individual civilian purpose. To this extent, therefore, their military establishments share some of the strength and some of the assumptions of their kind of in the Third World, and we may expect, indeed, a degree of reverse influence on them from their close associations with the armed forces of the client states.[21]

The other thing that follows from this close association with the government, of which they form part, is the nature of the institutional links between the military and the civilian decision makers. Here the spread of the presidential system, with its direct links between individual departments and the chief executive, gives a military a degree of insulation from the process of decision-making in civilian matters of which they do not fail to take advantage. In its most developed form in Latin American states three links ensure that the military are able to bypass the entire civilian establishment and enjoy a degree of autonomy in decision-making which is hard to believe. First, the president, as head of state, is commander-in-chief of the armed forces, and so the military enjoy direct access to him in that capacity through the chiefs of staff, which in turn form virtually a distinctive military cabinet. Second, instead of, as in Western Europe, the armed forces being represented in the cabinet by a civilian who controls them on behalf of the civilian government, they are represented by a serving general or admiral, who serves as a military ambassador to the civilian cabinet, keeping an eye on what it is doing. Third, in addition, the president in his capacity as commander-in-chief is surrounded by military aides who maintain a watchful eye on all his doings and report to the chiefs of staff on any political manoeuvres that may be in train to circumvent control which the military exercise in other ways. Clearly in more recently independent states institutional links of such elaborateness have not yet had time to develop, and in any case the persistence of the Westminster style of parliamentary democracy does a good deal to prevent its rapid spread in Africa, where some military establishments remain very small and military expenditure relatively insignificant. However, as the example of Suriname indicates, it is possible for the military to sieze power in the country in which the military establishment is minimal: the 300-member Surinamese armed forces siezed power in 1980 in a confused political situation and demonstrated that they had in fact all the force that they required in order to maintain it. And in the early 1960s the military forces of both Nigeria and Ghana were similarly regarded as much too small to intervene successfully, but by the end of 1966 they had both done so.[22]

Military influence in internal affairs therefore can be very invasive and depressive. This is less likely to be the case in routine foreign-policy making for two reasons. First, because the process of foreign-policy making is by nature intermittent, and the tedium and routine of day-to-day diplomatic intercourse prevents it from being of great concern to any but the specialists whose job it is to practice it. The military tend, therefore, to become concerned in foreign policy issues only at or near the point of decision, and unhappily it is the case that this occurs not so much when war is likely to break out as when peace has to be made, and particularly when there is a need for decision on a vexed boundary dispute with a neighbouring country, a common problem of new and of not-so-new states. Second, owing to the way in which the international system has grown up, it employs its own special language, which is an essentially legalistic one, and therefore these specialists are able to some extent to insulate themselves from interference from whatever source by the obscurity of the terms in which their dialogue is conducted. In effect, the fact that diplomacy is conducted in a specialised code accessible only to those that have taken the trouble to study it protects it to some extent from military interference, as indeed from the interference from either civilian politicians or of the public at large.[23] But the military retain their freedom to decide which matters, being matters of defence, come within their own sphere of interest, while there is always the danger, on the other hand, that the report of a move of some kind may lead to a sudden uprising of élite or public opinion which provokes the military into a hasty or ill-considered action, and this possibility always has to be borne in mind when dealing with Third World states.

One further advantage that the military enjoy is so obvious that it is often overlooked. This is the fact that, by long-established custom dating back to the days of the old European state system, they maintain their own network of diplomatic officers. These officers, who are attached to embassies and hence are termed 'attachés', are appointed to provide their countries with legitimate information about the armament and capabilities of the government to which they are accredited.[24] Officially they do not engage in spying activities, and are, indeed, liable to be expelled if they are caught in illegal activities or in breach of any special regulations that may have been imposed by the host government as to movement, and so on. They are, however, in no way debarred from reporting back to their superiors in the ministry of defence their impressions of any matters, including political developments, that may appear to be relevant to defence. In this way the ministry enjoys a source of information independent of the information provided by the ministry of foreign affairs, and at times, it seems, considered by them to be superior.

Part of the duty of a military attaché is to maintain liaison with officers of the armed forces of the host country. Especially where such links are reinforced by a formal alliance and the provision of military aid, this gives them a method not only of learning about political decisions taken within the military, but of communicating in return how their government is likely to react to those decisions. Thus it is widely believed that the Chilean high command sounded out the United States government as to how it was likely to react to the military takeover of September 1973,[25] and Argentine military officers tried to assess early in 1982 the posture of the United States in the event of a forcible Argentine capture of the Falklands.[26]

The intimacy of such relationships is the greater where the two countries concerned enjoy a formal alliance, or where there exists an established pattern by which the less powerful country relies on the more powerful one as a source of arms. Although this was not initially realized, the supply of arms and training by the United States to the Latin American countries was a powerful factor in strengthening the hand of the military establishments against their own governments. A wave of military coups in the early 1960s put military governments in power in several countries, and led ex-President Santos of Colombia to remark, 'Each country is being occupied by its own army'.[27] The ideology of anti-communism propagated (though certainly not originated) by US military instructors was followed by the emergence in some of the larger states of a doctrine of 'military developmentalism', by which the armed forces assumed the right to stay in power for a prolonged period to take control of the developmental process and to create thereby a strong country with a strong economy capable of maintaining strong military forces. At the same time, envy of the superior life-style of their US instructors and of the United States increased the sense of belonging to an élite with special privileges, and ensured that these regimes were even less sensitive than usual to the desires and wishes of the populations over which they had assumed control.

Some at the time saw these movements as 'Nasirist', and there is indeed an interesting parallel with the Free Officers Movement in Egypt, and the subsequent emergence of the Egyptian armed forces as the main political body of the United Arab Republic. As McLaurin, Peretz and Snider write:

> During Nasser's tenure, control of the military was ensured by three main approaches: outright takeover of key ministries by top Revolutionary Command Council (RCC) members, who then employed civilian experts in second-echelon positions; the placement of military personnel in the number-two slots in civilian-led ministries (for example, deputy minister or undersecretary); and beginning in the late 1950s, the appointment of a new breed of officer technocrats in top positions. The last was the most effective device of all since it meant that the military had trained its own experts to manage the complexities of a modern industrialized society, and thus need not rely on civilians.[28]

A similar pattern can be observed to a lesser degree in Syria and Iraq, though in the latter case qualified by the importance of the religious dimension.[29]

The Revolutionary Command Council referred to is the Egyptian version of the characteristic military–political instrument known traditionally in Latin America as a junta, as, for example, in Argentina from 1976 to 1982, where it operated on the so-called 'fourth man' principle. This means simply that the armed services controlled the administration through their respective heads meeting collectively, having appointed a fourth officer formally to head the government as president and maintain the day-to-day work of administration.[30] Such a junta operates primarily in relation to a military, not a civilian constituency. As Alexander Haig records, this relationship presents very special problems in relation to the conduct of foreign policy:

> On every decision, the government apparently had to secure the unanimous consent of every corps commander in the army and of their equivalents in the navy and air force. Progress was made by syllables and centimeters and then vetoed by men who had never been part of the negotiations.[31]

Under the military government in Peru after 1968 this process of consultation was both wider—extending further down the command structure—and more continuous, with the deliberate purpose of generating an organic consensus about the government's plans for the controlled internal development of its society.

In such circumstances, clearly, it may be much less important that the military authorities have access to their own diplomatic network than that they stand behind all authorities of the state as the ultimate decision-makers in all matters of both internal and external state policy. This means, in turn, that information which reaches them appears to be pretuned to a military wavelength, and that they receive in the main information that they expect and want to hear.

RELIGION

As noted above, the only interest grouping with a comparable degree of strength and independence within the political structure of most Third World states is the religious establishment. Religious establishments, however, vary very considerably and there are important differences between one state and another as to how well religious groupings are linked to the civilian and military organs of state, and what form of international communication system they enjoy on their own account. In addition, there are considerable differences in the extent to which states enjoy religious homogeneity. Religious establishments influence policy-making in the following ways.

First of all, they establish norms of behaviour to which society as a whole, including the decision-makers themselves, are expected to adhere. If they teach that it is wrong to kill, to take the most obvious example, then if a country is to use armed force as an instrument of policy, it must do so in a way sanctioned as an exception to this general rule, if it wishes to maintain the adherence of believers. Second, in its own structure of decision-making, it establishes a model for the lay world. If its decision-making structure is markedly vertical and hierarchical, the chances are that a similar pattern will be found in the civilian authorities; if, on the other hand, it involves the concept of a community of believers arriving at decisions by a process of discussion and resolution, the chances are that the civilian government too will accept some if not all of these features. Confucianism in Vietnam acted strongly, it has been argued, to predispose the Vietnamese to accept uncritically the state dogma of Marxism as having received the 'mandate of Heaven'. Third, by virtue of religion's role as a set of beliefs in forming social behaviour, religious bodies in most societies assume a particular function in the field of education, and in some societies retain this function without it ever having been transferred in whole or part to the civil authority. If, as in Indonesia under Sukarno, these bodies endorse the state ideology or accept it as their own that in turn compensates for any obvious deficiencies or inconsistencies it may exhibit.[33]

If an institutional structure of education exists in this sense. then the values inculcated by this system may include a wide range of individual behaviours which are considerably more detailed, and hence possibly more influential, than the more generalised statements of belief, obedience or obligation by the religious values system as a whole. Education, in short, makes these overall values specific. It gives them sets of labels, and it amplifies them in a way which ensures that they can be translated more easily into specific patterns of behaviour. Lastly, whether in the majority or not, religious bodies may, by their nature as religious bodies, have an international dimension in their own right. They may, in short, transcend the bounds of civil society and have links to similar organisations in other countries, or to a wider community of believers extending over a number of countries. Inevitably this wider dimension will inform their views on relations with these countries; the community of believers in short constitutes a special field of interest for the foreign policy-makers of that particular country. It does not follow that this community of believers will in fact be dominant in the minds of the policy-makers, but it is scarcely possible for them to accept their thought from the influence which this wider association implies. The most striking example is, of course, the immensely complex system of relationships incorporated into the institutional structure of the Catholic church.[34]

The impact of each of these on the processes of decision-making will naturally vary considerably with the nature of the religion concerned, the extent to which it finds adherence within the country in question, the strength or otherwise of its hierarchical structure and the way in which it may be varied within the assumptions of the group concerned. We can now turn to some more practical examples. In Europe, Christianity established the duality of church and state.[35] State structure owed a considerable amount to the influence of the church, which as the sole vehicle of culture during the Dark Ages transmitted to the nations and states of Europe the notion of a universal empire and the role of that empire in the organization of the faithful. Ironically, the church itself played a considerable role in transmitting the concept of sovereignty from the ancient world to the modern, and in turn it was this concept of sovereignty which was to lead throughout Europe to the church being restricted as far as possible to a religious role within an essentially secular state. This did not happen, however, until the diplomatic practices of the universal church had laid the foundations for the system of European diplomacy, which in turn became the foundation of the modern world order. The assumptions of sovereignty, diplomatic immunity, and so on, which were necessary to the foundation of what structure were in fact originally developed by clerics, and owed much to the assumptions of a universal world order which they had inherited from the Middle Ages.[36]

In Islamic states, which comprise 41 countries stretching today from North Africa through the Middle East to Malaysia and Indonesia in South-East Asia, as well as down into Central and West Africa, religious teaching does not distinguish between a religious and a secular sphere of interest.[37] Belief was immutable and allowed relatively slight variation by the teaching of individual mullahs. The ruler was Commander of the Faithful, so to this day civil–military relations operate within the religious dimension. The duty to wage war on behalf of the faith was taught as one of its fundamental articles, and may indeed in turn have influenced the militarisation of Christianity which took place so conspicuously between the fall of Rome and the time of the Crusades. Education, which in Europe had been secularized for the benefit of the state, remained essentially directed towards transmitting a religious orthodoxy. Its early promise of flowering of science and technology was curtailed by the break-up of centralised political authority and the increasing militarisation of life in general. Ironically, the major part of the benefit of this flowering therefore flowed westwards to humanize and enlighten Christian lands of Western Europe. The re-establishment of imperial authority by the Ottoman Turks finally put an end to the possibility of alternative ideas. Finally, in our own time the revival of religious fundamentalism within Islam, which began in southern Arabia in the first years of the twentieth century, has gained new force, and by stressing just those elements of Islam which least favour the possibility of fruitful change threaten to arrest the further development of communication between the Islamic states and the rest of the world.[38]

The effect of Buddhism, widely practised in India, China and South-East Asia has been somewhat different. Buddhism lacks the concept of deity central to other major religions, so it did not necessarily imply a single world order of divine origin embodied in one specific code of behaviour. It also lacked authoritative interpretation of such a code, in the form of the religious hierarchy of Christianity or Islam. Its spread was not a matter of military conquest but of proselytization by monks who travelled on their own initiative over vast distances and taught the virtues of withdrawal from the secular world. The major schools of thought within Buddhism, the Theravada in South and South-East Asia, and the Mahayana in north India, Tibet, China, Japan, Korea and Nepal, did not become oppressive religious orthodoxies, in the manner of Christianity or Islam, but their relative lack of cohesion had two very different results. On the one hand, Buddhism was able to adapt to very different situations and circumstances from those in which it had originated. On the other, it was able to integrate itself as a system of though with pre-existing religions in a fashion denied to religions of a more elaborated doctrine—in Indian and in Thailand with Hinduism, in China with Confucianism and Taoism, and in Japan with the worship of the emperor and Shinto. In political terms this meant that warring dynasties could conduct their feuds in countries in which the majority of the inhabitants remained essentially peaceful, and different concepts of world order could co-exist each of them regarded as being to some extent imperfect but neither totally superseding the other.[39]

The very different world orders implied by each of these three systems necessarily has had its effect on the way in which the states which have formed within them conduct foreign policy and regard their obligations towards one another, the way in which they communicate with each other and the extent to which they can be said to have interests and ideas in common. We must not forget, however, that at the edges of each of these spheres of influence other consequences flowed from the absence of certain acceptance. Thus Christianity was carried with great vigour into North, Central and South America by the Spanish conquerors, meeting with no effective challenge from an organized religious system which they were not capable of beating down by force of arms. It has not been totally unchanged by the process, but the change has been in the direction of making it a more assured support of the notion of unity, authority and stability. In Africa, where competing Christian denominations reduced the credibility of the whole exercise, Islam has expanded further during the twentieth century, but the Arabs themselves, with their record as slavers, have not won popularity and remain distrusted. This in turn put bounds to the further southern expansion of a religion whose capacity of proselytization had already proved to be remarkable. The Sahara Desert, therefore, effectively marks a break between the Islamic and the Christian spheres of influence. Nevertheless, in recent years, as between Islamic Sudan and Christian Ethiopia, it has been apparent that the old stresses are still very much present, and that the allegiance of religious groups is an important factor in the stability of regimes and the extent to which they can form foreign policy objectives.

PUBLIC OPINION

It is not at all clear how far in most societies we can conceive of society and public opinion apart from those who are articulated, and in pre-modern societies this tends to mean

government itself, and it does form the 'attitudinal prism' and so contribute to the process of policy-making.[41]

ECONOMIC STRUCTURES

At the same time, it has to be said that other forms of influence may also be brought to bear through these channels which are less attractive. The most important of these is the power of major financial interests. It is one of the extraordinary beliefs of some individuals in the United States, Britain and the Western Europe generally that the economic system is in some way independent of government, and that the economic sphere and the political sphere are naturally separate and should be kept separate. The kindest thing that can be said about this is that it exhibits a complete misapprehension of the role of the government in the economic process. Economics is the study of the process of production, distribution and exchange within a society, and since approximately 700 BC all such processes of exchange in developed societies have depended on the existence of a circulating medium, namely money. to which all values can be reduced and which facilitates this process of exchange. It does not seem to be understood that the value of money only exists because value is attributed to it by a government; that the invention of money, indeed, was the realisation that the authority of a government could facilitate the process of exchange by certifying that a particular object was worth a certain amount in terms of exchange. It is therefore quite impossible, given that the government is the guarantor of the medium of exchange, to separate economics from politics, since without the political structure economics, in the sense in which we understand it, cannot exist at all.[42] Moreover, once a medium of exchange was established, governments did not find it long before they found it desirable also to regulate the way in which exchange took place, by establishing markets, inspecting weights and measures, preventing disputes over bargains, enforcing a legal contract and undertaking certain public works, without which the economy could not function to the benefit of all those involved. This, Adam Smith, who is often cited as a prophet of the minimal state on a rather cursory reading of *The Wealth of Nations,* specifically recognized:

First, the duty of protecting the society from the violence and invasion of other independent societies; secondly, the duty of protecting, as far as possible, every member of the society from the injustice or oppression of every other member of it, or the duty of establishing an exact administration of justice; and, thirdly, the duty of erecting and maintaining certain public works and certain public institutions which it can never be for the interest of any individual, or small number of individuals, to erect and maintain; because the profit could never repay the expense to any individual or small number of individuals, though it may frequently do much more than repay it to a great society.[43]

From the beginning, these economic functions of government took place within an international context. The establishment of a monetary standard, in other words, was not done simply to facilitate exchange within the area covered by the sovereignty of the ruler concerned, in this case Croesus, King of Lydia. It also established a standard which was recognized by traders outside as being that established by the King of Lydia. Rival standards were established in Greece at Aegina and Euboea, and later at Athens. Within a very short space of time, they had been related to one another in the ordinary process of trade and barter, which proceeded to spread over a wider and wider area, facilitated by the political structure upon which it was dependent. It is therefore not possible to say that there ever has been a period in which exchange took place solely within the context of single national authority, and consequently international relations has always involved economic exchange. Indeed, from an early stage, the advance of economic contacts has tended to run in front of the establishment of the political ones, and in due course to lay the foundation for them.

The situation of modern new states is not therefore itself new. States have to accept the operation of the economic system as they find it. Trade is conducted in a number of standards, one of which, the United States dollar, at the present moment happens to dominate the others. The ascendancy of the dollar as a means of exchange, however, does not stem from the fact that it has the authority of its government outside its borders, rather it is because it is recognized for the purposes of exchange as being one to which all others can be related. This process of relationship is not done by the governments concerned, it is done instead by a network of financial institutions which in the process of making these decisions extend the political influence of the governments concerned along new and possibly unintended channels.

A government wishing to trade within this system has first to establish its creditworthiness within the structure; second, it must authorize financial institutions to develop so that a standard can be established; and, third, it must ensure that conditions of trading are maintained in its dealings with the outside world which encourage other states and sub-national entities who wish to do business with it or with its citizens. Failure to recognize these simple facts has been the cause of a great deal of trouble for governments of new states. With the emphasis on the assertion of political sovereignty, they have forgotten that they cannot legislate abroad the way they do at home, and they have attempted to blackmail and bamboozle the international financial system in to doing what they want, rather than by abiding by its rules and establishing their own position in it. It is understandable that they should wish to do so, since at first sight the system is complex and intricate, its term of credit seem harsh and the terms of trade seem to favour those countries that sell expensive manufactured goods rather than those that, as do most Third World countries, rely on the export of basic primary products. This has given rise in turn among their numbers for the demand for a New International Economic Order (NIEO) which will redress the balance in favour of producers as against consumers, and debtors as against creditors.[44]

Here we are only concerned, for the moment, with the impact that this system has on the process of decision-making in foreign policy. To begin with, it implies that a government can only use so much power in foreign relations as it is able to finance. Second, and more importantly, it means that no decisions can be taken in international relations without consultation with the relevant branches of government concerned with financial questions, the ministries of finance and the economy. Moreover, these organizations themselves spend much of their time in a process of intercommunication with their opposite numbers of other countries which establishes in effect a secondary diplomatic net, independent of the processes of diplomacy but in some respects equally important from a point of view of international relations. Except in countries of very strongly centralized economies, these processes operate to a considerable extent independently of others, and consequently are often overlooked.

4 How Foreign Policy is Made

FOREIGN SERVICES

There are similarities between foreign services which stem from two different sets of causes: the need, on the one hand, to engage in the international game of diplomacy, and the tendency, on the other, to maintain foreign-policy making as to some extent independent of the changing nature of government. In any case, most new states have inherited colonial traditions of foreign-policy administration. It is therefore important to understand what these are.

Diplomacy was and is shaped by the European tradition as it has grown up by steady increments since 1648.[1] Initially the principal states engaged in the European system were monarchies, and the basic assumptions about the way in which diplomacy should be conducted stem from this assumption. The monarch was a sovereign, independent and owing no subservience to higher authority. Consequently, his representatives were treated as being the sovereign himself in person, and granted reciprocally, by the states to which they were accredited, sovereign privileges and immunities for themselves, their staffs, their families and their belongings. This tradition has proved a valuable one to the maintenance of the structure of diplomacy, since in the absence of such a reciprocal observance of such immunities, it would be difficult, in the absence of a single world authority, for a system of communication of this type to exist between nations at all. This said, it is undeniably true that in modern times some of these privileges and immunities do sometimes appear somewhat archaic. When the traffic of, say, London or Paris is brought to a halt by the cars of diplomatic personnel who ignore local parking regulations, and when minor diplomatic personnel of obscure countries blatantly violate the laws of the country to which they are accredited and engage in espionage or activity of a criminal nature, then much ill feeling may be occasioned. Particular bitterness, for example, was caused in London by the shooting of a woman police constable by person or persons unknown from the Libyan 'People's Bureau' in 1984. The British authorities were punctilious in their observance of the obligations of the international system, and having previously conceded their diplomatic status, allowed those in the Bureau at the time of the incident to depart without searching their diplomatic baggage as laid down by the Vienna Convention of 1960. This added greatly to the public irritation but was seen by the government concerned as being necessary for the maintenance of the system of international diplomacy as a whole and its own diplomatic interests in particular.[2]

This traditional structure of diplomacy was associated with a particular sort of élite, a career foreign service, initially funded by its own private resources, which moved through the world of international diplomacy with an apparent effortlessness born of its cosmopolitan background and its peculiar facility in the understanding of foreign languages. This tradition has survived well into the twentieth century. It has even been imitated, to some extent, by a power with less interest in maintaining it, the United States, where from the beginning the requirements of a democratic policy-making process and a career diplomatic service have clashed in a way that has foreshadowed the problems of later new states and led to some bitterness. Historically, it was the Republicans in the United States, starting with Theodore Roosevelt, who realized the need for a professional foreign service which would have continuity beyond four or eight years of a president's office, and it was the Democrats who believed in the application of the 'spoils system' to the making of foreign policy, as to all else.[3] The result has been a somewhat uneasy compromise with the greater part of policy-making in the hands of a professional civil service, but the major embassies in the more important states have been held by political appointees, often appointed not because of their particular expertise but because of their wealth and the extent of their contributions to the ruling political party.

Like the United States, other new states have tended to use ambassadorial posts as rewards for political influence or for political contributions. Unlike the United States, they have also used them, beginning initially with the Latin American countries, as honourable posts to which to exile awkward political rivals.[4] The use of diplomatic exile in such a way undoubtedly helped lessen the internal faction-fighting of these states, though at the cost of creating a tradition of diplomatic asylum (i.e. the right to take refuge in one another's embassies in case of internal disturbance), which made political unrest itself a privileged activity of an élite group, which was predominantly, but not exclusively, military. In the Latin American countries the right of diplomatic exile, which is not recognised in other parts of the world, has actually been enshrined in international law by conventions guaranteeing the right of asylum.[5]

Unlike most other members of a state bureaucracy whose careers lie entirely within their own country, the members of of a foreign service must expect to spend a considerable amount of time abroad. Typically, short periods abroad (say three years at a time) alternate with somewhat longer periods in the foreign ministry. The periods abroad are spent in a series of posts of increasing rank, culminating, in successful cases, with the holding of major ambassadorships to important countries or to the United Nations. Such periods abroad may be highly remunerative, but the importance of this kind of structure goes far beyond that. Its most important characteristic is that the career diplomat spends a substantial amount of time in the rather peculiar and esoteric atmosphere of a foreign posting, in which he has more in common with his fellow diplomats from other countries and the government to which he is accredited than he has with his own country's nationals. In consequence, diplomats on overseas postings tend to develop a view of the world as seen from their own particular appointments,[6] and may well, in collaboration with their diplomatic colleagues, come to co-ordinate their views in a way that has important implications for the foreign-policy makers at home, who are thus denied, to some extent, the possibility of alternative points of view.

In modern times this tendency has been much offset by the

downgrading of diplomatic positions implicit in the improve-
ment of communications. No longer do foreign ministries have
to wait weeks, or possibly months, for the report of their
diplomatic agents abroad to reach them. Now much of their
information comes by electronic means and is instantly
available for scrutiny and analysis. More significantly much of
it now comes, as does that of other people, from the media. Use
of the media is in itself, therefore, part of the diplomatic
process, and a foreign minister, for political reasons, may well
choose to make an important diplomatic statement on
television or give a press conference rather than engage in the
lengthy formalities of diplomatic exchange. Nor is this
tendency to make pronouncements on foreign policy restricted
to foreign ministers: presidents, prime ministers and indeed
other officials with separate but overlapping responsibilities,
enjoy access to the media in a way that they do not through the
diplomatic network. More subtly, they can use this access to
the media to 'plant' stories about other countries in such a way
as to further their own political objectives; an excellent
example of such skilled use of the media being the attempt in
1985 of elements in the French government to transfer
responsibility for the blowing-up of the Greenpeace ship
Rainbow Warrior in Auckland harbour, by planting stories
suggesting that the British Secret Service were the real culprits.[7]
Dependence on the media as a source of information for
politicians and especially foreign ministers, accordingly has its
dangers. For though they are open to a great deal of
information, they are not informed by that network of what the
actual diplomatic position of their country is, and it may well
be that their initiatives, however well intentioned, will
therefore present serious problems to the professional makers
of foreign policy.

The third characteristic of a foreign service is its adherence
to precedents and principles. Foreign service has grown up as
a branch of the law, concerned with forms and precedents.[8]
Indispensable to its effective exercise is a detailed knowledge of
the past history of relations with all other relevant states, the
record of diplomatic exchange on a wide series of issues and a
series of annual reports as to the state of relations between the
country concerned and one's own. Obviously it is impossible to

maintain such a structure unless the Foreign Office itself is compartmentalized; typically, this compartmentalization takes the form of area responsibilities, relatively low-ranking foreign service officials being responsible for 'desks' concerned with one or more of a group of countries. Important major activities covering more than one country—economic, legal, and so on—are dealt with and co-ordinated by yet other desks with functional specializations. Above desk level, stretches the hierarchy of senior officials with regional and central co-ordinating responsibilities stretching all the way up to the minister, who as a political appointee, is responsible for ensuring that the operations of the ministry are in accordance with the political programme of the government which he serves.[9]

Behind all this lies the backing of a system of records. In the case of a recently independent state, however, the model lacks this essential foundation. There are no records, because diplomatic activity has not previously been a function of the government concerned, because the government itself did not previously exist. Not only, then, is the system of records lacking, but so too is the collective memory which informs policy-making and ensures that it makes some of the more obvious mistakes. Even in the case of countries that have been independent for a longer time, war or natural catastrophe—earthquake, hurricane or attacks of termites—has on a number of occasions resulted in the serious loss of national records.[10] All this is, of course, to assume that the records were there in the first place. There is, as we shall see later, strong evidence that the diplomatic agents of many Third World countries regard their positions essentially as sinecures. Their job, as they see it, is to look important, to go to diplomatic receptions, to exchange conversation with important people who they would not otherwise meet and to behave superficially in the fashion which they associate with the diplomatic agents whom they have seen visit their areas in the past. They do not devote a substantial amount of time to understanding the societies in which they are living, and they do not leave a foundation of adequate records either for their successors or for the foreign ministries on whose behalf they are supposed to be acting. The history of relations with newly independent countries of the past, therefore, is one of repeated attempts to reopen questions which had been regarded as diplomatically settled, to fail to recognize decisions that constituted important precedents for the future, or to inform their foreign ministries adequately about the likely consequences of actions which their governments might be proposing to take. Indeed, in some cases, it is apparent that diplomatic officials were not informed as to the action that was intended, as, for example, in the case of Japanese representatives in the United States before Pearl Harbor.[11]

HOW FOREIGN POLICY IS MADE AND WHAT FOR

The formal agency responsible in all countries for the making of foreign policy is generically termed the ministry of foreign affairs. In practice, the title of this ministry varies considerably from one country to another, even within the European state system in which the structures originally arose. In fact, the origin of a regular diplomatic service goes back even further, to the trading nation of Venice, whose power once stretched from the top of the Adriatic as far south as Crete and as far east as the Levant. The need of a trading nation to maintain regular diplomatic contacts to ensure the safety of its personnel was enhanced by the encroaching presence of the Ottoman Empire, and in consequence it was Venice that experimentally established the conventions of diplomatic intercourse with a non-European nation. It was not an easy task, and more than one Venetian ambassador lost his life in the service of his country before it was realized in Istanbul that this reaction was diplomatically unproductive.

From this rather unpropitious beginning, the system has now become worldwide. It first spread by way of the Italian city-states to the great nations of northern Europe. Niccolò Machiavelli was a diplomat at a time when the Italian city-state system began to be replaced by the new order of the greater European states, and his writings continue to have much relevance for diplomacy today. The emphasis in *The Prince* (1513) on the safety and security of the state, the amoral use of state power to further its ends, and the necessity for the Prince to be guided by a different set of criteria from other human beings, is one which seems to have been learnt all too effectively by his successors. But for a long time north European diplomatic practice remained relatively backward and their relations with one another intermittent. The Dutch and, following them, the English under William III, appointed consuls to deal with the intricacies of trade, but these, with the consular services of which they form part, were regarded and continue to be regarded as having a lesser functional status. It was only at the end of the seventeenth century that embassies ceased to be a delegation appointed on a special occasion and became a regular presence at a foreign court, charged with handling all manner of negotiations. The separation of domestic and foreign policy was not, indeed, necessarily seen as the most logical one: in Britain between 1681 and 1782 the ancient office of secretary of state, which included the conduct of foreign relations among its duties, was divided, but it was divided between a northern and a southern secretary, the northern being responsible for northern England and relations with northern Europe and the southern with southern England and relations with southern Europe.[12] It was only after 1782 that the present separation between Home and Foreign Affairs became established. The joining of these two functions is still retained to a modest extent in the duties of the United States secretary of state which are not concerned with foreign relations.[13]

At this time the notion of a formal bureaucratic structure, in support either of the minister of foreign affairs or of the ambassadors and ministers appointed by him, did not yet exist. Both those responsible for the conduct of foreign policy at home, and ambassadors overseas, were responsible for the hire of their own assistants, for whose payment they were responsible. In consequence, a career in diplomacy involved having extensive private means, and so the precedent was set that diplomacy became a giant system of outdoor relief for the upper classes. Something of this tradition, interestingly enough, has been carried forward into the foreign services of all modern countries. The United States is no exception. Since, as we have already seen, the spoils system was the norm in the nineteenth century, and until the time of Theodore Roosevelt there was no provision for a career structure in the State Department, the Department attracted only wealthy political appointees who came from a rather limited number of schools and universities, and in view of the replacement of the personnel every four years, or at a change of administration, continuity was notably lacking. For forty-seven years, under twenty-two secretaries of state, the sole source of continuity within the State Department was supplied by a single senior clerk, Alvey A. Adee, who retained the knowledge of the precedents and who gave to the United States' foreign policy a greater degree of continuity than it received from any other source.[14]

Some of the Latin American states, which as the first of the new states we may take as examples for later ones, were influenced by the United States model. Others, in particular that of the Empire of Brazil, were influenced, like their contemporaries, the new Balkan States of Greece, Serbia and Rumania, by European models. It is noteworthy that to this day the Itamaraty, the Foreign Ministry of Brazil, is regarded as by far the most professional and efficient foreign service in Latin America. It is the only major institution which survived virtually intact after the military revolution of 1964; indeed, as one author has shown, it was from the Itamaraty that personnel were drawn to staff other key departments of the military goverment. The professionalization of the Itamaraty owes a certain amount to the inheritance of the Portuguese traditions through the empire, but the modern foreign service of Brazil owes even more to the impetus of one remarkable character, the Baron of Rio Branco.

So important in the making of foreign policy is continuity that foreign ministers who stay in power for more than a few years have an unusual opportunity to influence foreign affairs. Rio Branco had had virtually no previous diplomatic experience, with the exception of a short spell as Brazilian vice-consul in Liverpool, which had left him with an abiding distaste for the United Kingdom. Nevertheless, during the ten years between 1902 and 1912, when he was foreign minister of his country, he was able to sign boundary treaties with all of Brazil's neighbours except one, Paraguay. By this process he was able to extend the bounds of his country much further outwards than would otherwise have been the case, taking advantage in particular of the endemic conflict and dissension in the neighbouring Spanish-speaking states.

The Rio Branco tradition of professionalization was strengthened by Brazil's participation in the League of Nations (from which it eventually withdrew when it was denied a permanent seat on the Council) and in the Second World War—in which it was the only South American state to take part as a combatant, sending an expeditionary force to the Italian front and, in due course, taking a leading role in the foundation of the United Nations.[15]

The foreign service of Chile also has traditionally been highly professional, though under the current military government, which has placed its country virtually in the position of a 'pariah state' by its treatment of its political opponents, this professionalization is much less effective than it might otherwise have been. Nevertheless, there are marked continuities in Chilian foreign policy between the pre-1973 and post-1973 governments, and these must be attributed substantially to the existence of an efficient career service. By contrast, Chile's neighbour across the Andes, Argentina, has a very different reputation:

Argentina long has had the reputation of conducting its foreign affairs in an unprofessional manner and of coming to the diplomatic bargaining table ill-prepared. Not too long ago, a former foreign minister told me that he had been unable to find critical background papers in the ministerial archives and that it was his common experience to attend international meetings without the benefit of briefing memoranda summarising the historical antecedents of the issues under discussion, the sort of memoranda that dot the records of the Brazilian and Chilian foreign ministries, not to mention the National Archives of the United States and the Public Record Office of Great Britain.[16]

The reasons for this are concisely set out by Milenky. Even the career officers are so badly paid that they generally hold another job, so that the workforce is essentially part-time. In addition, the staff have been repeatedly purged by successive governments, as in 1974 by the incoming Perón government, and again in 1976 by Videla, who also appointed two army captains, a naval captain and two air force captains to 'assist' the foreign minister in re-evaluating foreign policy. Continuity exists, and personnel have in fact been drawn from the foreign ministry to staff other departments, but the continuity is at a low level, and the individuals concerned have little or no influence on the central policy-making process.[17]

The advantage of the Latin American countries from the point of view of the student is that their relatively long independent existence and the relatively developed state of their archives enables us to test the efficiency of their diplomatic service by actual inspection of the documents. From this we can confirm four principal phenomena of the foreign services of new states already alluded to in Chapter 1, which appear to be widely applicable and which should be taken as being the norm in the foreign policies of new states.

Lack of a serious programme of work is the most important. Diplomatic relations are established with major states often very largely for cosmetic reasons. It does not follow that there is any direct diplomatic contact between the two countries concerned, merely that the new state wishes to signal its emergence into the international community by establishing formal diplomatic relations. This desire is compounded in the case of the decision-makers of the new state by their desire to be seen to be recognized as equals by the international community. Recognition is much more significant to new states than it is to existing ones, and more significant to states that have unstable regimes than it is to those that have an established degree of political continuity. Recognition, in short, is something which is extended from existing important states to new unimportant states or regimes, and in consequence is something which is highly valued, perhaps to excess.[18]

In the case of new states, the search for recognition begins long before independence, and the future foreign policy of the new state may well be set by the personal friendships and political alliances made at that time by its future leader and his political organization. Thus, as McMaster observes, the future pattern of Malawi's foreign policy, and the expectations of it by other African states, was set by conflict between the relative isolation of Dr Banda and the radical internationalism of the younger Kanyama Chiume, a personal friend of Oscar Kambona, later foreign minister of Tanzania, and Tom Mboya of Kenya, spokesman of pan-Africanism, who acted as the roving ambassador of the independence movement:

When the State of Emergency was declared in Nyasaland, Chiume was in Britain, and he did not return home until May 1960. During that time he visited the United States, Iceland, Ghana, Tunisia, Ethiopia, the Sudan, Jordan, Egypt and Sweden, publicizing the Nyasaland case and raising funds for the defence of the detainees. Most of his expenses were paid by the governments and political parties of the countries he visited, and in Ghana the governing Convention People's Party donated £5,000 to help retain Sir Dingle Foot to act for the detainees.[19]

On independence, Banda was to adopt a firmly pro-Western stance which owed much to his own personal conservatism and disrespect for his younger lieutenants, whom he kept busy roaming the world and well out of harm's way.[20] In any case, pan-Africanism, once independence was secured, was much more immediately attractive to the larger and more powerful states, like Ghana and later Nigeria, who saw in it a method of projecting their own power abroad. The founding of the Organization of African Unity did preserve the ideal of pan-Africanism, and met the immediate problem of the divisions disclosed by the Congo crisis of 1960–62. Not only was the continent divided ideologically between the radical Casablanca group and the conservative Monrovia group, but the Monrovia group was divided linguistically, the Brazzaville group of francophone countries forming a distinct bloc within it and retaining in addition strong formal ties with de Gaulle's France. The solution—to create a very weak umbrella organization that in effect preserved the colonial divisions to avoid exacerbating them—was perhaps far from ideal, but it did work.[21]

The foreign services of the new African states were drawn from the members of the independence movements that had created them, and, not surprisingly, political reasons were paramount in their choice. Diplomatic personnel overseas, including representatives before the UN and its agencies, are appointed for a number of reasons, not all of them particularly relevant. They may be appointed, as already noted in the case of the United States, for internal political reasons, as rewards for political supporters of fund-raisers. They may be used as a kind of refuse bin for political opponents, or potential troublesome elements, such as military commanders of high seniority who might be inspired to engage in a conspiracy against the government if they did not receive sufficient reward at a sufficiently long distance from the national capital. Or, third, they may be earnest career functionaries who are given the job because no one else wants it very much, or as a reward for long service, and who, lacking independent political bases, are therefore not likely to cut very much ice with the staff of the foreign minister. In any case, the relations between countries even of some intrinsic importance may not be very significant when they are a long distance apart. As John Kenneth Galbraith observes in his memoirs:

In India during my time there were some 50 ambassadors, including the High Commissioners, as they are called, from the other Commonwealth countries. They were a spectacular example of what economists, following Joan Robinson of the University of Cambridge, call disguised unemployment. The ambassadors from Argentina or Brazil could not have had more than a day's serious work a month. The more deeply engaged diplomats from Scandinavia, Holland, Belgium or Spain could discharge their essential duties in one day a week. Others from some of the lesser Latin American or Levantine republics were more heavily engaged but in genteel operations in the black market—in particular, the importation under diplomatic cover of watches, gold, pharmaceuticals and other items of high value and small bulk, which were at a premium in India. Thus these envoys pieced out their inadequate official earnings.[22]

Lack of systematic reporting is a natural consequence of a basically defective diplomatic system. As noted above, the major powers ensure that their envoys periodically return more or less detailed reports of the condition at their posts. To historians, indeed, such reports are of great value in filling out the details of internal politics, and it is easy to tell the difference between reports that are full, detailed and meaningful and ones which are merely perfunctory. Such a structure of regular reports has two advantages. First of all, it ensures that the envoy does in fact pay attention to the range of conditions which are relevant and not simply concentrate on those details which are merely of interest or amusement to him. Second, the structure of regular reporting compels both him and the staff of the foreign ministry regularly to review the state of relations with the country concerned. They can, moreover, in a diplomatic crisis, refer back to the immediate past reports for background information on how the crisis came into existence. This is undoubtedly of the greatest possible value when it comes to making decisions, and the lack of such reports, or the failure to consider such reports, is often responsible for ill-informed and hence panicky and dangerous crisis reactions.

Ironically, the practice of building up such reports originated at a time at which communications were bad and accurate information was generally deficient. It is therefore probable that many modern Third World countries have not effectively developed it. The reasons are obvious. The greater powers find newspaper and similar sources very inadequate as a source of information about the lesser ones. On the other hand, the doings of the greater powers are extensively reported throughout the world. It is therefore improbable that diplomatic envoys in general will be required to maintain the high level of reporting of affairs in the greater powers for a Third World government that they ought to do, and yet, it is quite evident that dependence on press reports and similar sources is not likely to be of sufficient foundation for the understanding of the political reasons behind the decisions of the major powers. A major exception is India, where the effective decentralization of decision-making to the India Office left the newly independent country a substantial archive of information which most other states would envy.[23]

Possession of records does not of course imply that they will necessarily be consulted, and the temptation must always be present to give undue weight to snippets of information, not because of their intrinsic value but because they have been hard to get or support preconceptions. Evidence at first hand is of course lacking as yet, but there very clearly existed a serious deficiency of understanding of British political process and British policy-making in the Argentine Foreign Ministry immediately before the Falklands crisis of 1982. In Carlos Moneta's words, 'the President himself, General Galtieri, publicly acknowledged that a military reaction was not expected from the British, and, in the event there was such a reaction, it was expected to be extremely moderate and designed only to reinforce London's negotiation strategy'.[24]

However, as Moneta points out, the military strategists made a much more serious error in failing to foresee accurately

concerned. But the informality of such records, the need for secrecy and the fact that such records as survive are likely to be treated as the private property of the individuals concerned, means that relatively few of them survive. Yet it is of course always possible that at this crucial stage before the state has formally come into existence important commitments have been made either directly or implicitly on matters of major public importance. It was, for example, in the early years of the Mexican revolution a continual accusation among all factions that others were seeking funds and support from the major oil companies in return for concessions.[26] It can be assumed that such bargains might well be made in modern circumstances also. It is not likely that, if they are, the records will be made easily available.

The new state is also affected by decisions made on its behalf by the colonial power before withdrawal. The extent to which these records survive depends a great deal on the nature of the colonial power and the way in whch it came to leave. Generalization here is difficult. Once independence has taken place, then an archive can be begun and records built up. Obviously, until several years have gone by a final system is unlikely to be established, even given the unlikely possibility that the archives will be staffed by trained archivists who have already worked in archives of international standing. In addition, the technical assistance necessary to maintain records is likely to be lacking. At least today, the technical facilities exist both to copy earlier records and to ensure the conservation of those that have survived. Two problems are familiar to historians of colonial states: the first exemplified by the example of Guyana, where many of the relevant records, owing to changes in European diplomacy, are to be found not in Britain but in the Netherlands; and that exemplified by Belize, where many of the earlier documents have perished altogether as a result of storm, flood or attacks of termites.[27] Even the oldest diplomatic archives in the world, those of the Vatican, are being slowly devoured by a voracious purple fungus which the Holy See lacks the financial resources to combat effectively.

In default of an efficient record system, the staff of the foreign minister are unlikely to be able to give effective guidance to their diplomatic agents overseas, and still less are they likely to be able to maintain the effective co-ordination of policies involving several agencies or several countries. It is of the greatest significance to any new state that it should ensure that its archives are in fact effectively maintained from the earliest possible moment, and funds should be given over to this purpose; it is, however, extremely unlikely that they will be. Fourth, and lastly, the operation of foreign ministries and diplomatic personnel is hampered insofar as the traditions of diplomacy result in them being relatively unconcerned about military or economic policy. Military autonomy in the new states ensures that military policy-making is effectively separated from civilian, but it is at least a tradition of diplomacy that military attachés are placed in missions overseas in order to maintain bilateral links with their opposite numbers in other countries. To this extent, therefore, the system already takes account of the need to co-ordinate civilian and military policy, even if it does not do so in all cases or always very effectively. The tradition, however, is that military personnel deal with the military. When, as in Argentina after 1976, a foreign ministry is purged by an incoming military government, it does not follow that military personnel given diplomatic positions will necessarily take up the range of civilian duties which a career foreign officer would be expected to undertake.[28] Least of all are they likely to do so in the economic sphere. In fact, in practice the rivalry between foreign ministries and finance ministries means that a great deal of diplomatic significance that takes place in the economic sphere is in fact undertaken directly by ministries of finance. But ministers of finance in new states tend to fall into one of two categories: either they are academic economists without much experience of the real world of economic management, or alternatively they are former presidents of the central bank who have been selected by the government of the day as non-political instruments of their will, under the erroneous impression that bankers necessarily know something about economic management, which is far from always being the case. In either case they lack the political base to hold their position when the going gets tough. Recent Latin American governments in Argentina, Brazil and Chile, therefore, have been characterized by a rapid turnover of ministers of the economy and finance, with the unsurprising result that the countries concerned are quite unable to meet either the economic targets set them by the IMF or the rather more modest expectations of the international financial community.[29]

To sum up, therefore, the character of the foreign policy generated by a machine of this kind is marked by three major characteristics. First of all, it is intermittent, it lacks continuity and policy is liable to change without notice or without adequate thought. Second, because in many cases the relationships between two countries do not involve anything of great substance, they tend to be strongly influenced by non-material factors such as pride, honour or dignity. Third, they tend to be reactive; that is to say, the foreign-policy maker of a Third World state lacking continuity and a real basis for association of policies with the country concerned is likely only to make a policy decision in relation to it when that country does something which appears to call for notice.

The purpose of the foreign policy thus generated is much more difficult to determine. On a rational actor model it should be designed in order to ensure the best interests of the state concerned. The evidence from Third World states, and given that their policy tends to be reactive rather than positive, is that this is in no way an adequate explanation. The organizational process model would suggest that the principal purpose of Third World foreign policy was to maintain the institution of the foreign ministry and the well-being of the élite which staff it, and there is, as we shall see, a great deal of evidence that this is the case. As a subset of explanations it can be seen that the maintenance of the institution of the foreign ministry also involved, at the level of bureaucratic politics, the well-being of those members in the ministry of foreign affairs. Where a basis for rational action exists and the rational actor model is appropriate, it tends to be on one issue at a time, and indeed if there is more than one issue at a time, one of the two or more issues will be given absolute priority over the others, as the system is not capable of accommodating more than one at a time.

Important decisions of this kind will therefore not be taken in the foreign ministry, but in the presidential palace by the president himself, generally in close consultation only with a very few advisers. In fact, President Sadat of Egypt consulted no one either in 1971 when he'decided to enter into union with Libya and Syria in the shortlived Federation of Arab Republics, or, more seriously, in 1973, when he selected 6 October as the date for launching Operation Badr, the start of the Six-Day War. He consulted only the foreign minister, Ismail Fahmi, when he decided to go to Jerusalem in November 1977, and when Fahmi resigned, appointed Mohamed Riad, his deputy to succeed him. The fact that mattered was that the decision was supported by the minister of war and commander-in-chief, Mohamed Gamassy, who expressed the support of the armed forces in a good-will message and turned up to show his public support for the president at his departure.[30]

Conversely, in Indonesia Sukarno's decision to oppose the creation of Malaysia in 1963 by 'confrontation—a typical euphemism for war in the jungle of Sarawak and Sabah (North Kalimantan)—was widely regarded in the West as simply a nationalistic bid to distract attention from the internal economic failings of his government. However, the policy was in fact strongly supported by the Indonesian military establishment, then led by General Nasution. When in 1965 the policy had failed to work, and he was being increasingly pressed by the Indonesian Communist Party (PKI) to form a workers and peasants militia, ostensibly for service in Malaysia, the armed forces were branded as 'capitalist bureaucrats' for opposing the idea, and a group of conspirators began planning the abortive putsch of 1 October which was to lead to the fall of Sukarno, the assumption of power by the army and the massacre of hundreds of thousands of Indonesians on suspicion of being communists. Political power since that time has been grasped firmly by the military junta which rules Indonesia and which, having ended confrontation, has taken upon itself to modernize the economy and bring the country into firm alignment with the West.[31]

As the Indonesian example also shows, where the military hold power, regional political changes that affect their perception of national security will affect both their external and internal policy. As Alfred Stepan demonstrates, this was particularly marked in the case of the military government in Peru after 1968. In the first phase of its existence, its stance of controlled left-wing reform was easily maintained as there were no significant external threats on Peru's borders. Chile moved from a reforming Christian Democratic government, under Eduardo Frei, to a radical socialist one under Salvador Allende; Bolivia imitated Peru's policies under the brief regime of General Torres; Ecuador, whose border losses in 1941 still rankled, was still weak and Brazilian expansion was still far away. By 1974 things had begun to change drastically: Brazil was booming, Allende had fallen and Torres was in exile, pro-Brazilian governments were in power in Bolivia, Chile, Paraguay and Uruguay, while the Argentine government, under the nominal leadership of 'Isabel' Perón, had moved to the right. Worst of all, Ecuador was booming too, and with the money from its new oil revenues was setting to work to build up its air force by buying Mirage interceptors from the French, while as the hundredth anniversary of the War of the Pacific (1889) approached, there was concern lest the Chilean military regime might do a deal with Bolivia that would allow it access to the sea and threaten Lima's control of Tacna. With concern for the foreign-policy environment now paramount, the military pressed for retrenchment in domestic political reform, ultimate withdrawal from the task of government, and a lower profile in foreign policy which would enable them to reduce the extent of their commitments. The serious illness of President Velasco in March 1973 enabled these changes to be accompanied by his removal, which happened, ironically, in the middle of the week that the Group of 77 were meeting in Lima in 1975, when he was displaced by his prime minister, General Morales Bermúdez; the conference was therefore opened by one president and closed by another. Following the change, the radical officers who had been reaching the top of the seniority list were retired before they could become serious contenders for the Presidency.[32]

Hence, in all further discussion of Third World foreign-policy making three things have to be borne in mind. First of all, a Third World state acts for its own reasons, not those of the superpowers, nor even those attributed to it by one or other of the superpowers. Second, just as the superpowers erroneously see Third World states as being like them, so the Third World erroneously see superpowers as being like themselves. The Argentine example is instructive here; it was impossible for Argentine military decision-makers not to regard the armed forces as being the major institution within the United States, just as they would be within Argentina itself—a view, incidentally, improbably supported by members of the peace lobby and those on the far left of American politics. Third, new states generally have a poor perception of the outside world. Even if the ministry of foreign affairs does work efficiently as an organization, there is a strong tendency not to listen to it if it gives the 'wrong information'.

5 Capabilities

The capabilities of a state are, like those of an individual, determined by wealth, status and power. Like an individual, too, a state can 'trade off' any one of these resources against the others.[1] Thus Japan, deprived by the Allies in 1945 of the capacity to wage war, has chosen in the course of time to maximize its wealth. India, a poor country, has sought in the non-aligned movement a world leadership role which has brought it status; to do this, however, it has foregone the possibility of going fully nuclear, a potent and very expensive form of power. And Israel, perceiving itself as threatened by a ring of enemy states, has sought to maximize its power to resist attack. In the search for security, wealth has been dissipated and the country's international position has declined.

None of these three variables is a simple one, but that of power is probably the most misunderstood. Power is not simply military force. It is not necessarily the use or threat of force at all, though in the wild uncertainties of the international system states tend to act as if it were, and spend vast resources arming themselves against all kinds of improbable contingencies. Power is in fact simply the ability to get other states to act in accordance with the policy-maker's goals. Provided they do act as the policy-maker wants, there is no need for this state to resort to military force.

There is, however, a conceptual problem. If state A acts on state B in order to secure a policy objective, how can we determine whether or not that action was responsible for the outcome? The answer is obvious if no change of policy occurs. If a change does occur, the answer is different depending on whether or not state B had other reasons for seeking that policy objective. If it acted in opposition to previously stated

99

positions, it is a reasonable assumption that the action of state B was relevant, but it is still not certain that this was the reason for the change of policy—internal considerations could also have been influential. The result of this dilemma is that states tend to be alternately credited with far more influence than they in fact possess or denied any influence whatsoever on the policy processes of other countries. It is not a problem which can be easily resolved in general terms; it is one which is specific to the actual cases investigated. The further problem of what precisely constitutes an effect, what degree of modification of policy is sufficient to indicate influence, is one which will also have to be tackled. And for many reasons these things are difficult to assess. States, unlike people, live in a geographical relationship to one another which determines many of their capabilities and limitations. People can move but states cannot. Hence many of the variables which we are about to discuss have a very different meaning depending on the location of the states concerned.

Population constitutes the first resource of a state, and one which many new states see as a resource and not as a liability. An excellent example is the case of Brazil whose booming population (119 million at the 1980 census) has been increasing, despite poor health conditions, drought and famine, for many decades at a rate of over 2.5 per cent a year. Successive governments in Brazil, however, have not sought to encourage any system of population limitation, unlike India (population 683 million at the 1981 census) where a programme of compulsory sterilization was introduced during the first period of Indira Gandhi's prime ministership, as the most controversial part of a powerful drive to restrict growth of a population much of which was already starving.[2] In Brazil's case, admittedly, ideological (i.e. religious) considerations might have been a factor were it not for the fact that other Latin American states, also Catholic in religious persuasion, were persuaded that limitation of the population would in fact be a valuable step to take in order to equalise the distribution of economic resources.

However, gross population size is one of the major marks of a great power. It is largely on account of its overwhelming population (estimated in the West at some 1,100 million at the census of 1982) that the People's Republic of China is seen as a possible third superpower.[3] Nothing else to date in its economic structure, capabilities of production or sophistication of technology has been particularly remarkable, and the contrast is made the more striking by the country's close proximity to that technological giant, Japan. Certainly, historically, when arms capabilities were substantially equal, there was a rough correlation between size of population and political influence. States with large populations tended to be regarded as more powerful than states with small populations, if only because of the theoretical ease which which they could put an army in the field. There is, however, a big difference between the gross population size and the ability to arm one's forces, as the case of Brazil shows. Today Brazil has the largest army in Latin America, numbering approximately 182,750. This army is extremely powerful in internal politics, and in 1985 handed over power to civilians after an uninterrupted period of rule of some twenty-one years—a time quite exceptional by the standards of most countries.[4] Yet the army of Brazil, big as it is by Latin American standards, is not much larger than that of Cuba, with a population of only 10 million, is trivial in physical numbers compared with the population of the country which supports it, and in comparison, for example, with the 135,000-strong army of Great Britain, would not form a very remarkable adversary, all other things being equal. Brazil is not therefore a superpower, though it would very much like to be one.

All other things are not equal, though, and a larger population does make it easier to defend a national territory; that is, provided that the numbers involved are not absurdly disproportionate. Britain, with an army of 135,000 has to defend only 93,000 square miles of territory; Peru, with an army of 39,000 (on a population base of only some 14 million), has to defend a national territory of more than 750,000 square miles. Yet because of Peru's geographical situation and the policies of the governments that surround it, it does not feel the need to maintain the gigantic air and sea defence establishment with which Britain backs up its relatively formidable ground forces, and even if it did, it could not easily find the economic resources to do so.[5]

Gross population size can be a disadvantage when the inability to feed that population impairs the economic resources necessary to arm it, and this is far more generally the case in Third World countries. Again there is no direct correlation between size and the ability to arm troops. Libya, for example, although large in area, is by no means the largest state in Africa (that distinction goes to Sudan), has a tiny population (3 million) and is a poor country in all respects but the fact that it has substantial oil resources, but by trading off those oil resources it is able to maintain a disproportionately powerful armed establishment and indeed to support other countries with it.[6] Nigeria, in West Africa, has a much larger population than any other state in Africa. Yet although it maintains substantial armed forces, and has frequently since independence been under a military government, it does not have a belligerent record. Nigeria's large size in terms of population, therefore, is not a guide to its position in the hierarchy of states even though in the regional context it is certainly significant and has rather ill-defined ambitions to exercise a wider role on the continent which led it to send troops to withstand Libyan expansionism in Chad.[7] Again, Nigeria presents a striking contrast with South Africa which although it has a relatively small population and its effective military capability is vested in the tiny white minority in a potentially hostile black majority, nevertheless manages to maintain very much more powerful military forces than those of Nigeria. The problem of divided populations, or substantial ethnic minorities, will be considered further in the next chapter.

TERRITORY

Territorial extent is often viewed as being a sign of status among states. However, as with population, this can be very misleading. It is true that the territorial extent of the Soviet Union is more than twice that of the United States, or indeed of any other country in the world, but this does not mean that the Soviet Union is twice as powerful as the United States. Almost equal in size to the United States is China, which hence is commonly regarded as a potential superpower, but also Brazil and Canada, which are not. In the case of Canada, the disparity between area and population is particularly marked. The United States, comprising the fifty states and the Federal District of Columbia, covers a land area of 3,539,289 square miles with a population at the census of 1980 of 226 millions; Canada with an area of 3,851,809 square miles had a population in 1981 of only 24,343,181.[8] Yet it can be argued that the great territorial extent of Canada, or for that matter of Australia, both of which have relatively small populations, is nevertheless significant in giving them more standing and more capabilities in world politics than otherwise would have been the case.

Part of the reason for this is simply economic. The greater the extent of a country, the more probable it is that it will contain valuable natural resources, and these resources, if exploited, can help bring in a substantial income. But in the case of a new state inadequate mapping and limited exploration often means that there is very little realization of the real value of its territorial possessions. Thus, whereas the United States gained in northern Minnesota by territorial adjustment with Canada a very substantial reserve of iron ore which it was relatively swift to exploit, Mexico lost to the United States in 1848 the entire territory of modern California, which within a year was discovered to be rich in gold and the scene of the famed California Gold Rush. It cannot be doubted that had the value of this area been understood at the time, the Mexican government, however weak, would have endeavoured to obtain a more favourable bargain from the United States.

The desire to exploit natural resources was one of the major reasons for European colonial expansion. It does not follow, however, that the cause of humanity in general will necessarily be any better served by their national control. A Third World state often lacks the resources, capital and expertise to exploit its own resources, but also lacks the patience and foresight to wait until it can do so. In consequence, foreign companies have often been invited back to exploit such resources without reasonable assurance that the people of the country concerned will benefit, and where this has not been done, the country concerned remains a target for the strategic plans of other states with an eye to its natural resources. As late as the early 1960s, states becoming independent still had very little knowledge of the full value of their territorial possessions, unless those possessions had been explored by European or other colonial powers. Now, however, the situation is changing rapidly. Mapping by sophisticated earth satellites enables slight variations in colour of soils or even of vegetation to be used to detect potential ore-bearing territory. Access to this advanced technology, which at the present moment is substantially in the hands of the established powers, can be of great potential value to a Third world country.[9]

It is doubtful, however, if this more accurate knowledge will totally prevent actions such as Morocco's penetration of the eastern Sahara in conjunction with the nominal state of Mauritania,[10] because, for better or for worse, territorial extent still exercises its mystique over politicians and decision-makers. When Argentina and Chile came almost to the point of war in 1977 and 1978 it was over the possession of three utterly valueless islets in the Beagle Channel, which had no conceivable economic value whatsoever, and were of infinitesimal value even from a strategic point of view.[11]

The strategic value of territory, as this reminds us, does not necessarily coincide with its economic value. Possession of territory has various military advantages. Sheer depth of territory is of value in defence against attack by outside powers, unless they enjoy, or suffer from, the possession of advanced military technology in the field of aircraft or rocketry. Depth of territory protected the Soviet Union against the mechanised push of Hitler's armies in 1941, just as historically the plains of Hungary had provided the opportunity for the Austro-Hungarian Empire to defend itself against the incursions of the Turks before they reached the vital centres of political control.[12] Historically, too, the possession of high ground was a great advantage in land-based conflict, and it still is of some value to this day. The most striking example at the present time has been afforded by the acquisition by Israel of effective control over the Golan Heights following the six-Day War in 1967. Previously this strong point, part of Syria, had given the Syrians an opportunity to fire down upon Israeli settlements without fear of effective retaliation. The capture of this territory gave Israel a strategically secure frontier in this region and helped relieve the anxieties of its defenders.[13] Possession of the territory, however, has not yet been ratified by any form of international agreement, and to this extent constitutes a liability to Israel also. If so, it is one which they are prepared to accept for the sake of its advantages.

Nevertheless not all territory is valuable, and in any case value is something that is in itself always hard to define. Some areas of a country, particularly that of the national capital, are of great symbolic and political importance, and loss of these areas would constitute a major blow to the country's credibility as a viable state. On the other hand, large areas of tundra or desert, like the Ogaden or the Western Sahara, have perhaps no intrinsic economic or strategic value, and disputes over such areas, if they are not based on a mistaken perception of their real physical worth, depend on the attribution to them of a symbolic value as representing the overall determination of the state to defend its national territory.

There have been marked changes however in international practice in relation to the drawing of territorial boundaries since 1945. In nineteenth-century Latin America it was belatedly decided in 1848 at the First Congress of Lima, that territorial disputes would be regulated between the independent states on the basis of the Spanish colonial boundaries as at 1 January 1810, a decision known as the *uti possidetis juris*.[14] Unfortunately, by that date, virtually none of these boundaries was intact, and for the rest of the century there continued to be a series of conflicts between neighbouring states in order to secure satisfactory territorial frontiers. Fortunately for the peace of the region the natural geographical obstacles of the Andes, and other major mountain ranges, were effective in preventing the conflicts from being totally destructive, and many of the modern boundaries lie in areas remote from centres of population. In 1935, for example, the Chaco War between Paraguay and Bolivia effectively came to an end when Paraguayan forces had driven the Bolivians out of the disputed area and had reached the foothills of the Andes. On the other hand, at approximately the same period, Colombia was prepared to accept a quite artificial frontier in the area of the so-called Leticia Trapezium in order to gain access to a deep water port on the River Amazon—a case of economic value overcoming a strategic disadvantage.[15]

Possession of an irregular frontier with many salients or re-entants, in the absence of satisfactory physical features protecting it, is a disadvantage rather than an advantage for a country. The Versailles Treaty of 1919, by giving Poland a corridor to Danzig (Gdansk), separated part of East Prussia from the rest of Germany and formed an excuse for Hitler's subsequent attack on Poland.[16] The Caprivi Strip, which gives South Africa access to Zambia through Namibia, would be quite indefensible. A disjoined piece of territory is always particularly vulnerable. A major example, between 1947 and 1975, was the artificially shaped state of Pakistan, whose two halves were separated by Indian territory. The revolt of Bangladesh in 1975 was aided by India, which was able, by securing Bangladeshi independence, thus substantially to weaken Pakistan as a military enemy.[17] Pakistan, however, is itself large enough to restrict Indian access to its north eastern states to a relatively narrow corridor, which remains India's major strategic weakness. A smaller example was afforded during the Angolan Civil War by the seizure of the Cabinda Enclave by forces of the South African backed UNITA movement; the significance of this lying in the fact that the Cabinda Enclave, separated from the rest of Angolan national territory, was a major centre of oil exploration and exploitation.[18]

In the case of the African states, fortunately, the decision was taken early in their independence by the Organization of African Unity (OAU) to respect the colonial boundaries with which they had been established.[19] Since no substantial breaches of these boundaries had occurred by that time this settlement so far has been amazingly effective. A major exception was the war between Ethiopia and Somalia over the possession of the Ogaden, in which Cuban forces lent support to the Ethiopians in their battle against their Marxist neighbours, and were very successful.[20] It is unlikely that the Ogaden is of any economic value, and possession of it is merely a strategic liability. For the paradox is that a country may be weakened by the possession of territory which other nations want, even though that territory may not be of very much value of any kind.

COMMUNICATIONS

Communications are of such particular importance in the development of states and their contact with the outside world that they deserve special treatment. Here again there have been important changes in the period since 1945.

The easiest method of communication throughout all but the last few years of the human race's history, has been by water. To this day it is still cheaper to carry goods from New York to San Francisco by water rather than by land or by air. But the opening up of the United States was aided by the unique advantage of two major river systems both capable of navigation to a considerable distance inland. These are the St Lawrence seaway system and the Great Lakes and the Mississippi-Missouri-Red River system. By contrast, with the major exception of the Amazon, much of the territory of Brazil was closed off from water transport by the edge of the Brazilian Plateau, which forms ridges of mountains that lie close inshore for many hundreds of miles. And the opening up of Argentina occurred from not less than three centres, and followed a very different course depending on whether traffic could expand along the Parana-Uruguay and Paraguay river systems, or whether it had to cross the Andes and the land barriers beyond. On the west coast of South America river transport was of no value whatsoever, the waters running rapidly off the high Andes straight into the sea, with scarcely enough time to do more than irrigate tiny patches of coastal settlement among the deserts of the Andes rain shadow. The pattern of geographical settlement in Latin America, therefore, followed the coast, and such navigable river systems as existed.

Colonial expansion in Asia followed a similar pattern, the acquisition of Singapore in 1816 by Sir Stamford Raffles being a major step in the consolidation of British control of the Straits Settlements and hence of the Malay Peninsula, and the capture of Saigon at the mouth of the Mekong River, giving the French control of their Indo-Chinese protectorate.[21] In West Africa European settlements grouped around the various river systems creating the curious set of enclaves of former British and former French territory which have been preserved in the structure of the modern states of Nigeria, Ghana, Sierra Leone and The Gambia.[22] River systems in this sense formed a natural basis for the control of an area of territory, and this is still to some extent true in the case of modern states.

Away from water, tracks rather than roads have historically formed the chief routes of communication, with pack animals rather than wheeled vehicles forming the chief means of carrying goods. In mountainous areas such as the Andes and Himalayas such tracks still exist and are still used. Every year more people are kicked to death by donkeys than are killed in air crashes, though whether this supports the argument that air is the safest mode of transport is another question. With the development of reliable motor transport and asphalt-surfaced roads in the early years of the twentieth century, road transport has taken on a new lease of life, and today roads form the chief basis of modern industrial transportation in all parts of the world. They do, however, have their disadvantages; their development, as in the Brazilian Amazonian Region, is incredibly destructive of wild life and makes a major breach in the local ecosystems.[23]

By contrast the railway lines which carried the economic development and formed the basis of communication of the nineteenth and early twentieth century penetrated virgin forest without disrupting it permanently to the same extent, and were much more efficient in transporting low-value products at a relatively low cost. It was the railway network which made possible the development of the Argentine Pampas into the huge meat-producing area that it has become, and the railway which also made possible the exploitation of the copper mines of Katanga in inland Zaire, of bauxite in Jamaica, of coffee and more particularly bananas in Central America, of rubber in Malaya and tin in Bolivia. The railway formed a thin chain linking a series of separate settlements each of which expanded naturally in their own economic hinterland. By contrast, modern road systems cut a great swathe through the jungle, and throughout their length the land is partitioned up and sold off. Settlement is diffused over a wide area, and the problems of government and administration, to say nothing of defence, are correspondingly multiplied.

Nineteenth-century communications systems were built with the extensive use of private enterprise, though the direct contribution of government to their initiation and development is often played down by modern commentators, particularly in the West. After all, a railway system cannot be constructed without rights of passage over land, and it is government which licenses the development of railways and so creates economic value in the surrounding land which makes settlement worthwhile. In fact, early attempts to build railways in Latin America in the nineteenth century were often taken by local initiative, as, for example, in Peru and Guatemala, and it was only to accelerate the process that it was decided to hand the whole process over to the new firms of specialist contractors who had grown as a result of their work in the first instance in Europe.[24] Such firms of specialist contractors still exist, and are called upon by many Third World governments when it comes to constructing port works, railways, airports or other fixed installations needed for communications purposes. But a government today can, with its own local resources, employ men and women if it lacks the machines to build roads, and to this extent, therefore, the technological revolution in road transport has put the control of communications back in the hands of Third World governments, from which it had never really departed. Though not all Third World countries by any means understand the long-run value of communications, it is significant that while the railways of Western Europe have been closed down, often with political pressure from road-building interests to accelerate the process, the value of railways as low-cost, high-bulk carriers has been evidenced by the construction of new railways in industrializing countries. Australia, Canada, China, Japan and the Soviet Union have all found it economically desirable to expand rather than to contract their rail networks in recent years.[25]

However, it must be admitted that not all developments of Third World communications systems are in the interests of the countries concerned. The fatal lure of national prestige led the government of Kwame Nkrumah in Ghana to embark on a whole string of ill-considered projects with a superficial development appeal. Super highways, where there were too few motor vehicles, a shipping line at the time at which shipping was becoming increasingly unprofitable, and a prestige airport where relatively few aircraft wished to land, all

weight such as computers and transistor radios from Hong Kong—it is still a flimsy basis for a successful exporting economy, and unlikely to be of much value unless backed by a substantial additional structure of development.

Developments in communications can herald important developments in international relations. American scholars have used the exchange of mail, tourists, emigrants and students as indices of the warmth or coolness of relations between countries.[27] This makes sense—after all, it is hard to interact if there are no lines of communication along which interaction can proceed, a fact long since recognised by established powers in the negotiations setting up diplomatic relations with new states. Conversely, establishing lines of communication with military potential has always been perceived as diplomatically significant. Thus the development of the railway to the Bolivian frontier at Corumba has enabled Brazil to bid for the exploitation of that country's mineral wealth, and in return offered it an alternative route to the outside world, lessening its dependence on Chile and Argentina. The offer by Brazil to build a road through the Essequibo region of Guyana and establish industries there effectively checkmated Venezuela's long-standing claim to two-thirds of Guyana's national territory. Construction of a road down into Ladakh in 1962 enabled China to assert its effective control of the Himalayan passes, and threw India into a profound state of alarm. And more recently, construction of Mount Pleasant airport on the Falklands has been perceived by the Falkland Islanders as their lifeline with the outside world and simultaneously by Argentina as a threat.[28]

ECONOMIC RESOURCES

It is one of the ironies of history that the colonization of the Third World was undertaken by Europeans in the belief that it was rich. Certainly, when Europeans reached India, Sri Lanka or Indo-China, they found very wealthy civilizations with every evidence of conspicuous consumption. But gold, silver and jewels are a poor basis for an economy, and the Spanish obsession with bullion (silver and gold) had serious long-term economic consequences for its colonies in Latin America. Certainly the economic motivation in early colonial expansion was very marked in the case of some other states: the Portuguese sought the Spice Route to India, the French sought sugar in the West Indies, and so forth. It has therefore become a truism that colonization took place for the purpose of exploiting the natural resources of the colonies, and the fact that other reasons for colonial expansion could and did exist is therefore easily overlooked. Not least among these possibilities was that of sheer prestige seeking.

In consequence there are at least three possibilities among economic relationships betwen metropolitan states and colonies. First, there were those colonies such as Mexico or Peru which produced wealth which was then re-exported to the colonizing country. Some of the richest of these colonies were in fact relatively small, such as the sugar-producing islands of Jamaica, Guadeloupe and Martinique.[29] Second, there were colonies, like the Falkland Islands, which formed self-contained economic systems, producing enough to defray the costs of their administration, but little in the way of surplus.[30] Third, there were those colonies, like German South West Africa (subsequently Namibia), which ran at a loss.[31]

Germany's defeat in the First World War was followed by the transfer of imperial control of this region, together with that of Tanganyika, to Great Britain. Britain subsequently transferred responsibility for Namibia to South Africa, who thus benefited from the discovery of diamonds in 1907 and the ability therefore to monopolize the world's supply of that valuable industrial commodity. Britain remained responsible for Tanganyika, which has, since independence as Tanzania continued to be one of the poorest countries in Africa.[32] Most of French Equatorial and French West Africa never ran at a profit. Ironically, the one promise of economic return came at the very end of the colonial period when oil was discovered to the south of Algeria, and the region concerned united with the province of Algeria shortly before that too had to be conceded to the forces of independence.

Colonial rule, therefore, wherever possible involved the development of natural resources. The effect of this varies considerably depending on whether these resources are renewable or non-renewable. The loss to the country concerned from the exploitation of non-renewable resources, such as coal, iron ore, gold, silver or other minerals, is unlikely to be in any way compensated for by leaving behind a functioning industry. On the other hand, no newly independent government would wish not to have functioning industries of this kind, given the enormous profits which potentially they are capable of yielding. Hence the government of Jamaica has continued to develop its bauxite mines, the government of Bolivia continues to be dependent upon the export of tin and so forth. Nothing can be done about any losses that have occurred in the past, so realistically they seek to maximize their gain for the future. The problem with this is that they are making use of a non-renewable resource and that places a time horizon on their efforts for development which requires them to reinvest as heavily as possible during the period of maximum gain if they are to benefit as fully as they would wish.

Renewable resources are another matter. It is not quite true to regard the establishment of plantation agriculture as a renewable resource, given that, as in Brazil, it involves first the destruction of the natural vegetation cover and its replacement by one that may well not be so beneficial to the soil or so well adapted to local conditions. At the worst, the wholesale cutting down of trees and the destruction of the undergrowth which accompanies land clearance has resulted in the laying bare of huge tracts of land to the forces of wind and water. Soil erosion of this kind has been widespread in Africa, and on the poor laterite soils of Brazil it looks as if it will be very serious indeed. However, if this aspect is controlled, and plantations properly managed, it is not only possible to crop them effectively over a long period of time, but it is also possible, if necessary, to diversify their production or to change the basis of it entirely. Limits are, of course, imposed by the available sunshine and rainfall, and the question of whether or not there are markets for alternative products on the necessary scale. But a government should be able, with intelligent planning, to make efficient use of its land resources in this way provided that it maintains the necessary degree of control over a product.

This, however, is seldom the case. The growth of plantation

agriculture, like the growth of mines and the oil industry, occurred at a time when private enterprise was the norm and it was believed that natural resources should be exploited for the good of mankind wherever they occurred. The effect of this has been to establish substantial vested interests in Third World countries who in conjunction with government, can exercise great political influence. A classic instance is that of the coffee interests in Colombia, which regulate the production of coffee between big and small growers, maintain reserves to equalize the price on the world market and deal as a block with coffee growers in other countries in order to maintain the best possible price on the world market. It would be very difficult for a Colombian government to legislate against the interests of this powerful political block, and certainly they do not attempt to do so.[33] Instead the maintenance of a high return on coffee exports through the International Coffee Agreement (ICA) has become the main plank of Colombian foreign policy, which requires it simultaneously to maintain good relations with other major producers such as Brazil and Kenya, and with its major market, the United States.

In El Salvador, where the government is almost equally dependent on the production of coffee, this has established a very powerful landed interest with extremely conservative ideas about the distribution of land which has the highest population density in the Americas. Their resistance to any hint of land reform has been total, and has been largely responsible for the vicious civil war which raged throughout that country in the early 1980s.[34] This internal situation has had important external effects, given that successive governments in El Salvador have invoked the aid and assistance of the United States government in resisting the socially generated forces which they are seeking to fight. In this way a local problem has become internationalized.

A different reaction to the dependence on a single crop can be seen in the case of Brazil after the series of frosts which have devastated the coffee harvests throughout the 1970s, and which originally were seen as being freak weather conditions unlikely to recur. After several recurrences, probably caused by the progressive deforestation of the Amazon region and the consequent destabilization of the climate, the growers concerned have diversified out of coffee. For many of them soya beans have proved a satisfactory alternative crop, but it would obviously be dangerous in the long term if Brazil was to become as dependent upon an alternative agricultural product, and in any case there is no guarantee that the market for soya bean will in fact remain as good as it has been in recent years. Meanwhile the main effect has been to accelerate other economic developments, industrialization and the exploitation of off-shore oil reserves, which strengthen Brazil's position in the world economic system to the point at which it can 'go it alone' in negotiations over debt rescheduling.

A further consequence of reliance upon agricultural production is its need for a substantial economic infrastructure of roads, railways and ports to handle low-value bulk products. A striking example of dependence upon such an elaborated infrastructure is provided by the banana industry of Central America and Ecuador. Bananas have to be picked unripe, handled with relative care and placed in controlled conditions on board specially designed vessels at the earliest possible moment.[35] The result is the creation of dependence by the growers on this elaborate system of distribution in which the end-product and its cost determines to a great extent the economic return which is received by the growers concerned, but only because it has been many times multiplied in the course of establishing the system as a whole. In the case of the Argentine railway network, established in the first instance for the movement of cattle to the meat-processing plants of Buenos Aires and other major centres, a constant complaint since 1945 has been the unsatisfactory nature of the railways for providing inter-communication between districts in the provinces. All routes lead to Buenos Aires and thence to the sea, and the radial pattern thus established is not necessarily the one that would have been chosen had Argentina designed a railway network for the twentieth century.[36]

Many Marxist writers argue that Third World countries have in this way been linked into the world economic system in such a way as to establish a condition of neo-colonialism and dependency.[37] Indeed, the dependency thesis, first developed in Argentina and popularized by Brazilian writers, achieved great popularity among Third World countries writers in the 1970s, as it seemed to provide a simple explanation for all their economic difficulties. These difficulties, therefore, could be blamed upon the system and not on policy decisions made by themselves. Dependence on an ultimate market is of course a fact of economic life. There is no value in a product unless someone wants to buy it, and the huge systems by which coffee, bananas and other products are produced have grown up purely and simply because a market existed and was seen to exist for the products concerned. There may well be other markets which have not yet been found. An excellent example of a new product found in the late 1970s has been jojoba oil, which is being produced commercially now on a large scale in Australia and for the softening of fine leathers has been able to replace whale oil, and so perhaps help arrest the catastrophic decline in whale species. It is probable that new discoveries will continue for some years to come to be made in this kind of way establishing the existence of new markets which had not previously been seen to exist. Certainly any crop that can be used to help the world's food shortage is likely to be of long-term value, though the old distribution of demand is critical since the problem of world hunger is closely linked to the inability of countries who suffer from it to produce enough to satisfy their own needs, still less to produce enough to export to buy in crops from abroad.

The extent to which any individual country is dependent, however, depends very much on the nature of its product. If that product is valuable or essential or in high demand and it is one of relatively few producers, then its bargaining position is much better than if its product is commonplace or of low value or in little demand. An interesting example of the former situation was afforded in 1952 by Bolivia, when at a time when the other major world tin producers were disrupted by civil war or the threat of it, it decided to embark upon a social revolution. This experiment was treated with relative enthusiasm and encouragement by the government of the United States, despite its ideological antipathy to it.[38] On the other hand, proposals for a similar degree of land reform in Guatemala in Central America in the same period led to indirect intervention by the United States in order to put a stop to it.[39] Guatemala's main export, coffee, was neither sufficiently distinctive nor sufficiently critical to give it any leverage on the situation. In addition, the country's strategic weakness was much greater and so too was its proximity to the United States, but this does not take away from the distinctiveness of the Bolivian case.

An important role in the creation of dependency is played by the middle men who market the product and arrange for its transportation. Dependency theorists describe the trading middle class which undertakes these operations in conjunction with foreign interests in Marxist terms as the 'comprador bourgeoisie' or more generally the 'national bourgeoisie'.[40] These individuals and families play a crucial role in the development of extractive and exporting industries. The personal rewards which they gain from their participation in the process of dealing with overseas interests gives them great political strength within their own country, and they are therefore able to ensure that the system makes the kind of decisions which are most specifically in their own interests. Once this process has been established, it is very difficult for this financial interest, backed as it is by the enormous financial resources of international corporations, to be challenged successfully by any other internal interest. An uncertain question is the extent to which the individuals are actually aware of what they are doing. Businessmen in general are not particularly knowledgeable about political structures, still less the way in which international relations operate. They tend to respond pragmatically to individual opportunities to make money; it is therefore possible that the cumulative effect of a number of small decisions, each of them separately seen in purely economically rational terms, produces the overall effects which we have been discussing here.

This fact is very important when we turn our attention from economic resources to financial ones. The ability to mobilise economic resources costs money. There are a limited number of ways in which these financial resources can be obtained. The principal ones are taxation, banking and borrowing abroad. Since governments have in theory unlimited sovereign power, they can also have resort to confiscation, a measure commonly used against domestic interests, but when used against foreign ones subject to particular hazards. We will deal with each of these in turn.

First of all, then, let us consider taxation.[41] The ability to tax depends on the ability of the citizenry to pay, but generally new states have relatively underdeveloped taxation systems. In states which became independent in the nineteenth century, direct taxation was almost unknown, and the major sources of income consisted of duties on imports and exports. Concessions were frequently given to foreign corporations entitling them to exemption from import duties on machinery and capital investment and from export duties for a limited term of years, after which the newly established industries were expected to pay for themselves. Not surprisingly, this led to competition between countries to offer easier and easier terms, and in dealing with modern multinational corporations where an economic resource which is widely distributed is concerned—such as, for example, oil—this means that each individual country is very weak indeed in obtaining a satisfactory return for the alienation of its unique resource. Despite the ever present losses through corruption, taxes on imports and exports are relatively easy to collect. An income tax, on the other hand, presents very considerable problems; to be fully effective it has to be levied upon the rich, and the rich are disproportionately politically influential. To persuade legislatures, still less dictators, to tax themselves is always a difficult art, and none more so than in the field of individual taxation. Corporation taxes, which should be easy to collect, are in practice not so. The corporations concerned, particularly if they operate in more than one country, are able to engage in a variety of devices to minimize their tax burden. One which attracts particular hostility from Third World governments is the practice of transfer pricing, by which a company buys and sells goods to its own subsidiaries in other countries, setting in many cases purely nominal prices so that widespread tax avoidance can take place.[42] Obviously where a country operates in many countries it is very difficult for the government of any one country to find out just what is going on, particularly where the home government of the TNC concerned is not prepared to co-operate. The lesson is therefore, that in assessing the capabilities of a taxation system one has to have regard not only to the known wealth of the country but also to the ability to extract that wealth in the form of taxes, and these two can be very different things.

Earlier new states generally lacked an adequate banking system of any kind. It was not, indeed, until the 1920s that major expansion of Latin American banking systems took place, and former colonial states that have become independent since 1945 still continue in many cases to be full of subsidiaries of banks established in the time of the colonial power. The establishment of a central bank for note issue and overall supervision of the banking system, is one of the first acts of sovereignty, if it has not already been undertaken. The existence of an adequate banking system then enables the mobilisation of capital. This directly benefits the government by enabling it to encourage the carrying out of developments which are socially and economically useful and indirectly by improving the general prosperity of the country and enabling it to draw upon these resources through the taxation system. As the case of Latin American states shows, however, the existence of adequate banking systems does not necessarily mean the effective internal mobilization of capital. Capital tends to flow where the returns are best, and if there is any degree of anxiety about the security of returns, then this too is a factor that will have to be taken into account in determining the placing of funds. In consequence, well into the twentieth century, many Latin American states have suffered from an acute shortage of capital, while extensive funds in the hands of the rich were invested overseas in United States stocks and bonds, on the European market or merely stored away in numbered Swiss bank accounts.[43] It can be said, with confidence, that most new states are capable of generating very useful amounts of capital for internal development from their own resources; the fact that they do not do so is largely due to political considerations.

Even more tempting for newly independent governments is the attraction of borrowing overseas. Not only is there some historic tendency to orientate borrowing towards the North American and European capital markets, but the sums of money involved can be gigantic by the standards of the Third World states, and a great deal of the capital thus raised sticks to the fingers of politicians and others who have anything to do with making the decisions. In the 1970s financial institutions,

who should have known better, rushed to Mexico, Brazil,
Venezuela, Indonesia, Rumania, Poland and other countries,
to press upon them huge loans, often without regard to the
overall balance of the economies concerned or the fact that it
would be unlikely that it would ever be able to pay a reasonable
rate of return both to themselves and to their successful
rivals.[44] The tendency to contract heavy loans soon after
independence and be unable either to repay or to service them
is such a marked feature of Latin American history, again, that
valuable experience could have been learnt from it for other
new states, and in some cases clearly has been. And the
development of the international financial system means that
loans are no longer given on such appalling terms as, for
example, ensured that from a loan of 16 million pesos Mexico
in 1825 received only 5.4 million pesos of disposable funds.[45]

But the sophistication of the international financial system,
which means that rates and terms of loans are today much
more attractive, also has its disadvantages in that the overall
criteria of being a desirable country in which to invest are now
set by the international community specifically through the
agency of the International Monetary Fund (IMF). Thus it is
no longer possible, as was once the case, for a new state unable
to raise funds in the United States to turn to Europe, or vice
versa; the co-ordination of the financial system is such that the
banks concerned operate under one general system of
assumptions. These assumptions are crucial, for they are all
designed to make it possible for bankers to get their money
back again. Thus the IMF, confronted yet again with a plea
from a Third World country to defer repayments on its loans,
responds invariably with the same financial requirements: a
squeeze on public expenditure, renegotiation of terms of
repayment, no resort to measures which would impede the free
repatriation of capital out of the country and so on. At the
other end of the scale the consistent effect of these measures is
to make it more, rather than less, difficult for the country
concerned to develop, as the Latin American states made clear
in the Declaration of Cartagena in 1984 and repeated at Lima
in 1985.

There are a few new states like Singapore, who owe their
particular position in the developing world to their ability as
financial brokers, having emerged into independence with the

expertise already at their fingertips. Other states have found it convenient to attract funds rather than industry on an off-shore basis: thus Liberia and Panama have long offered 'flags of convenience' to shipping of all nations, the Cayman Islands offer the opportunity to transfer money freely and untraceably from one place to another, and states like Liechtenstein offer the opportunity to register companies outside the control or legislation of major states and so avoid the many restrictions which guarantee the well-being of investors as well as of employees in those firms.[46] However, these resources are positional goods; that is to say, only some states can enjoy the benefits of them as their value lies in not being shared with others.[47] If every state offered equally advantageous rates for the opening of business or the operation of shipping lines, then it would become unnecessary to seek out those states offering special advantages. Hence a new state that wishes to tap resources of this kind must discover something that is not currently on offer.

As for the rest, nothing that politicians can do can possibly create mineral resources where they do not exist. This lesson has been painfuly and expensively learnt by Cuba, which has since the late 1960s been forced to go back to the monocultural production of sugar in order tó earn its way, even if it is for sale within the Eastern Bloc rather than as before 1959 to the United States.[48] Nor can politicians ensure the development by outsiders of potentially valuable mineral resources where they are in competition with existing low cost producers. Guatemala endeavoured to secure the development of extensive nickel resources with attractive inducements. But with the coming of the recession in the late 1970s the producers concerned found it paid them not to use the resources, even though they had already invested a substantial amount in the necessary plant and infrastructure.[49] Recession hits the periphery of the business network first, and most Third World countries are peripheral in this economic sense. Politicians enjoy much more ability to intervene in agriculture. Those that have the ability to feed themselves are in an unusually advantaged position however, because, more often than not, what ability to intervene a state possesses is directed towards the growth of export crops. This is because the state's interest in the higher revenue is in this instance in direct confrontation with the interests of its citizens in being adequately fed. This lesson of unequal development has recently been taken up by War on Want, whose most recent campaign has been directed towards making people aware of the structural inadequacies of the system which helped create regional famine and accentuate hardship where hardship exists.

When major crises of this kind occur countries can, and do call upon the United States and Western Europe to help them. It is in fact widely believed that the wealthier have a duty to help their less fortunate counterparts in the Third World. Dependency theorists, however, argue that the aid which is given is an illusion. By solving, for the moment, the acute problem of crisis it prevents a radical review of the underlying causes of the situation, which in their view is the fact that wealth is being exported from these poor nations to the wealthier ones through the processes mentioned above.[50] In its most extreme form, this thesis holds that underdevelopment is not simply the absence of development, nor even the distortion of existing development patterns by the effects of the powerful economies upon it, but the actual reversal of development— the condemning of Third World countries to a state of underdevelopment by the effect of their insertion into the world capitalist system.[51] When such writers talk about the Third World as underdeveloped, they mean that a process has occurred which has actually underdeveloped it.

Examples can be found which support this view. In Ethopia, for example, while famine relief was being rushed to the country, it was discovered with some surprise by Western journalists, that food was actually being exported from the country in order to import Western goods. But these goods were not necessarily ones which aided tne economic infrastructure, like ploughs, shovels or spades. Instead tney were luxury items like Scotch whisky, evidently for the consumption of the small wealthy élite. This example is particularly interesting as it occurs in a state which, for nearly ten years, has had a Marxist government dedicated to the pursuit of equality and presumably educated in the views of the dependency theorists. It is hard to avoid the conclusion, therefore, that politicians have to take some hard decisions, and that one of the decisions that they will have to take if they wish to exert influence in the world instead of being dependent upon it, is to act on occasions to their own personal disadvantage and to that of their families and friends.

What then is the New International Economic Order for which the new states of the Third World have been calling? The term originated after the oil crisis of 1973 gave Third World states the idea that their control of many primary products gave them effective leverage in dictating the terms of trade to the developed countries of the United States and Europe. It was popularized by the Charter of Economic Rights and Duties of States proposed by Mexico at UNCTAD III at Santiago, and its subsequent acceptance by the Third World majority of the UN General Assembly.[52] But though it was clear what problems it was designed to correct, it was much less clear what was to be put in its place.

The instability of the international financial system after the abandonment of the gold-related standard in 1973 brought even more rapid inflation, increasing dependence on private borrowing in an attempt to get away from IMF controls, and increased penetration by TNCs. The optimum solution would be a genuine world bank and an international currency, which the Third World states want to be linked to the price of primary materials. For the moment this is impractical, though attempts since 1984 to increase the role of the World Bank relative to that of the IMF are designed to help. Inflation has meanwhile strengthened the already strong tendency for the wealthy élites to invest their capital in the advanced industrial countries, so depleting the internal capital market, but as we have already seen, the condition of further loans or the rescheduling of existing ones is that the investors must get their interest, and the international community frowns on any measures that would arrest the free movement of money.

Change of the terms of trade in favour of the producers of primary products is also difficult. To begin with the leverage of the primary producers is weaker than it seems, as there are so many products. The collapse of the tin market in 1985 showed the limits of cartelization; tin is no longer in as great demand as it was, since substitutes have been found for most of its traditional uses. The United States, moreover, is itself a substantial producer of petroleum, copper, manganese and many other raw materials, and its strategic buffer stocks have helped cushion it from changes in the world market. Lastly it is the chief source of aid, and can, and does make use of this fact to deal with its sources of supply separately.

Dependence on markets in the advanced countries could, it is thought, be reduced by the development of regional integration through regional organizations such as the Andean Pact (the Latin American influence on the entire concept of the NIEO is very strong). But such organizations have limited effects for two reasons: the fact that the economies of the countries concerned are not complementary and the desire of each country to protect its own uncompetitive sectors.

Competitiveness could, it is believed, be increased by insistence of transfer of technology as an integral condition of trade. It is, however, very hard to legislate for the transfer of technology. Nor is the information of much use to a country that lacks the industrial development to exploit it effectively. But the fact that in the Far East where a substantial base already existed development has outstripped that of Europe suggests that the idea is basically sound if only it can be used. Investment in education and training in technology would have a substantial effect. But here a major problem is the attitude of entrenched political élites who do not want their position threatened by new contenders for power. Again the decisions taken by such people tend to be essentially cosmetic; symbolic modifications which maintain the flow of funds, rather than fundamental ones that will increase the overall stock of wealth for all. It is very hard for them to believe that the international financial community will ever really turn the tap off, and all recent experience suggests that on the contrary they will do almost everything else but do that, even if it means that they are in effect paying themselves the interest of their outstanding loans with their own money.

6 Limitations

DECOLONIZATION

Decolonization has been a major topic of international discussion for the past generation. In political terms it is a finite process. Now that the process of decolonization is almost complete, states which have become independent recently have tended to be very small, either in size or population. Some of them, the island states of the Pacific, appear to create quite new problems, combining very small populations with exceedingly dispersed territories: the island state of Tuvalu, formerly the Ellice Islands, consists of nine coral atolls with a total land area of some 10 square miles and a population of 7,349 (1979 census) spread over something like two million square miles of water. These states are often regarded as being in a category of their own, termed 'microstates'.[1] It is generally agreed that they are unlikely to be able to defend themselves unaided against a determined state opponent. More seriously it may be, that like the Seychelles in the southern Indian Ocean (which consists of 94 islands with a land area of 171.4 square miles and a population of 64,303 (1980 estimate) spread over some 400,000 square miles of ocean), they may be the target of privately organized *coups d'état* such as that which brought Albert René to power in 1977. They may even, like the smaller islands of the Caribbean, be subject to attack from subnational groups of gangsters. Sir Eric Gairy, for example, was believed by the Bishop government in Grenada to be capable of mounting such a coup with the aid of his friends in the United States underworld.[2]

Certainly, small size, whether of population or of territory, places crucial limits on the economic and physical resources of a country. Certainly, too, it places a range of options outside the microstate's capacity, particularly, without the aid of a great power—which is likely to demand something in return—in anything relating to advanced technology, especially weaponry. Most seriously, as David Vital points out, in strategic terms it is weak, not simply because of its intrinsic lack of strength but because with small size goes the inability to risk defeat. The small state, unlike the large one, has very little chance of recovery from an early defeat. The reason is that its forces lack a safe base from which they can respond to an unexpected attack or one for which they are unprepared.[3]

The disparity between a very small population and a large area to defend, however, is so great that defence in the traditional sense is scarcely an option. So, can such states survive? In practice, yes. For the problem is not in fact confined to the microstates. Indeed it is true of very many states that have recently become independent, and of many of their predecessors of the nineteenth century as well. A major feature of nineteenth century Latin American states was their inability to control their national territory.[4] This inability to control effectively much of the territory they claimed, was not only crucial in determining the boundaries that eventually emerged, it also had important internal consequences, which in turn were reflected in external policy. Specifically, they generated a strong internal struggle between those committed to a policy of centralization and those who supported federalism or regional automony. Federalism was an ideological justification for the independence of regional leaders (*caudillos*) but it became in itself a powerful force shaping people's conception of the just political order.

In other territories, the struggle between the centre and the periphery, between unity and disunity, goes back, as does the Latin American case, into colonial times and beyond. Burmese resistance to colonization took the form of endemic rebellion in the Shan States. It continues to be a problem for present-day Burma, and has indeed since 1962 been met by the institution of a military-backed Socialist Republic which has, as far as possible, endeavoured to seal its country off from external influences in a manner strangely reminiscent of Paraguay under the rule of Dr Francia (1813–45).[5] In Africa two major secessionist movements have had repercussions on the international system. The most spectacular was the threatened dissolution of the former Belgian Congo, now Zaire, within days if its independence in 1960. The state of Katanga, backed by the financial interests in the Union Minière, declared its independence, and succeeded in maintaining its isolation from, and resistance to, the central government until after the fall and death of Patrice Lumumba and the intervention of the United Nations, where there were consistent allegations of covert aid by Western governments to the secessionists.[6] International aid, on the other hand, was certainly not made available to the rulers of Biafra when they attempted to secede from the federal state of Nigeria in 1966. The fear of dissolution of the Federation has however continued to be used as justification for a series of military governments in Nigeria, which has been unable to re-establish civilian rule on a permanent footing. In the meantime, the number of states within the Federation has been increased from the original three regions of independence days to nineteen in the most recent military constitution, but 'unity' has been preserved.[7]

The struggle between centre and periphery, therefore, has led all over the world to rulers seeking at all costs to strengthen the power of the state and to eliminate those factors which they see as leading to weakness. This has tended to give them a strong dislike of opposition in any form. Of course, until the twentieth century, in most parts of the world the concept of a 'loyal opposition' scarcely existed; opposition was by definition disloyal and was characteristically met by military force. But the development of the concept of the loyal opposition in the European states of the nineteenth century was transmitted to the newly acquired colonies of France and Britain by direct instruction when the members of the colonies' élite travelled to the metropolitan motherland to pursue their education. The problem was that the concept—however warmly encouraged, and it was not always warmly encouraged in practice—was in direct conflict with the actual practice of colonial government. Early British colonial practice had been to reproduce the institutions of the motherland among European settlers, as in the parliaments of Ireland, the Bahamas and the North American colonies. It was these assemblies that formed the seedbed for the growth of democracy in the United States of America. But in the nineteenth century the acquisition of

leadership in power on the day of independence thereafter enjoys all the advantages of primacy. For this reason, the evident desire of colonial Powers to hand over to 'friendly' governments seems quite sensible. What they seem consistently to have failed to estimate accurately, however, was the limited range of possibilities at their disposal. Thus Britain's foolish attempt under the Macmillan government to create a Central African Federation which would keep the former colonies of Northern Rhodesia (Zambia) and Nyasaland (Malawi) under white settler control was deservedly unsuccessful. Learning the wrong lesson from the fiasco, the first Wilson government (1964–70) then compounded the disaster by refusing to use against the white settlers in Rhodesia (Zimbabwe) the force which previous governments had found no difficulty in using in territories where those seeking independence were of a different complexion. The long term consequence was that the Thatcher government had to accept in Zimbabwe a far more left-wing government than it would have liked, and this despite what Mrs Thatcher herself termed 'the supreme negotiating skill of Peter [Lord] Carrington.'[11]

A major role in the continued pressure for the independence of Zimbabwe was played by those African states that had already attained independence. It was inevitable that in the foreign policy of such new states a major plank would be to encourage the independence of their neighbours in every way possible, as the maintenance of existing colonial empires appeared to them a guarantee of continuing risk for themselves. The larger new states went further: they put forward claims to neighbouring territories that they desired to annex, and where possible made good on their claims. China annexed Tibet, and claimed Taiwan, which had been in Japanese hands until 1945. India took over Hyderabad and much of Kashmir, captured Goa, and more recently has formally incorporate Sikkim. Indonesia successfully used military force to assert its claim to Dutch New Guinea (West Irian) and Portuguese (East) Timor, but failed to prevent the consolidation of Malaysia or to gain control of Sarawak and Sabah (North Kalimantan). Medium sized powers were less successful. Argentina claimed the Falkland Islands, Venezuela most of the territory of its neighbour Guyana, North Vietnam the rest of former French Indo-China, Thailand the province of Siemreap annexed by France in 1907 and reunited to Thailand briefly during the Second World War. Small states such as Guatemala, which had tried to take advantage also of the Second World War to annex Belize (then British Honduras) found itself having to rely, for what it was worth, on the good will of the international community and the wishes of the United Nations.

The United Nations was the one arena where states nominally met as equals, and it was inevitable that the ex-colonial states should attach an exaggerated importance to its votes and resolutions. In New York a vote was a valuable commodity which could be traded for prestige, good will and even on occasions hard cash in the form of economic or military aid packages. But the United Nations had been effective between 1945 and 1960 for reasons that were largely fortuitous; in the rivalry between the superpowers its will coincided with the interests of the United States, its leading proponent and paymaster, and strong secretaries-general were able to make of their office an important positive force for peace. After the Congo/Zaire crisis, these factors were eroded. The new Third World majority in the organization was able to create in the Special Committee on Decolonization (the Committee of 24) a forum for their claims to universal decolonization. But the realities of the postcolonial order—a fragmented world divided between authoritarian governments keen to maintain their distance from both East and West—were deeply disillusioning to the United States and Western Europe. Both increasingly ignored the weak Third World-appointed secretary-general and obeyed only those resolutions of the United Nations that happened to suit them. The United States, whose leaders had in 1945 seen decolonization as a universal ideal, was particularly offended when in the early 1980s the Special Committee on Decolonization turned its attention to Guam and the Pacific Trust Territory, both of which formed an important part in its chain of Pacific defence.[12]

The United States and the Soviet Union, as in this example, both set a bad example in the application of a double-standard to the question of decolonization and the rights of independent states, and each find unexpected thorns in the bouquet of platitudes customarily offered up in discussions on the subject.

Of the members of the non-aligned group, Afghanistan, Angola, Congo, Cuba, Ethiopia, Mozambique and Syria are in fact aligned—with the Soviet Union. Other states, India, Libya, Mexico and Nicaragua, for example, while pursuing an independent course, have a marked tendency to judge the two superpowers in very different terms, as their votes show. The fact is, the governments of almost all Third World new states retain the principle of decolonization as a basic principle of their foreign policy. But it applies only to states designated as imperialist. Since the Soviet Union cannot be imperialist, and Third World states cannot, by definition, be colonialist, it is scarcely surprising that consistency is difficult to attain. Israel was a creation of the United Nations and a classic instance of the principles on which decolonization is based. But the large size of the Islamic Conference and the fact that Israel has no automatic bloc and is seen as closely aligned with the United States and as a bridge for that country's influence in the Middle East, combine to make the issue of the Palestinian Arabs a major example of the double-standard.

One of the few issues on which there is almost universal agreement is the illegality of apartheid in South Africa and the Nationalist regime that has enacted it and maintains it. Britain, in particular, has been comprehensively discredited by the obsessive refusal of the Thatcher government to recognize this fact. The United Nations has retaliated in kind, by refusing to support even Britain's reasonable argument for the self-determination of the Falklands.

CLEAVAGES

The new state passes into independence retaining two sorts of social cleavages: those which, like the Indian caste system or the religious divide between Hindus, Muslims and Sikhs, predate colonial rule, and those which colonial rule itself engenders. The leaders of these states face a difficult problem in establishing their legitimacy. On the one hand, it is an advantage, both in internal and external relations, to be the formal successor of the colonial power; on the other, it is essential as soon as possible for them to dissociate themselves from their predecessors. In this process, as with Kwame

Nkrumah in Ghana, when after 1957 it was the first newly independent black African state, old symbols of chiefdom and traditional authority may be of use, but have to be employed in such a way as not to reawaken slumbering traditional allegiances. If the style is traditional, however, the methods tend to be those of the former colonial rulers, and the result is that the new state actually undergoes a form of 'internal colonialism' in which the capital and urban sectors rapidly 'colonise' the rural provincial hinterland.[13]

The establishment of a one-party state was seen in Ghana and has been represented latterly in Zimbabwe as a 'necessary' adaptation to post-colonial 'realities'. Yet few of those who advocate or who tacitly accept this point of view have stopped to think why, if a multiplicity of parties is so undesirable, is it necessary to have parties at all. The fact is that there is no 'need' to have a one-party state; the prohibition of other parties is merely a useful device to help consolidate a specific ruling clique in power under the semblance of legality. By eliminating a focus of criticism, it becomes easier to use the post-colonial battery of emergency power, decree law, arbitrary arrest, torture and expulsion of political opponents. This in turn means that the country's foreign policy-making process, insulated as it is from internal criticism, becomes also increasingly isolated from actions whose public criticism might damage the appearance of the new government in the international arena.[14]

There are four types of cleavage in newly independent states.[15] To begin with there is a cleavage between the ideal 'nation' in whose name power is exercised and the actual institutions and personnel of the state (the nation/state cleavage). Second, there is the gross disparity between the view from the capital and the view from the provinces, compounded by the strains caused by accelerated urbanization and immigration of rural elements to seek work in the new government-sponsored industrial zones (the urban/rural cleavage). Third, there is, as ever, the gap between rich and poor, a gap which in independent Third World states has been particularly marked owing to their relatively early stage of industrialization and the need to import desired consumer goods (the rich/poor cleavage). Last but not least, there is the religious-ethnic dimension, which in some states (e.g. India) stems from the remote precolonial historic past, but in others (e.g. Nigeria) is the product of the consolidation of colonial boundaries without reference to the existing divisions at the time.

Such social cleavages tend to occur together and to reinforce one another. When they do so, we speak of them as being 'congruent'. In general, the greater the degree of congruence, the more serious for the future of a stable political order. Sharp lines of division may not seem to matter when they delimit a small minority, as long as that minority can be kept in subjection. But even that situation is an unstable one. Cross-cutting lines of cleavage, on the other hand, present constant problems but offer the best hope of the evolution of a political order allowing wide participation under some form of agreed rules. In any case, there is always a strong tendency for the ruling élite to assume that its own particular culture is the only proper basis for a national culture, and so to use the education system and the media to impose its own language, norms and taste on the inhabitants of the country at large. In the nature of the case, such a culture is likely to reflect strongly the colonial tradition, since in colonial times the education system was largely geared towards turning out recruits for the civil service, the public utilities and the armed forces. It is these individuals who form the core of the ruling élite in the post-colonial state, regardless of the ideological pattern of its government, and again in the nature of things they tend—all other things being equal—to set the standard for their successors.

Not all internal cleavages act as a limit on the power of the newly independent state. Initially, as with the Ibo in Nigeria, independence can liberate productive energies, cut short in that case by the assertion of Northern primacy implicit in the original structure of the Federation. The ones which are of particular importance to us as those that give rise to insurgency, and those which run across national boundaries, thus facilitating the rise of a secessionist or irredentist movement within the country or a demand for intervention from outside it.

Strictly speaking, secessionist movements want a new state, completely separate from the one in which they presently live. In practice, governments tend to regard all movements seeking autonomy as potentially secessionist, and oppose them accordingly. They can therefore be considered together. Secessionist movements are fairly widespread in today's world, and many can be named that have recently taken up arms to secure their ends.[16] In Europe the Basque secessionist movement ETA (Euzkadi Ta Akatsuna) seeks a united Basque state and independence from Spain. In the Middle East the Palestine Liberation Organization (PLO) seeks an independent Palestinian state, and the Kurds a united Kurdistan formed of territory at present held by five countries: Turkey, Iran, Iraq, Syria and the USSR. In Asia the Sikhs and the Nagas seek autonomy, as do the Shanti Bahini of Bangladesh and the Shan, Karen, Mon, Arakan and Kachin peoples of Burma. The Tamil Tigers of Sri Lanka and the Moros of the Philippines seek independence, as do the Acheh in Java, the Fretelin (Revolutionary Front for an Independent East Timor) in East Timor and the Free Papuan Organization (OPM) in West Papua, all from Indonesia. In Africa the inhabitants of Tigray and Eritrea seek independence from Ethiopia, the Polisario Front from Morocco, and SWAPO (South West African Peoples Organization) from South Africa, whose *de facto* control of South West Africa (Namibia) has been repeatedly challenged by the United Nations. The chances of success of all such movements are strongest, as in the case of SWAPO and the Polisario Front, where they operate against a single state organization and enjoy widespread international support for their objectives. The Basques and the Kurds may be tolerated in France and the USSR, respectively, as long as their activities are confined to their neighbouring states, but clearly they are very much less likely to get all they want. In southern Asia, the fact that all states of the region are threatened to some extent by secessionist or autonomist movements gives them a common interest in supporting one another, or at least, as in the case or Rajiv Gandhi's policy towards the Tamil secessionists in Sri Lanka, avoiding putting pressure on a friendly government despite internal political pressures to do so.[17] The policy of the Indian government towards the Nagas is of particular interest as it demonstrates a clear continuity with the colonial policy towards insurgency in the frontier regions, and the methods employed bear a striking resemblance to

British methods in the former North-West Frontier and North-East Frontier Agencies.

If secessionist movements seek to leave an existing state, irredentist movements seek to reunite ethnic or religious groups by acquiring territory from a neighbouring state. Some potential irredentist movements have been forestalled by peaceful means, as with the union of former British and French Cameroon (now Cameroun) or of former British and Italian Somaliland (now Somalia).[18] In a few cases, irredentism is the official policy of a government, as in the case of Pakistani claims to Kashmir, annexed by India on partition in 1947, despite its predominantly Muslim population. Where irredentism takes the form of insurgency within an area in the name of union with a larger territory, the options for the government of that larger territory are more complex, and the movement may hope for varying degrees of support, depending on circumstances. They may receive active support from the state apparatus, as in the case of Somali support for the recovery of the Ogaden from Ethiopia; tacit support, as with Namibia's neighbours Angola and Zimbabwe; or disapproval, as with the Republic or Ireland and the Provisional IRA in Northern Ireland, whose ultimate objectives go beyond the 'liberation' of Northern Ireland to the establishment of a secular Marxist Republic in Ireland as a whole. The fact that despite governmental disapproval, the Provisional IRA can clearly count on a great deal of support within the Republic and even among the Irish-American community in the United States, is an illustration of the formidable difficulties such movements present to the host government.[19]

Irredentist claims complicate the settlement of boundary disputes, and such disputes are a major affliction of new states, leading them to expend a great deal of their scarce resources in maintaining an otherwise unnecessary military establishment which will always pose a potential threat to the civilian political order. The large number of surviving boundary disputes in Latin America illustrate how intractable such problems can be. there the situation has been particularly difficult to resolve, owing to the vagueness and imprecision of colonial boundaries and the lack of an agreed transfer of power at the end of colonial rule.[20]

Most seriously, such disputes can offer an excuse for international action to rectify it. The United States intervened in 1903 to ensure the independence of Panama and to secure the advantages of the Hay-Bunau Varilla Treaty, and by doing so deprived Colombia of a unique natural resource. But it was much easier for it to do so since persistent neglect by the political élite of upland Bogotá had left the relatively internationally minded inhabitants of Panama discontented and ripe for secession.[21] Neglect of remote areas by capital-centred élites was similarly a factor in the movements that gave rise to the secession of Bangladesh from Pakistan, and the attempted secession of Eritrea from Ethiopia, and the equatorial provinces from Sudan during the harsh Islamic rule of General Nimeiry.[22] If such a state of affairs exists, it is contrary to all we know of human nature to expect the government of a neighbouring power not to take this fact into account in planning its foreign policy. And it will be tempting for the governments affected to blame those neighbours, rather than themselves, for the problem. In this way they conceal from themselves a significant weakness in their own position, and their ability to conduct their relations with the outside world is corresponding impaired by their failure to understand it correctly. In extreme cases they may, and do, deny that a problem exists at all, thus demonstrating in the clearest possible fashion the subordination of foreign to domestic policy-making; a subordination which in this extreme case is likely to ensure disaster.

The attitude of the capital and its élite to the challenges presented by secessionist and/or irredentist movements are, however, only a logical extension of its general ignorance of and lack of concern for the problems of remote country areas. Today, as in the time of Karl Marx, urbanized intellectuals still tend—erroneously—to think of those who live in the countryside as needing to be rescued from 'the idiocy of rural life'.[23] There is no doubt that in most countries outside Western Europe and North America there is a drastic difference in the standard of living between town and country; this is the case, for example, even in the Soviet Union, where the workers on collective farms earn much less and have many fewer social and educational advantages compared with the workers who live in towns.[24] In Mexico, as in other relatively developed Third World countries, children living in the countryside have poorer access to formal education and social pressures to work may leave them with only a couple of years of formal schooling. There, as in Central America and the Andean states, functional illiteracy often goes with incapacity to use the Spanish language effectively, the dominant tongue used in government and legal proceedings. The rural dweller is therefore at a relative disadvantage compared with those who live in towns and share from birth the assumptions and advantages of the dominant culture.[25]

However, to assume from his lack of formal schooling that he is stupid, lacking in the skills necessary to survive in the rural environment, or unaware of his position in society, is quite unjustified. Undoubtedly this impression is strengthened in the minds of town dwellers by their equation of slowness with dullness. But the guerilla movements of the 1960s were—if unsuccessful—a reminder that farmers and farm workers, if, by nature of their tie to the land, slow to engage in militant political action, are likely when they do so to adopt an extreme radicalism born of their desperation to secure needed change through any other means.[26] Rural discontent, therefore can be a very serious problem for any government that chooses to neglect its underlying causes, or tries to override them by the use of forceful repression. Needless to say, a persistent rural insurgency such as that of Burma, Colombia or Angola, considerably weakens a government's standing in the outside world. For foreign policy-makers it has two implications besides. Rural insurgency as often inspires emulation in neighbouring states as it leads to the flight of refugees, so its successful handling involves collaboration with neighbouring states. But an urbanised state élite frequently comes to despise a neighbouring state in which rural insurgency is endemic as itself inferior, and consequently such collaboration is not always easy to obtain, just where it might be most useful.

When we turn to the division between rich and poor we are on more familiar ground. It was Marx who predicted that in capitalist societies the division between those who owned capital and those who owned capital and those who sold their labour power would continue to widen, culminating in a social revolution in which the proletariat would sieze control of the state apparatus, destroy it and establish a communist society. This prediction forms the basis for the legitimacy not only of the regime currently in power in the Soviet Union but of Soviet-style regimes in other states. Until 1959 all such regimes had come to power with the direct aid and assistance of the Soviet Union (though in the Chinese case only after a period of hostility which had forced autonomy on the movement), and in the majority of cases (Yugoslavia and China excluded) by direct imposition using the coercive apparatus of the Red Army. The Cuban revolution of 1959, though it was not presented as a socialist revolution and did not follow the course predicted by Marx, was the first to give rise spontaneously to a regime claiming to be Marxist-Leninist, and the collapse of the Portuguese empire in Africa in 1975 in due course gave rise to Marxist-Leninist governments in Angola, Mozambique, Guiné-Bissau and the Cape Verde Islands.[27]

Both communism and its converse, the irrational fear of communism, however, became a significant political pheno-menon in Europe and the United States as early as 1918. Following the founding of the Third International in 1920, new communist-inspired revolts occurred in the Baltic area and China,[28] while in Latin America the organization of commu-nist parties was greeted by the ruling élites with an alarm quite out of proportion to their actual numbers or efficacy in a continent still largely undeveloped in economic terms. A supposed 'communist revolt' in El Salvador in 1932 was ruthlessly suppressed, much to the relief of the ruling oligarchy of coffee planters, who for thirty years were able to close their eyes to the sharp inequalities of wealth in their country and the need for peaceful social change in a state which had in the meanwhile the most overcrowded population in Latin America.[29]

In the immediate postwar period it was generally assumed that the new states were bound in the long run to follow the same course of development as the existing industrialized states. Brazil in the 1930s and India in the 1950s set to work to industrialize the way Britain, the United States and the Soviet Union had done before: by concentrating on coal, steel and textile manufacture. Little care was taken to equalize wealth. Incentives for industry were actually encouraged, and it was assumed that the wealth generated would in due course 'trickle down' (hence the 'trickle down theory') to the poor though the generation of secondary and tertiary employment. However between 1964 and 1980, in the Brazilian 'economic miracle' associated with the name of one minister, Professor Antônio Delfim Netto, the Brazilian economy grew steadily at a rate of over 10 per cent per year, yet the disparities between rich and poor widened substantially.[30] By contrast, given the historic commitment of its governments to social reform, the growth of the Mexican economy between 1940 and 1976 was accompanied by strenuous efforts to share out the wealth, which ensured that when after 1976 these efforts tailed off, there was far less social unrest than might otherwise have been expected and the government remained firmly in charge.[31] Yet, ironically, the Mexican government, which had sought some idea of social equality but had prevented organized political opposition from becoming a reality, had to contend with an active guerrilla movement in the State of Guerrero, while the Brazilians, who had not prevented organized dissent, developed a strong constitutional opposition and had no significant guerrilla challenge. In the African states President Nyerere's Tanzania, where social equality under 'African socialism' has been a major plank of policy, has not suffered from the unrest of the rest of the continent, but neither has Kenneth Kaunda's Zambia nor, despite one abortive military coup, the firmly capitalist regime of Kenyatta and Moi in Kenya, where those white settlers who stayed on have kept their relative wealth.[32]

The cleavage between rich and poor, therefore, seems in practice to be less significant in the history of social unrest in the Third World than might be expected given Marx's predictions and European experience. Some of the reasons are clear. The post-colonial governments had a convenient scapegoat in colonialism, and in 'neocolonialism'—defined as the maintenance of control over the policies of a former colonial territory through covert, especially financial, means.[33] Aid from the developing countries helped at the same time to enable those governments to do far more than their own resources would have allowed, the expensive prestige projects so dear to the hearts of political leaders everywhere being paid for by the foreign taxpayer. An optimistic belief in the possibility of self-betterment spread to Africa as it earlier had to Latin America and to South Asia.

It was, in fact, the ethnic dimension which acted most widely as the underpinning of conflict in the new states. 'Ethnic' is used here in a loose sense to refer to cultural differences perceived to exist by the parties concerned. It comprehends both what I have already termed 'nationalism' and what, for no good reason, has often been termed alternatively—in Africa in particular—'tribalism'.[34] In India and Pakistan the sense of ethnic identity was reinforced by the religious cleavage, as between the relatively poor but politically dominant Muslim North of Nigeria and the Christian Ibo, who had come to play a particularly prominent role in the economic life of the country. In Indo-china the Meo of the uplands fought to resist what they took to be further colonization by the lowlanders, and the Christians and the Cao Dai supported the South against the atheistic regime in Hanoi.[35] In Lebanon a vicious civil war continues to rage between Christian and Muslim militias,[36] while the carefully balanced constitution of independent Cyprus was carelessly destabilized by the incompetence of the Greek colonels, and their clumsy meddling used as a pretext for the Turkish invasion of 1974.[37] In each of these cases there is also an element of economic subjection and superordination, yet it is clear that the driving force in the conflicts concerned was fundamentally 'ethnic' and/or 'religious'; terms which, in any case, are largely synonymous.

At their most serious, as in the case of Cyprus and Lebanon, such cleavage can effectively destroy the capacity of a state to act as an independent actor in world affairs. In fact, these two states have become the reverse, areas subject to intervention by two or more external powers, acted upon but unable to act. Intervention can however only happen where there are neighbouring states both able and willing to intervene. The religious cleavages of Belgium and Northern Ireland might in less favoured circumstances invite more than verbal intervention, but not within the well-defined European context. In any case, intervention in a civil war is a dangerous policy for the intervening power. As the Vietnam War and the long-running

Afghanistan insurgency have shown, even apparently over-whelming force has to reckon with the subtleties of the human will, and US intervention in Cambodia precipitated a disaster there, and drove it into a paroxysm of fear, without saving the situation across the frontier in Vietnam. External intervention may be the one thing needed to unite warring factions and create a sense of country where hitherto it did not exist. The alternatives may be worse. Though the Tanzanian intervention in Uganda did succeed in its narrow objective, the expulsion of Idi Amin, Uganda itself continues to be dangerously unstable. Ghanaian participation in the UN action in Zaire, a much less extensive commitment, politicised the armed forces and was itself a material factor in the destabilization of the Nkrumah government.

MILITARY LIMITATIONS

Conflict and war is often seen as being the main characteristic of the international system. Certainly the history of the world is often written as if it were merely a chronicle of wars and conquest, and in the twentieth century two great world wars have been succeeded since 1945 by the division of the world into two great armed camps, while a multitude of small wars, foreign and domestic, rage throughout the world. If peace is seen as being merely the absence of war, the world is not at peace, yet if, as many believe, peace is something positive, an active desire for co-operation and co-existence, ironically a case can be made out that the world is perhaps nearer to peace than it has ever been in an age in which contacts are multiplying even between states that previously were on distant or even hostile terms.

The pursuit of neutralism and non-alignment by the rulers of new states has reflected in many cases a genuine realization of the terrible consequences of war. Its widespread approval, however, also reflects the military limitations under which new states have to operate in a world where the terms of the international system are already established and—apart from Antarctica, where by an international agreement all claims have been 'frozen' until 1992 at the earliest[38]—there is no more 'vacant' territory to be shared out.

Military limitations consist first in the absence or limitation of the capabilities discussed in the last chapter. A small population, a weak economy, few economic resources, poor communications and indeterminate or indefensible boundaries all imply restricted military capacity. So too do governmental instability, contested leadership, irredentist claims, social cleavages and insurgency, discussed above.

Military capacity is an elusive concept. If we look at a single state, we find that its capacity to defend itself will almost invariably be much greater than its capacity, if any, to engage in war of aggression. In each case, its power will depend on the numbers of its forces, their training and morale, the weapons with which they are equipped, their ability to deploy them in battle and many other factors. Modern war is mechanized to a degree that makes it highly dependent on the ability to mobilize economic resources; without vast quantities of petrol, tanks and armoured cars will grind to a halt, and without ammunition, machine-guns cannot be fired. Smaller states are almost invariably dependent on outside supplies for much that they need, and this dependence climbs rapidly within hours of the beginning of a conflict. Hence military capacity cannot be discussed without relation to other states. The theory is that states are sovereign, independent entities, and this would imply that they were capable of defending themselves against all comers. In practice this is not an option for any state, even the superpowers, whose external policies since the onset of the Cold War in 1947 have on both sides been directed towards creating a system of alliances which enable them to extend their defensive capability as far outside the perimeter of their territorial holdings as they can manage.

For a smaller state, entering into an alliance has both advantages and disadvantages. The advantages are obvious: protection in numbers, the support of a major power, a stable basis for foreign policy. The main disadvantage, as France and Britain discovered in the Suez crisis of 1956, is that individual diplomatic initiatives have to be concerted with the alliance partners or they are liable to fail, and that if the alliance is to be retained, policy will therefore have to be reshaped to fit it.[39] To a limited extent the same pressures act in reverse on the dominant powers in the alliance, as the United States discovered in 1982 when confronted in the Falklands crisis with a clash between two powers, each of which was allied to the United States through a different alliance system.[40] But they do not necessarily suffer the other disadvantages, the most obvious of which is the degree of economic dependence which a modern alliance creates on the few countries which are major arms suppliers. Where these are the superpowers themselves, the pressures are particularly strong, as the superpower's policy-makers obviously wish to compensate for what they see as excessive expenditures on supporting their allies by getting them in return to buy the products of their own arms industry. In any case, given the increased complexity of modern weapons systems, economies of scale have inevitably meant the concentration of arms production into a decreasing number of major suppliers.

In recent times, the purpose of alliances, as with all military deployments, has been seen as being the avoidance of war. This has not always been the case: as recently as 1939 Hitler concluded an alliance with the Soviet Union which was intended to do just the opposite, to allow him safely to attack and annex part of Poland. Inevitably in the Soviet Union the suspicion of alliances lingers on, and we cannot be sure that new states with less experience of modern war will not still believe it is a glorious thing. In the Middle East, in particular, the rhetoric of holy war against 'imperialist' Israel suggests otherwise. But if alliances are defensive, then their intended effect is to deter a potential aggressor by making it clear that force will be met with sufficient force to ensure that victory cannot be gained. Both the United States and the Soviet Union have repeatedly said that the reason for arming themselves with nuclear and conventional weapons, constructing alliances and engaging in seemingly endless self-justifications of their failure to make any meaningful moves towards mutual force reductions, is to preserve peace. The result is that today, as any day for the past twenty years, the world stands within a few minutes of total destruction should any significant part of this massive armoury ever be brought into play.

The theory behind this extraordinary situation is that of

deterrence. Thermonuclear weapons, it is argued, are so frightful and indiscriminate in their effects that no sane person will ever wish to resort to them. Consequently, by maintaining an armoury sufficient to ensure the destruction of the power that does resort to them, it can be deterred from choosing that as a viable course of action. Deterrence theory, therefore, assumes rational actors operating with full possession of the facts with sufficient time in which to make a rational calculation of the variables involved and act accordingly. Such, as we have already seen, is not in fact a model of international behaviour which adequately explains the way states act in practice. Indeed, its fundamental logic is more flawed than that, since it assumes that an irrational decision to employ nuclear weapons, on the one hand, will be countered, on the other, by a rational decision to do something quite irrational, and indeed immoral; namely, to annihilate the entire population of the world. It is the belief that in some circumstances the deterrent therefore might not deter that keeps military strategists talking of what in practice would be a quite meaningless alternative: 'limited nuclear war'.[41]

States which form part of an alliance with one or other superpowers, and which do not have nuclear weapons of their own, which includes a number of new states, are sometimes talked about as 'sheltering' under the 'nuclear umbrella' of their alliance partner. To avoid what are seen as the dangers of this subordinate position, Britain and France, which are members of NATO, and China, which was formerly allied with the Soviet Union, have acquired a nuclear capability also, the prime purpose of which is to deter aggression against their own states. Though their policies have been very different, the end result has been the same, to complicate further the already very complex calculations of force capabilities between the superpowers.

India, which has tested a nuclear device but has chosen not to develop nuclear weapons; South Africa, which is believed to have tested a nuclear device at sea; and Israel, which has been the recipient, both intended and perhaps unintended, of much potentially fissionable material and in an unprecedented pre-emptive strike 'took out' the Osiriak nuclear reactor in Iraq on the pretext that it was being used as a cover for the development of a nuclear weapon, all have the knowledge and resources to develop and deploy nuclear weapons. So too, it is believed, will Pakistan, Argentina, Brazil and some other states in the very near future.[42] Notably, these states tend to occur in pairs (e.g. India/Pakistan, Israel/Iraq, Argentina/Brazil), suggesting that rivalry and fear of being left behind in a regional arms race are the main factors driving nuclear proliferation. The pressure for absolute neutrality in the nuclear world, has on the contrary, been strongest where geographical factors seem to create a common interest in denuclearization—as in Latin America, the South Pacific and Antarctica, each of which is now covered by denuclearization agreements.

Access to nuclear weapons, however, requires very considerable resources and the diversion of a substantial proportion of these by a state into an essentially unproductive area which offers little 'spin-off' in terms of employment. Some well-established advanced industrial powers (e.g. West Germany and Japan) certainly have the capacity to enter the nuclear field, but for various reasons have either been unwilling or unable to do so. Hence, though among those states that are currently on the nuclear threshold, some, like India, Pakistan and Israel, are 'new states', in that they have gained independence since 1945, they have pursued nuclear capability for rather special reasons and we cannot generalize from this that other new states will want to do the same.

As regards the likelihood of new states wishing to engage in conventional war, opinions are divided. Quincy Wright, in his *A Study of War*, thought that new states were more likely to use force than older, established states.[43] It is certainly true that India, which has consistently argued for non-alignment as regards the superpower confrontation, has been prepared to use its own conventional forces in its own interests, not just to protect itself from what it saw as Chinese incursions into Ladakh but also to annex Hyderabad and Goa, challenge Pakistan for the control of Kashmir and assist in the secession of Bangladesh, as well as within its own frontiers to suppress the Nagas and to occupy the Golden Temple at Amritsar when Sikh nationalists turned it into an armed camp.[44] Israel, which had to withstand simultaneous attack from five of its

they are backed by a stronger power (like Serbia in 1914),[49] so modern alliances tend to be optional;[50] yet this incurs the risk that a potential aggressor may not in fact be deterred.[51]

Considering states on their own, however, it is clear that the smaller a state is, the smaller both its defensive and its offensive capacity will be—all other things being equal. Some theorists have evolved from this fact theories of 'geopolitics' which seek to relate the power of states to their capacity to control territory, and to explain the relationship between big and small powers in terms of what in extreme form can become simply geographical determinism. For this reason such theories are now not given much credence in Western Europe and the United States. They are, however, still taken extremely seriously in parts of the Third World, particularly among the military who so often serve as policy-makers.[52]

At the beginning of this century, the dominance of Great Britain as an imperial power led Admiral Mahan of the United States to formulate a theory of world power in terms of the expansion of empires by control of the sea.[53] This view, taken very seriously at the time not only in Great Britain but also by, among others, Theodore Roosevelt in the United States and Kaiser Wilhelm II in Germany, is now much less regarded than the history of European expansion suggests it should be. But it was in opposition to this that the British geographer Sir Halford Mackinder (1904) formulated his theory of geopolitics which sought to explain the same history in terms of control of land. For Mackinder, the world was dominated by land areas, the major one of which, Asia-Europe-Africa, he termed 'the World-Island'. Control of the World-Island is, he argues, the control of the world, and it depends, like the control of any land area, on the control of its key region, the 'Heartland', which he identified with the region of the Caucasus Mountains.

Who rules East Europe commands the Heartland:
Who rules the Heartland commands the World-Island:
Who rules the World-Island commands the World.[54]

In practice, either the region of the Heartland has not been correctly identified or the statement itself is not true. But this has not stopped the drive of great powers for specific key geographic objectives in the region identified by Mackinder, such as Russia's for the Dardanelles and Imperial Germany's for the Berlin to Baghdad railway, nor the general recognition that certain key passages by water (the Straits of Gibraltar, the Gulf of Hormuz, the Gulf of Aqaba, the Straits of Malacca, the Suez and Panama Canals) or by land (the Netherlands and Belgium, the Sinai Peninsula) in other parts of the world confer particular advantages on a great power that controls them.[55]

Britain's long struggle to prevent Russia gaining control over Afghanistan in the nineteenth century was motivated not only by fear for India but also concern over the long-term effect that such an accretion to Russian power might have. Russian presence in Afghanistan since the coup of 1972 has been seen in the United States as in Britain and Pakistan, as a fulfilment of this old fear. On a smaller scale, geopolitical reasoning has been popular both in Cuba and in Brazil; the Cubans believing that their island is, as indeed it was in Spanish colonial times, the key to the Caribbean,[56] and the Brazilians seeking to extend their influence over the 'Heartland' of South America, which their military strategists identify as being in geographical terms the Charcas Valley or, in political ones, Bolivia.[57]

As these examples show, possessing what is regarded as a strategic location is for a Third World country not a blessing but a curse. Bolivia has been subjected to repeated political intervention by both Brazil and Argentina, and a series of military coups has left it dangerously enfeebled politically, with an economy wrecked by drug trafficking and suffering from the highest rate of inflation in the world (in 1985 five digits were lopped off the currency).[58] The USSR has been prepared to spend billions to maintain its presence in Cuba and billions more to safeguard its presence in Afghanistan. In the process the interests of the local inhabitants have alike been interpreted by each superpower as being identical with its own strategic interests. In the complex rivalries of the Middle East, where the central struggle between Israel and the Palestinian Arabs inevitably has echoes of another theorist of geopolitics, Karl Haushofer, who saw rivalries between nations in terms of *Lebensraum* (lit. 'living space'), both superpowers have been concerned. Both have repeatedly found the temptation to become more closely involved quite irresistible, though so far by good fortune rather than by good judgement they have done so mainly through support for proxies and the risks of symmetrical superpower intervention have been avoided.

Afghanistan has been particularly unlucky. However smaller states directly adjoining great powers (Canada, Mexico, Cuba and the Bahamas for the United States; Norway, Finland, Poland, Czechoslovakia, Hungary, Rumania, Turkey, Iran, Afghanistan, Outer Mongolia and North Korea for the Soviet Union) are under strong pressure to align themselves with their powerful neighbour. As this list shows, the USSR has in the post-1945 period essentially reversed the so-called *cordon sanitaire* of small states by which the Western powers had in the 1920s sought to prevent its ideological influence spreading westwards,[59] and in 1961 the Soviet Union had a particularly strong incentive to support Cuba given the preexisting alignment with the United States, through NATO, of two of the Soviet Union's neighbours, Norway and Turkey—and particularly the latter, where, as Kennedy was to find in 1962, the USSR was keen to engineer a trade-off.[60] A state in this position, seeking to change sides and distance itself from its large neighbour, obviously faces the certainty of intense hostility, up to and including the risk of direct military intervention. In practice, it is unlikely to do so, not so much because of its neighbour's power, as because of its influence.

Such influence, where it is long-standing and continuous, is often termed 'hegemony'. It works in a variety of ways, directly and indirectly, to limit the range of possible choices open to policy-makers in smaller states. They make the choices they do, because their view of the world is so heavily conditioned through upbringing, education and habituation by the media, that they see no alternative. For such hegemony does not simply stem from the hard facts of geographical proximity, still less the naked use of military force, but from a combination of many factors including economic and cultural penetration. Hence its nature varies very considerably. For example, both Mexico and Canada are economically tied to the United States economy, extensively pervaded by the US cultural influences and each is allied with the United States. Canada exists only because of the former strength of Britain; Mexico, historically antagonistic to the United States, neutral in the First World

War because of internal turmoil, ignored German overtures and a 'Cuban solution'. Both were drawn by 1940 into the US orbit. But for historical, cultural and geographical reasons, each has a distinct subset of national interests—Canada in the Arctic and Mexico in the Caribbean—and each has sought through assertions of neutrality in specific cases, links with Europe, and the search for an international role through the United Nations and its agencies to gain sufficient 'distance' from US policymaking to be able to act as a 'power broker' in the game of multilateral politics.[61] This may be only a qualified independence, but it is a very useful and indeed necessary role in ameliorating the dangers of bipolar confrontation.

Neutrality is a different condition altogether. Finland's neutrality depends on two things: its proven willingness to fight in 1939–40 for its own independence and the high cost incurred at that time by the Soviet Union, and a bilateral agreement by which Finland undertook to avoid presenting a threat to the Soviet Union.[62] In general it is probably true that in the last resort a state that wishes to maintain its neutrality must, like Switzerland or Sweden, arm itself and be prepared to defend it, independently of all others. In practice, a state with very weak military forces, such as Ireland during the Second World War, may be able to maintain its neutrality if its violation appears to offer insufficient advantages to warrant it, or like Spain to the Axis (under a sympathetic government but neutralist and ravaged by civil war), it would form a diversion from the central threat.[63]

Historically the right of great powers to intervene militarily in small ones was recognized by diplomatic practice until the First World War. In theory it has been denied by the United Nations Charter since 1945, except where undertaken at the invitation of the government of the country concerned (the US in Lebanon in 1958; Cuba in Angola and Ethiopia in 1975, etc.), or in the case of measures of collective security undertaken with the authority of that organization, the only significant case of which was the Korean War (1950–53).[64] United Nations peace-keeping forces in the Middle East have been present by the invitation of the host countries, and had to be withdrawn when requested, as was done by President Nasir in the run-up to the Six-Day War in 1957.[65] Collective intervention can be authorized by a regional pact such as the Organization of American States (OAS), but only in respect of its members and not in theory if contrary to'a resolution of the UN itself, though this has not yet happened. Thus the US intervention in the Dominican Republic in 1965 was valid (however foolish or unnecessary it may have been), but the US intervention in Grenada in 1983 was not, as the Organization of Eastern Caribbean States (OECS) did not have the authority to authorize an intervention and, in any case, broke its own rules by not allowing Grenada to vote on the matter.[66] Soviet intervention in Afghanistan in 1979 was stated by the USSR to have been validated by an invitation to intervene from the Afghan government, but since the government in question was not in the country at the time and only achieved power after the event, this too seems dubious.[67] Third World states cannot therefore in practice rely on their legal standing in international law to protect them from *faits accomplis* of this kind. It is, however, true to say that overt interventions of this kind are comparatively rare.

Where there exists a large 'grey area' is in the field of covert or indirect intervention. 'Intervention' is a term that is often much misunderstood. Strictly speaking it means to 'come between' two contending parties in such a way as to alter the balance of advantage between them; a state can therefore 'intervene' in either an international or another country's internal conflict situation. We can distinguish various kinds of intervention, but one common factor, if the word is to retain any real meaning at all, must be that the action concerned must be specific and of finite duration. The pursuit of normal diplomatic relations beween countries may have some very unpleasant results, but it is not intervention.[68]

Diplomatic intervention, therefore, which is also quite proper in international law, is the indication through diplomatic channels that certain courses of action will or will not receive the support of the great power concerned, with a view to ensuring that a certain policy is carried into effect.

Economic intervention is a phrase that has been widely misunderstood and distorted almost out of recognition. To intervene economically is to offer economic inducements for a specific policy, or to threaten to cut off trade links or financial aid. In theory all these actions are quite properly within the competence of the government concerned, though questions of compensation might arise where a legal contract is involved. When it involves more subtle pressure; when, for example, a government orders its central bank to cut off funding or credit it is widely regarded in the Third World, however, as an immoral if not actually illegal act and is bitterly resented as a sign of the extent to which the great powers control the world financial system. The potential effects on the economy of the Third World state concerned can undoubtedly be severe, and the theory that such a 'destabilization' of the economy can bring about changes in government structure to the advantage of the great power concerned was apparently adopted by the US government in the early 1970s and followed up by a range of measures designed to bring about the collapse of the Chilean economy and with it the Marxist government of Salvador Allende.[69] The fall of that government in 1973 was therefore understandably blamed on the government of the United States, though the immediate instigators were of course the Chilean armed services themselves.

The obvious disadvantages with such a procedure are that the consequences are very unpredictable. Similar pressure on the government of Cuba both before and after the abortive invasion of 1961 served merely to strengthen the regime. And as this case shows, the temptation is strong to proceed either to direct or indirect military intervention. By indirect intervention we mean support for irregular military forces either within the state concerned or operating across its frontiers from a safe base in a third state. It is quite contrary to international law to arm and train forces for the invasion of a neighbouring state, or to support an enemy in arms against it. Yet this kind of indirect warfare has in fact become a major feature of the international scene, examples being the civil wars in Angola, Cambodia and Nicaragua, in each of which outside powers are sponsoring rebellion against the government of the day that is in the first and last cases, recognized as such by most of the outside world and by the United Nations. Hence no policy-maker can afford to ignore this possibility, and we may be sure, in fact, that it is ever present in their minds when weighing up the international situation.

To sum up, therefore, the policy-makers of new states see a world dominated by superpowers, in which they are much more conscious of their weaknesses than their strengths. So they act, in the main, cautiously. On the other hand, their main domestic constituency, the educated élite, naturally believe that political independence should be used to benefit them, and resent the fact that their government is locked into a world financial and economic order which seems to them heavily loaded in favour of the wealthy and powerful. Their most powerful constituency, the military, have exaggerated confidence in their own abilities, but their practical weaknesses mean that their aggression tends to be directed more towards their own government than towards the outside world. Their larger constituency, the masses, feel that their country should cut a respectable figure in the world—a view encouraged by politicians at election times, who with their inexperience of the world are often inclined to promise much more than they can achieve. Faced with the hard realities of world politics, those politicians, once in power, can only resort to gaining the maximum internal political capital from the few things they can do, such as making impassioned speeches, visiting other political leaders, voting at the United Nations, and expressing their sympathy for popular causes.

7 Playing the Game

The last question that the decision-makers of a new state have to answer, after taking account of its environment, its capabilities and limitations, and the rules of the international system, and before becoming too accustomed to any of them is: which game to play? There is no doubt about the pay-offs which are desired. As we have seen, they consist of wealth status and power. All these will accrue to the ruling élite in the event of them being gained by the state, so the interests of the two are parallel though never identical. As we have seen, too, it is not necessarily impossible to pursue all three of these goals simultaneously, but at any one time it may be necessary to trade off one against another: to use power to acquire status, to dispense wealth in order to accumulate the resources of power and to assert status in order to compensate for inadequate resources. Such trade-offs will affect the position of individual members of the ruling élite, and are therefore a subject for internal political settlement. But this still leaves open the question as to how these objectives are to be secured, and what roles they are to adopt.

Being leaders within their own states it is perhaps natural that their vanity and inexperience often leads them to try to assume leadership roles in the international arena. There are however, only a limited number of such roles open to be filled and the decision-maker who seeks to fill one of them must have resources and capabilities commensurate with the role in question or he will at best look absurd and at worst injure the interests of his country beyond redemption.

It is obvious, for example, that the two superpowers enjoy a stable relationship with one another which gives them a mutual interest in the maintenance of one another's position

Ideological polarization, which maintains this position, does so by helping keep their allies and client states in line, thus preventing the reemergence of the shifting alliances associated with the traditional European 'balance of power' system. The leaders of France and Britain have tried to play at being superpowers long after they had the resources to do so, and have succeeded in making themselves look absurd. But by definition a third world state will not be a superpower, and, as we have already seen, China, the most likely state to evolve into one, has so far foregone the role.

The highest aspiration of a third world leader, therefore, will be to lead a regional power. Two regional powers, Australia in Oceania and South Africa in Sub-Saharan Africa, are usually regarded, on account of their economic development, as part of the First World, as is Japan, which since 1945 has been precluded by its Constitution from exercising military power. Third World states that have acted in a regional role in the same period include Brazil in South America, China in East Asia, Indonesia in South East Asia, India in South Asia, Iran in South West Asia, and Egypt in North Africa. It may only be coincidence that most states likely to be able to assume such a role are states that have reemerged rather than emerged from colonial status. Establishing links with and maintaining friendly governments in such important states has since 1945 been a principal concern of the diplomacy of both the United States and the Soviet Union.

Other third world states with more limited resources and capabilities have leaders who must at the least defend the national frontiers, confront the historic enemy (if any), and cut a reasonable figure in the company of foreign dignitaries. This last point is more serious than it seems: President Carlos Julio Arosemena of Ecuador, for example, was deposed by the military of Ecuador in 1963 when at the airport to welcome the President of Colombia, he was overcome by alcohol and fell flat on his face on the tarmac.[1] Conversely a well-timed foreign tour, taking in a speech to the United Nations on the need for a New International Economic Order and a visit to Washington to sign new loan agreements followed by a 'photo opportunity' in the White House Rose Garden, means votes in the mid-term municipal elections for a third world President and his party.

Today even the leaders of the smallest and weakest states can enjoy these and similar benefits to their internal political standing, since every state that is a member of the UN has a vote and those votes are useful to the superpowers as well as to countries like Britain who have got themselves into diplomatic difficulties (Belize, the Falklands) for which they need support. Thus Dr François Duvalier's Haiti was persuaded to vote for the exclusion of Cuba from the inter-American System by a well placed loan, though in 1965 the resolution in the OAS in support of the US intervention in the Dominican Republic was carried only with the support of the vote of the disputed government of the Dominican Republic itself.[2] Any sign of notice by statesmen abroad is gratefully noted in such countries and turned as rapidly as possible by propaganda into the hard coin of political support at home.

Leaders of smaller states can, of course, always hope to multiply their influence, if not their power, by working with the leaders of other countries to form a group. At any given time since the Bandung Conference of 1955 there have always been prominent in the international system a number of political leaders who owe their world renown to their group role: Marshal Tito of Yugoslavia, Gamal Abd-el Nasir of the United Arab Republic (Egypt), and in part Dr Fidel Castro of Cuba. The most effective 'grouperpowers' have been those acting on a regional basis to try to solve a particular regional problem. Recent examples are the 'front-line states' in the settlement of the Rhodesia question and the emergence of Zimbabwe, and the Contadora Group (Colombia, Mexico, Panama and Venezuela) in the early Eighties and the confrontation between the United States and revolutionary Nicaragua.

Next there is the *choice of roles* for the leader himself. Here there are many possibilities: the Redeemer of his People, like Kwame Nkrumah; the World Leader, like Jawaharal Nehru; the Benefactor of the Fatherland, like the megalomaniac Rafael Trujillo of the Dominican Republic; the supernatural being, like the elder Duvalier in his role as 'Baron Samedi', the king of the Un-Dead; the Commander of the Faithful, like the Ayatollah Khomeini; the New Machiavelli, like Luis Echeverría of Mexico, who gained three votes for the post of Secretary General of the United Nations; or the New

Napoleon, like Nasir. And one other role at least is open to the
leader of a relatively small state, though at a high cost, and that
is the role of revolutionary leader, spreading the message
abroad as well as at home. As we have already seen, the
successful revolutionary leader, if his defeated rivals have
support in the international community, will himself be driven
to seek help abroad. If the traditional patron state is prepared
to retain its links then well and good; if not, the alternative is a
reversal of alliances, and that means gaining the tacit support if
not the active help of the rival superpower. Again the examples
of Nasir in 1956, Castro in 1961, Gaddafi in the 1970s, the
Nicaraguan junta in 1979 come to mind. A major exception has
been the Islamic regime of the Ayatollah Khomeini in Iran,
which has continued to regard the Soviet Union as the 'lesser
Satan' and has instead appealed for support to the considerable group of Islamic states that surround it on East, South and
West.

Lastly new states may, and do, seek to win influence through
gaining laurels in cultural and more particularly sporting
competitions, such as the Olympic Games or the World Cup,
which though established in the first instance by citizens of the
older states offer outstanding individuals from relatively poor
countries the chance to shine and to win renown for their
national flag. It is true that by doing so they accept to some
extent rules that have been laid down by older states and the
older states tend to interpret the rules in a fashion which is to
some extent binding upon the newcomers. But this does help to
some extent to turn what might otherwise be irreconcilable
differences into simple disputes about the application of rules,
though for many third world countries, for whom games form
a surrogate field in which they can compensate for their relative
lack of influence in international affairs, it is a very serious
occupation. In 1969 a disputed decision in the third qualifying
round for the World Cup gave the stimulus for a war between
the Central American states of El Salvador and Honduras in
which over 5,000 were killed in thirteen days.[3]

In the field of diplomacy this facility to interpret the rule of
international discourse also applies, and has been used to
ensure that newcomers to the international system abide by the
traditional pattern. An interesting example in 1957 was the

occasion on which in the early days of its independence Ghana sent a Diplomatic Note to the United Kingdom.[4] This occasioned great surprise in London, for Ghana, as a member of the Commonwealth, was expected to treat the UK as a fellow Commonwealth member, and it is a distinctive characteristic of relations within the Commonwealth that they avoid much of the formality which attaches by diplomatic tradition to relations between non-Commonwealth countries or between Commonwealth countries and non-Commonwealth ones.

I have throughout likened the behaviour of states in international relations to a game. There are, however, in general no umpires in the international system, and neither the decisions of the great powers, nor, when unwelcome, those of the United Nations, are accepted as authoritative and binding on parties to a dispute. The fundamental assumption that international relations is the sum total of a series of bilateral relations is still a very strong one, and continues to dominate politics in a world of many states. Above all, if only for the sake of simplicity it tends to dominate the thinking of new states, who in any case often emerged with a ready-made antagonist in the form of the former colonial power. It took a hundred years of peace for the 'first new nation', the United States, to cease to regard the rest of the world in terms of its original struggle with Britain, and it was Britain, not the United States, that led the process. The Irish could, as individuals, fight in the British Army in World War II, and even receive their pensions from London, but Ireland as a state could not formally enter the war.

It seems, then, that some major decisions are taken at what traditionally have been regarded as the pre-decision stages by the decision-making school of theorists. The first step is to identify one's principal opponent. The *identification of an opponent* enables one to apply a bilateral game model to the situation and to organize relations with other countries around a single principal polarity. It was regarded by Kennedy's decision-makers as the first step in coping with the Cuban Missile Crisis of 1962.[5] But this is by no means a creation of the Cold War, the bipolar world or the world of the superpowers. Most of the older states have an old antagonist (e.g., Britain and France), or indeed an old enemy (as in the case of India and Pakistan). In 1942 many Mexicans, with historical memories of their territorial losses in 1848, were amazed to find themselves at war on the same side as the 'gringos' and not against them. These traditional rivalries and hostilities form the core conflict around which all other negotiations and understandings are based; it is in terms of the knowledge and understanding gained in the bilateral conflict that other subordinate relations are organised. Making use of our own knowledge of games, we can therefore analyse the process of decision-making in terms of a series of bilateral relations in the way that such analogies would suggest would be most profitable.

As the case of India and Pakistan shows, the relative newness of states does not necessarily preclude them having an ancient antagonist. One need only think of the frontline states in confrontation with South Africa to realize how easily this polarity has been translated into the bilateral diplomacy for countries of the African continent, and by way of that into a multilateral policy for the Organization of African Unity. The confrontation with South Africa, therefore, has acted to consolidate the rather tenuous links which the African countries enjoyed at independence and to give them a degree of solidarity in international relations greater than might otherwise have been attainable.[6]

Ancient antagonisms are useful in avoiding responsibility as well as placing it. For example, the failure of the British negotiations to enter the European Economic Community in 1962 is invariably in Britain attributed to a veto by the French president, Charles de Gaulle.[7] The notion of a veto, melodramatic as it is, not only places responsibility on a single antagonist (now conveniently dead) but it avoids any sense that Britain, by its dilatory, hesitant and indeed antagonistic behaviour, might have demonstrated itself to be a power which the other European Community countries did not wish to have enter at that stage. This is not the only example of British intransigence leading to unnecessary international difficulties focused on a single political opponent—the Suez crisis of 1956 is an outstanding example. Anthony Eden, obsessed with the belief that Nassir was a dictator who had, like Hitler, to be resisted at all costs, was drawn into a joint military action with

France and Israel which not only was bound to fail, but also was inadequately underpinned diplomatically to have any positive value.[8] Among new states, the reciprocal example was the Egyptian obsession with the destruction of Israel which, following its fortuitous and largely spurious success at Suez, led Nassir into the débâcle of the Six-Day War, and Anwar Sadat into the further disaster of the Yom Kippur War.[9]

A foreign opponent, particularly an easily identified one, has particular value within the domestic context. For, as already suggested, the principal objectives of all foreign policy-makers are domestic ones. They want to stay in power, to enhance, if possible, their own position, or at least to hold their place on the greasy pole of political preferment. Their principal objective in all cases, therefore, will be to secure a desired outcome which will confer credit upon them. It is true that in international relations the situation, and in particular a crisis situation, is generally at least in part attributable to an outside power, and to this extent beyond the control of the politician. But it lies within the control of the politician to defined the situation by telling his people what for the purposes of the exercise counts as the desired outcome, to define the objectives of prospective action, and hence to state the issue on which action is required. What constitutes an issue is capable of considerable interpretation, though in not all circumstances is the freedom for action as wide as it is in the great majority of cases. In short, the issue in a conflict is not necessarily the cause of the conflict, but only that aspect of the conflict which is highlighted or chosen by one of the two contending parties to be the one through the emphasis of which it is most likely to secure its general objectives.

Definition of the situation was crucial to the Israeli decision to invade Lebanon in 1982.[10] The civil war there had been raging since 1975 and had been accompanied by the steady rise to ascendancy of the Maronite Christians, who in confrontation with the Syrian backed Sunni Muslims had been effectively able to hold their own. The costs in lives had been high, and the destruction of Beirut as the entrepôt of the Middle East had been almost complete, but one of the incidental results was that the Palestinian forces in Lebanon no longer enjoyed a secure base and were pinned down in Beirut. They were consequently separated from Israel by a zone of peace in southern Lebanon which the Israelis effectively controlled and so no longer presented an immediate danger to it.

The Israelis, however, were not prepared to give effective support to the Christians, despite the fact that they certainly did not want the Syrians to move south on the pretext of restoring order. A first attempt to invade Lebanon in strength in 1978 was checked by pressure from the United States, Israel's major backer and arms supplier; but Israel left a proxy in charge there in the shape of the irregular forces of Major Haddad. Taking advantage of the continued fighting, Israel mounted regular reprisal raids evidently aimed at rooting out and destroying the headquarters of the Palestinians. This virtually impossible task had by no means been accomplished when in August 1981 the prime minister, Menachem Begin, brought Ariel Sharon into his cabinet as defence minister. It was Sharon who redefined Israeli security as requiring to the north a wider sphere of influence secured by Israeli arms, and who took advantage of Washington's past hesitations and the sympathies of the secretary of state, Al Haig, to launch the full-scale invasion of Lebanon of which he had long dreamt. Inevitably it was a disaster in every respect. It destroyed Israel's credibility as a small power resisting overwhelming aggression, demonstrated that its government, if not its people, was prepared to connive at the sort of atrocities (e.g., the Shatila massacre) that it had rightly invited the outside world to condemn in others and wrecked its already overextended economy and credit. It did all this, moreover, without in any way strengthening the position of Israel itself; indeed by bringing the Syrians into Lebanon the entire sequence of events had even succeeded in weakening it.

Defining the issue follows, and is inseparable from the nature of the instruments which are available to be employed. Of the range of diplomatic instruments available—diplomatic persuasion, alliance politics, appeal to an international forum, adjudication and war—only the last was in practice usable for Israel; hence the ease with which a difficult diplomatic position was redefined into terms which appeared to offer prospects for a successful outcome. After all, had not the new state of Israel won every war in which it had taken part, despite the overwhelming odds confronting it? That it might not be equally well equipped with its distinctive citizen army to undertake what amounted to a police action on a long term basis was not adequately realized, it seems. Nor on this occasion could information be controlled, so that the action could be presented in an acceptable fashion to the outside world.[11] Israel's previous military engagements had been too brief to give much time for news gathering, and Israeli sources of information were so much more informative than Arab sources, that Israeli governments had always previously been able to gain every advantage from their de facto ability to control the flow of news. But in Lebanon, where news had been the life-blood of commerce, its importance was recognized by all sides, and exploited accordingly, and it was not long before the Arab view of Israel as a militaristic, imperialist power bent on endless conquest came to be taken at face value, both from the sheer weight of its presentation and the compelling argument that not to accept it would be to run the risk of having to look for oil supplies elsewhere.

The importance of presentation is fundamental to all conduct of diplomatic negotiations. The appearance of smooth, orderly negotiation is in itself an image which the diplomats maintain in order to preserve their professional expertise. But the presentation of issues becomes of crucial importance in crisis situations. A crisis is not, contrary to popular belief, something that breaks upon an astonished world unprepared. A crisis has to be *defined* as a crisis before it *is* a crisis.

In theory a crisis is a sudden combination of events which brings with it the threat of armed conflict and so disturbance to world peace. But the fact is that most conflicts in the Third World do not directly endanger world peace. The very fact that in 1986 there are over thirty wars going on in the world does not mean that the peace of the rest of the world is threatened. Even the superpowers do not have the capacity to become involved in very many conflicts at one time. Thus President Gerald Ford in 1975 defined the Angolan conflict as one that did not require the intervention of the United States; the conflict continues but it has never since looked remotely like becoming a crisis for the rest of the world.

It remains true, though, that it was a crisis for the newly-fledged government of Angola to find itself confronted by a substantial guerrilla force armed and backed by its powerful southern neighbour, South Africa. It called for and received substantial aid not only from the Soviet Union but among other pro-Soviet states from Cuba, which still maintains (1986) some 5,000 troops in Angola. Cuba is thus generally regarded in the West, particularly the United States, as a 'proxy state' for the Soviet Union. But the Cubans themselves claim to have acted independently of the Soviet Union in sending volunteers by chartered ship and public transport who were able to make use of the modern weapons that the Soviet Union had supplied. They did so, they say, to return the gift of freedom to the land from which so many of their own ancestors were, as slaves, taken by force.

The point about Cuban—as opposed to direct Soviet—intervention in Angola, of course, is that it was very difficult for the United States to define as a crisis such a remote 'threat' from its miniature neighbour (Cuba is just about the size of Pennsylvania but has a smaller population, 9.7 million). A crisis may it is true develop not because of the intrinsic importance of the situation as a whole but of a single *incident* within it, as when, in the same year, the Vietnamese government attacked the US ship *Mayaguez*, leading to a strong response from the United States. The arrest of a foreign national, his/her maltreatment or torture, an act of deliberate insult to the symbols of another country—all are the types of incident that in the past have led to crisis between states. But the other state always has the option of overlooking them, if necessary by finding excuses to do so, as did the British Government of Mrs Margaret Thatcher when it decided to overlook the arrest and torture of Sheila Cassidy and restore diplomatic relations with the military dictatorship of General Augusto Pinochet in Chile.

When difficulties arise between states that are not crises and are not exacerbated by embarassing incidents they can be, and are, treated as *problems*. Problems are the basic stuff of diplomacy, for a Third World state in particular. Lacking the necessary resources to take forceful action, and the necessary leverage to engage powerful allies, such a state has little alternative to settling down to a long run of diplomatic exchanges.

nternational relations lies less in the long-term attempts of
;overnments to secure the objectives (important though these
nay well be) than in the short-term effects that they have on the
nternal political system. These scenarios, it is suggested, are
•rimarily important for their dramatic quality. The long-term
ustification they create is for a series of confrontations, each of
vhich has, in the manner of all confrontations, a strong
•otential for the building of an image of success for individual
•oliticians and individual governments. The careful choice of
uch image-building confrontations, the designation of such
onfrontations as crises, to be managed and hence overcome
•y the skill and resolution of the diplomats and politicians, is of
he essence of international politics. The disjunction between
he image of policy and its actuality, moreover, explains why
;overnments from time to time make such extraordinary
nistakes, and indeed undertake disastrous forays into the
nternational arena when common sense would have suggested
he importance of avoiding anything of the kind. The history of
nternational politics, in fact, forms a sequence or series of such
onfrontations, which in successful cases have been arranged
o as to produce an overall positive effect on the international
nvironment. Such care in sequencing is needed not only to
.void the complications of being engaged simultaneously on
wo or more fronts with inadequate resources, but more
mportantly to maximize the dramatic possibilities in each
ituation. The ability to manage such dramatic confrontations,
noreover, is enormously enhanced by the ability of most Third
World states to exercise a high degree of control over the
nternal distribution of information. Any external confronta-
ion, therefore, however minor, can be turned to good account
.nd represented as being a diplomatic triumph for the
;overnment concerned, up to the point at which the invading
orces actually occupy the national capital and prove that they
vere wrong all the time. In such a closed atmosphere it is
oossible for very erroneous conceptions of the environment to
;ain ground and to be accepted as truth, a process helped and
ndeed accelerated by the phenomenon of 'groupthink' which
operates to ensure that group solidarity within a ruling body
:an, and in certain circumstances does ensure, that any
eservations there may well be about the current project are not

voiced owing to a belief in the superior wisdom of the group and the social pressures of not wishing to be thought of as a dissentient.[14]

The now classic example of such a sequence, culminating in a disastrous misperception of the world which went wrong, is that of the military government of Argentina after 1976. This government came to power by military force at a time in which the country was in a state of crisis. The military authorities believed that this crisis was due to subversion, and, seeing themselves as possibly the ultimate defenders of Western civilization against the insurgents, proceeded to crack down on them severely in the repression known as the 'Dirty War'. Towards the end of May 1977, however, their concentration on internal affairs was increasingly disturbed by a development in the international community which had been begun many years before. The long standing dispute with Chile over the Beagle Channel Islands had been taken to international arbitration under an agreement long since subsisting between the two countries, and it was at this point that the results of the arbitration were made known, awarding the islets to Chile. Though the islets themselves were of no significance, this award affronted the susceptibilities of the military government, which chose to ignore the award and proceeded to mobilize its forces for a confrontation with Chile which, if fought on land, it was confident of winning. Before the confrontation could result in open warfare, a more compelling offer of mediation was offered by the Vatican, and the issue removed from the arena of international conflict in a manner which enabled both Argentina and Chile, both under strongly Catholic right-wing governments, to sink their differences in a common accord to stand against the Left.

The problem with this was, however, that the government had been deprived of a valuable image-building confrontation in the outside world, and finally turned its attention back to the long standing dispute over the Falkland Islands in the search for a new image-building confrontation with Britain. This confrontation risk had earlier been handled by Britain with great subtlety. Perceiving the threat as a potentially real one, the Labour government in Britain arranged for a flotilla of ships to stand by, and without formally conveying to

Argentina the news that they were doing so, let it be known through third parties that they were prepared to meet force with force.[15] The issue was thereupon driven underground until after the election of Ronald Reagan as president to the United States, when, believing themselves now to have a strong ally in Washington, the military government once more advanced down the path of confrontation, with the results which are well known to the world.

Confrontation with Chile, a very respectable adversary, would have been very satisfying both from an image-making point of view, and from the point of view of hereditary rivalry, but it involved conflict with a fellow Latin American country, and it was not wholly certain, given the strength of the Chilean navy, that Argentina would in fact be able to win the confrontation, given that it would have to be fought in Tierra del Fuego in which naval power would be of great significance. Conflict with Britain, a formidable adversary, was in the image sense even more desirable, but, though Britain's ability to deploy naval forces at a great remove had been publicly downgraded by Mr Nott's own defence review, the confrontation still had to be undertaken with a prior assurance that there would be no serious attempt to resist. This assurance was not present in 1977; in 1982, owing to a combination of misleading information from both London and Washington and the groupthink by then far advanced in the closed confines of an authoritarian military regime, the situation was disastrously misread. The consequences were the total destruction of the credibility of both government and regime—and, incidentally, the saving of that of Mrs Thatcher.

Miscalculation of this kind has been by no means confined to Argentina, and it is interesting to see how in other circumstances it has been possible for the government concerned to recover so easily from its mistakes. The Chinese punitive expedition into Vietnam in February 1979 was widely recognized in the West as a disaster. The Chinese from the beginning stated that their purpose was only to make a momentary intervention and then retreat, but it became obvious before they had succeeded in doing so that it had been no easy task.[16] Nevertheless, the control of information within China was such that the Chinese themselves were in no way aware of the fact that their government had made a serious diplomatic miscalculation, and the relative strength of Vietnam and China were such that the Chinese at least had no fear of a serious Vietnamese reprisal. They certainly did not achieve their objectives, but despite losing an estimated 10,000 troops, avoided losing international prestige through a swift withdrawal.

In the case of Iraq's attempt to sieze the Iranian oil-fields, when, after being repeatedly denounced by the Iranian government led by the Ayatollah Khomeini, in September 1980 Saddam Hussein appears erroneously to have believed that his neighbour was in a state of internal chaos which would make it unable to resist, the attack led to a full-scale war.[17] That war, in turn, enabled Iran, through the appeal to a combination of religious sentiment and nationalism to rally its forces and reconstitute its armies, so that the new Iran proved to be if anything a more powerful military machine than the Shah would have been able to provide. In the short-term, it was certainly stronger, insofar as the religious zeal of its soldiers seems to have compensated with their lives for the inadequacies of their training, preparation and armament. The Gulf War, which is still going on, has therefore been one of appalling attrition and has been disastrous for both sides. It certainly has not strengthened their regime in Iraq against those of its neighbours in the Middle East. Since both sides can freely buy arms on the open market, no one has rushed to give more than the minimum assistance. In fact both superpowers seem to have been content to sit back and watch two normally troublesome countries wholly engaged in doing the maximum damage to one another.

To serve a successful image-building purpose, confrontations need neither be military nor conducted in a bilateral context. Diplomatic negotiations of all kinds are image-building occasions, whether they are about bank loans, fishing rights, or the sale of sheep meat. Mrs Thatcher may not have needed the Falklands War; her repeated forays into European summit diplomacy to obtain budget rebates on behalf of the United Kingdom have proved powerfully supportive from the point of view of her own political position. They admirably illustrate, however, the dangers of seeking confrontation in a multilateral context. Where the outcome depends, as in this case, on a consensus of agreement, the parties seeking the confrontation stand to lose by the creation of coalition against it, and such has proved to be the case.

For Third World politicians, however, with much more effective control of the media, it is much easier to supply the interpretation along with the report, and the events themselves need not be so demanding; as we have seen, a simple visit to Washington or Moscow, a speech in person at the United Nations, are good examples of the sort of media event on which third world international relations subsists, and whose prime purpose is the strengthening of the leader's domestic political position. Attacks on foreign leaders by US congressmen or British MPs, which presumably have a beneficial effect for those politicians, have a very two-edged effect abroad. Often they act to strengthen rather than weaken the position of the leader attacked. With skilful handling the leader can, after all, turn the occasion into a dramatic confrontation with a politician from a powerful state, a (harmless) surrogate for confrontation with the state itself.

Such events are useful because they have little or no real significance other than publicity, and consequently are not open to the usual objections of most foreign policy initiatives—that they may go wrong if the other party refuses to stick by the rules or conventions. They are as scripted and predictable as a state visit, where prodigies of effort are devoted to ensuring an anodyne series of statements, the principal purpose of which is to accompany the pictures of the two leaders together. The development of press photography and more recently television has enhanced the value of these occasions, as the overriding imperative for pictures and the very short time in the average news bulletin in which information can actually be conveyed plays directly into the hands of the news managers, who have, in any case, ensured in advance that the event will be seen the way they want it to be. Summit meetings are therefore of particular value when all outstanding issues have already been settled, and the occasion can be used for the purely ceremonial purpose of signing agreements painfully arrived at after months and perhaps years of negotiation behind the scenes. It was a measure of the failure of diplomatic relations between the superpowers that at the Reagan-Gorbachev Summit in 1985 this groundwork had evidently not been done, and from the standpoint of the US government that meeting served only to demonstrate a commitment to peace without actually conceding anything on the question of arms limitation. The joint statement by the Latin American leaders at Lima earlier in the year, on the occasion of the inauguration of President Alan Garcia (the Declaration of Lima), was, on the other hand, a well mounted demonstration of their growing solidarity on the debt issue, well calculated to exert pressure on the international financial community in forthcoming debt settlements.

Such settlements are the stuff of diplomacy, and it is the very length of time that it takes to reach an acceptable conclusion that tends to discredit diplomacy in the eyes of the public at large. As we have seen, some new states, the so-called revolutionary states such as, in their time, the United States, France or the Soviet Union, or today Cuba and Libya, have gone further. They have tried to reject the entire world diplomatic order as being either irrelevant to their needs or even a positive hindrance to their acceptance as an equal. There are, of course, some grounds for regarding this as a reasonable complaint, but to regard the world as a confrontation between the established powers and the new emerging forces does not necessarily mean that in that confrontation the new forces are going to win.[18] The historical precedents, as we have seen, suggest that the world order is very resistant to change—much more so, perhaps not surprisingly, than any individual country or group of countries. It would be too pessimistic to accept that new states have only one role in that order, that of victim. But it would be too optimistic to expect them to be able to do very much to influence matters, either, certainly the history of the 1970s seemed to confirm their fundamental weakness. At the same time as the first projections were appearing about the possible combined effects of the increase of population, energy use, exhaustion of resources and pollution, the United States was responding to the oil crisis of the early 1970s in a way that was to lead within a very short time to an increased energy gap.[19] Then the attempts of the energy-rich countries to recoup their position by forcing an increase in the oil price and a change in the terms of trade was met with such resistance that in the early 1980s major world oil-producers such as Mexico, Indonesia and Rumania found themselves bankrupt.

Such violent fluctuations make things difficult for the advanced industrial countries, but their effect on some of the poorer ones has been nothing short of catastrophic. The bitterness to which this has given rise is something to which the advanced countries must realistically give attention, if they do not want to be presented with even more serious problems for the future. They must try to see the problems of the new states in their own terms, remembering that their political weaknesses also limit their capacity to explain their interests adequately.[20] Above all, they must remember that among them war is not yet seen as an unrealistic option.

Notes

1. THE ILLUSION OF FOREIGN POLICY

1. Joseph Frankel, *The Making of Foreign Policy: An Analysis of Decision Making* (London: Oxford University Press, 1963), p. 1.
2. Martin Burch and Bruce Wood, *Public Policy in Britain* (Oxford: Martin Robertson, 1983).
3. R. Hambleton, 'Towards Theories of Public Learning', in Christopher Pollitt, Lew Lewis, Josephine Negro and Jim Patten (eds.), *Public Policy in Theory and Practice* (Sevenoaks, Kent: Hodder & Stoughton with The Open University Press, 1979), p. 4.
4. Alberto, A. Conil Paz and Gustavo E. Ferrari, *Argentina's Foreign Policy, 1930–1962* (Notre Dame, Ind.: University of Notre Dame Press, 1966), pp. 137–80; Alan Thomas, *Third World: Images, Definitions, Connotations* (Milton Keynes: Open University Press, 1983); Leslie Wolf-Philips, 'Why Third World?', *Third World Quarterly,* January 1979; Peter Willetts, *The Non-Aligned Movement: The Origins of a Third World Alliance* (London: Frances Pinter, 1978). See also Peter Lyon, *Neutralism* (Leicester: Leicester University Press, 1963).
5. *The Annual Register, 1979*, p. 85.
6. Graham T. Allison, *Essence of Decision: Explaining the Cuban Missile Crisis* (Boston: Little, Brown, 1971), p. 13. Hedley Bull, 'International Theory: The Case for a Classical Approach', *World Politics* 18 (1966), 361–77, reprinted in Klaus Knorr and James N. Rosenau (eds.), *Contending Approaches to International Politics* (Princeton, NJ: Princeton University Press, 1969), argued that owing to the uncertainties of competing models this one had positive merit. F.S. Northedge (ed.), *The Foreign Policies of the Powers* (London: Faber & Faber, 1968), is a good example. See also Arnold Wolfers, 'The Actors in International Politics', in William Fox (ed.), *Theoretical Aspects of International Relations* (Notre Dame, Ind.: University of Notre Dame Press, 1959).
7. Raymond Aron, *Main Currents in Sociological Thought: 1* (Harmondsworth: Penguin, 1972), p. 70.
8. Allison, pp. 253–5.
9. *Ibid.*, pp. 67–96; see also James March and Herbert Simon, *Organizations* (New York: Wiley, 1958).

10. *Ibid.*, pp. 144–81.
11. James N. Rosenau, 'The Premises and Promises of Decision-Making Analysis', in J. Charlesworth (ed.), *Contemporary Political Analysis* (New York: The Free Press, 1967), pp. 189–211.
12. James N. Rosenau (ed.), *Linkage Politics: Essays on the Convergence of National and International Systems* (New York: The Free Press, 1969).
13. Harold and Margaret Sprout, *Foundations of International Politics* (Princeton, NJ: D. van Nostrand, 1962), p. 46–7.
14. Michael Brecher (ed.), *The Foreign Policy System of Israel* (London: Oxford University Press, 1972), pp. 11–12. See also Michael Brecher, B. Steinberg, and J. Stein, 'A Framework for Research on Foreign Policy Behavior', *Journal of Conflict Resolution* 13 (March 1969), 75–102; Michael Brecher, *Decisions in Israel's Foreign Policy* (London: Oxford University Press, 1974) and *Crisis Decision-Making: Israel 1967 and 1973* (Berkeley, Cal.: University of California Press, 1980); Richard Snyder, H.W. Bruck and Burton Sapin (eds.), *Foreign-Policy Decision Making: An Approach to the Study of International Politics* (New York: Free Press of Glencoe, 1962).
15. Bahgat Korany, 'Foreign Policy in the Third World: An Introduction', *International Political Science Review* 5 (1984), 1: 7–20.
16. For example, *ibid.*, 248–9.
17. Roland Perry, *The Programming of the President* (London: Aurum Press, 1984); Joseph Spear, *Presidents and the Press: The Nixon Legacy* (Cambridge, Mass.: MIT Press, 1984).
18. Compare, for example, K.J. Holsti, *International Politics: A Framework for Analysis* (Englewood Cliffs, NJ: Prentice-Hall, 1967), pp. 128–32, where the assumption is that 'political units' seek objectives.
19. Clinton Rossiter, *The American Presidency*, 2nd edn (New York: Time Magazine, 1960), pp. 13–16.
20. Peter Calvert, *Politics, Power and Revolution: An Introduction to Comparative Politics* (Brighton, Sussex: Harvester, 1983), p. 126.
21. Fitzroy Ambursley and James Dunkerley, *Grenada—Whose Freedom?* (London: Latin American Bureau, 1984), pp. 89 ff.
22. Hugh O'Shaughnessy, *Grenada: Revolution, Invasion and Aftermath* (London: Sphere Books with The Observer, 1984).
23. Ambursley and Dunkerley, p. 92; cf. *The Guardian*, 10 November 1983, citing US military estimates that 160 Grenadan soldiers and 71 'Cubans' were killed.
24. John H. Herz, *International Politics in the Nuclear Age* (New York: Columbia University Press, 1959), p. 64.
25. See Mattei Dogan and Dominique Pelassy, *How to Compare Nations: Strategies in Comparative Politics* (Chatham, NJ: Chatham House, 1984).
26. *The Annual Register, 1982*, p. 200, gives figures.
27. Calvert, *Politics, Power and Revolution:* cit. sup.
28. Peter Shearman, 'The Soviet Union and Grenada under the New Jewel Movement', *International Affairs* 61 (Autumn 1985), 4: 661–73, citing United States, Departments of State and Defense, *Grenada Documents:*

An Overview and Selection (Washington, DC: Departments of State and Defense, 1984); see also O'Shaughnessy, pp. 109–11, 224–6.

29. Tony Thorndike, 'Grenada: The New Jewel Revolution', in Anthony Payne and Paul Sutton (eds.), *Dependency under Challenge: The Political Economy of the Commonwealth Caribbean* (Manchester: Manchester University Press, 1984), p. 116.

30. See Peter Calvert, *The Falklands Crisis: The Rights and the Wrongs* (London: Frances Pinter, 1982), p. 158; cf. Fred Halliday, *The Making of the Second Cold War* (London, Verso, 1984), pp. 22–23.

31. Hugh Seton-Watson, *Nations and States: An Inquiry into the Origins of Nations and the Politics of Nationalism* (London: Methuen, 1977), p. 1.

32. Gabriel A. Almond and James S. Coleman, *The Politics of the Developing Areas* (Princeton, NJ: Princeton University Press, 1959).

33. See also Peter Calvocoressi, *World Order and New States* (London: Chatto & Windus for the Institute for Strategic Studies, 1962).

34. Martin Wight, *Systems of States* (Leicester: Leicester University Press and London School of Economics and Political Science, 1977), p. 16.

35. Calvert, *Politics, Power and Revolution*, pp. 41–4.

36. D.W. Brogan and D.V. Verney, *Politics in the Modern World* (London: Hamish Hamilton, 1963), p. 19.

37. International systems theorists include Morton A. Kaplan, *System and Process in International Politics* (New York: John Wiley, 1957); see also Kaplan (ed.), *The Revolution in World Politics* (New York: John Wiley, 1962); Klaus Knorr and Sidney Verba (eds.), *The International System: Theoretical Essays* (Princeton, NJ: Princeton University Press, 1961); James Rosenau, *International Politics and Foreign Policy* (Glencoe, Ill.: The Free Press, 1961).

38. Paul Reuter, *International Institutions* (London: Allen & Unwin, 1958), pp. 80–3; cf. Hedley Bull, *The Anarchical Society: A Study of Order in World Politics* (London: Macmillan, 1977), pp. 262–3.

39. Peter Calvert, *Revolution and International Politics* (London: Frances Pinter, 1984), p. 163.

40. Joseph Frankel, *The State and the Realm of Values* (Southampton: University of Southampton, 1965).

41. Martin Wight, *Power Politics*, 2nd edn (Leicester: Leicester University Press for Royal Institute of International Affairs, 1978, ed. Hedley Bull and Carsten Holbraad), pp. 101–2. On the Hobbesian view in a recent practical context, see Jeane Kirkpatrick, 'The Hobbes Problem: Order, Authority, and Legitimacy in Central America', *Across the Board* 18 (Sept. 1981), 22–31.

2. THE RULES OF THE GAME

1. For conflicting views on the definition and nature of the state see, *inter alia*, C.B. Macpherson, 'Do We Need a Theory of the State?' *Archives Européennes de Sociologie* 18 (1977), 2; Karl Deutsch, 'The Crisis of the State', *Government & Opposition* 16 (1981), 3: 331–43; Harry

Goulbourne (ed.), *Politics and State in the Third World* (London: Macmillan, 1980); Gianfranco Poggi, *The Development of the Modern State: A Sociological Introduction* (London: Hutchinson, 1978). For alternative views of international politics as a game, see, *inter alia*: John Spanier, *Games Nations Play: Analysing International Politics*, 3rd edn (New York: Holt Rinehart & Winston/Praeger, 1978), and Raymond Cohen, *International Politics: The Rules of the Game* (London: Longmans, 1981).

2. Caroline Thomas, *New States, Sovereignty and Intervention* (London: Gower, 1985).

3. Evan Luard, *A History of the United Nations, Volume I: The Years of Western Domination, 1945–1955* (London: Macmillan, 1984), pp. 23, 31; see also Marshall Singer, *Weak States*, p. 35, who notes that it was not until 1956 that the principle of general membership of the UN was accepted.

4. See, *inter alia*, Katherine C. Chorley, *Armies and the Art of Revolution* (London: Faber & Faber, 1943); Feliks Gross, *The Seizure of Political Power in a Century of Revolutions* (New York: Philosophical Library, 1958); D.J. Goodspeed, *The Conspirators: A Study of the Coup d'Etat* (London: Macmillan, 1962); Calvert, *A Study of Revolution*.

5. Steve Chan, 'Mirror, Mirror on the wall—Are the Freer Nations More Pacific?' *Journal of Conflict Resolution* 28 (Dec. 1984), 4: 617–48.

6. Bernard Diedrich, *Somoza and the Legacy of US Involvement in Central America* (London: Junction Books, 1982).

7. Clive Archer, *International Organisations* (London: Allen & Unwin, 1983).

8. Evan Luard, *The United Nations* (London: Macmillan, 1979).

9. Harold Karan Jacobson, 'New States and Functional International Organisations: A Preliminary Report', in Robert W. Cox (ed.), *International Organization: World Politics* (London: Macmillan, 1969), pp. 74–97. To international lawyers these bodies are known as 'public international unions'; see D.W. Bowett, *The Law of International Institutions*, 4th edn (London: Stevens & Sons, 1982), pp. 6–9.

10. Ernst B. Haas, *Beyond the Nation State: Functionalism and International Organization* (Stanford, Cal.: Stanford University Press, 1965); Amitai Etzioni, *Political Unification: A Comparative Study of Leaders and Forces* (New York: Holt Rinehart & Winston, 1965); David Mitrany, *The Functional Theory of Politics* (London: London School of Economics and Martin Robertson, 1975); Robert I. McLaren, 'Mitranian Functionalism: Possible or impossible?' *Review of International Studies* 11 (Jan. 1985), 1: 139–52.

11. Elizabeth Barker, *Britain in a Divided Europe 1945–1970* (London: Weidenfeld & Nicolson, 1972).

12. Valentine Herman and Juliet Lodge, *The European Parliament and the European Community* (London: Macmillan, 1978).

13. Louis T. Wells, Jr, 'The Multinational Business Enterprise: What Kind of International Organization?', in Robert O. Keohane and Joseph S. Nye, Jr (eds.), *Transnational Relations and World Politics* (Cambridge,

Mass.: Harvard University Press, 1973), pp. 97–114; J. Spero, *The Politics of International Economic Relations*, 2nd edn (London: Allen & Unwin, 1982); Susan Strange, 'The Study of Transnational Relations', *International Affairs* 52 (July 1976), 3: 333–45.

14. On ITT see James F. Petras and Morris H. Morley, *How Allende Fell: A Study in US–Chilean Relations* (London: Spokesman Books, 1974), pp. 29–35, 41, 65–7.

15. On the workings of the HEIC, for example, see Maurice Collis, *Siamese White* (Harmondsworth: Penguin, 1941).

16. Robert J. Donovan, *Eisenhower: The Inside Story* (New York: Harper, 1956), p. 25.

17. Paul Wilkinson, *Political Terrorism* (London: Macmillan, 1974).

18. Paul Wilkinson, *Terrorism and the Liberal State* (London: Macmillan, 1978).

19. Michael Akehurst, *A Modern Introduction to International Law*, 3rd edn (London: Allen & Unwin, 1977), pp. 72–5, 88–102.

20. *Ibid.*, pp. 20–1; Ullmann.

21. C.V. Wedgwood, *The Thirty Years War* (London: Jonathan Cape, 1938).

22. George Scott, *The Rise and Fall of the League of Nations* (London: Hutchinson, 1973), pp. 11–50.

23. Akehurst, *International Law*, p. 109.

24. *Ibid.*, pp. 15–16, 28, 43, 198; cf., 194; see also Herman Weber, 'New Standards for International Behaviour and Integration', in Rüdiger Jütte and Annemarie Grosse-Jütte, *The Future of International Organization* (London: Frances Pinter, 1981), esp. pp. 161–2.

25. Note on the Central American Court in Connell-Smith, pp. 51–2;

26. Luard, *History of the United Nations*, pp. 66–8; Bowett, *International Institutions*, pp. 266–82.

27. Bowett, *International Institutions*, p. 273, records only 13 Judgments and 12 Advisory Opinions in the twenty years 1945–64.

28. Akehurst, *International Law*, pp. 76–82; on application see, *inter alia*, Tom J. Farer, *The Future of the Inter-American System* (New York: Praeger, 1979).

29. Amnesty International, *Torture* (London: Amnesty International, 1973).

30. On extraterritoriality in Thailand, established by the Bowring Treaty of 1856, see Fred W. Riggs, *Thailand: The Modernization of a Bureaucratic Polity* (Honolulu: East–West Center Press, 1966), pp. 20–1, and Gerald Sparrow, *The Land of the Moon Flower* (London: Elek Books, 1955), esp. pp. 41–2, 116. Extraterritoriality was established in China by the (French) Treaty of Tientsin (1858) for which see Li Chien-nung, *The Political History of China 1840–1928*, trans. and ed., Ssu-yu Teng and Jeremy Ingalls (Princeton, NJ: D. van Nostrand, 1956), p. 86.

31. Li Chien-nung, *Political History of China*, pp. 37–42 discusses the cession of Hong Kong; Macau, which passed under Portuguese control under the Ming dynasty, was not formally ceded and theoretically remained Chinese. See also Joseph Y.S. Cheng, 'The Future of Hong Kong: A Hong Kong "Belonger's" View', *International Affairs* 58 (Summer 1982), 3: 476–88.

32. *The Times*, 18 June 1982.
33. Akehurst, *International Law*, p. 17.
34. Calvert, *Revolution and International Politics*.
35. Boris Goldenberg, *The Cuban Revolution and Latin America* (London: Allen & Unwin, 1965).
36. Ruth First, *Libya: The Elusive Revolution* (Harmondsworth: Penguin, 1974), p. 16.
37. Hamilton Jordan, Jr, *Crisis: The Last Year of the Carter Presidency* (New York: Putnam, 1982). For background of the Iranian Revolution see also Fred Halliday, *Iran: Dictatorship and Development* (Harmondsworth: Penguin, 1979); Roger Homan, 'The Origins of the Iranian Revolution', *International Affairs* 56 (Autumn 1980), 673–7.
38. Akehurst, *International Law*, pp. 30–1.
39. Samuel Eliot Morison and Henry Steele Commager, *The Growth of the American Republic*, 4th edn (New York: Oxford University Press, 1950), II, pp. 415–16.
40. Humphreys, *Diplomatic History of British Honduras*, p. 79.
41. Richard Langhorne, *The Collapse of the Concert of Europe: International Politics 1890–1914* (London, Macmillan, 1981), p. 120.
42. Franz Ansprenger, 'Namibia and Apartheid: What Type of Conflict? What Kind of United Nations Action', in Jütte and Grosse-Jütte, *Future of International Organization*, pp. 181–200.
43. M.J. Heale, *The Making of American Politics* (London: Longman, 1977), p. 70; Ralston Hayden, *The Senate and Treaties 1789–1817: The development of the treaty-making functions of the United States Senate during Their Formative Period* (New York: Macmillan: 1920), pp. 154–6.
44. Jozef Goldblat (ed.), *Non-Proliferation: The Why and the Wherefore* (London: Taylor & France, 1985), pp. 263–4 and ff. Cuba has neither signed nor ratified the Treaty.
45. Fred L. Israel (ed.), *Major Peace Treaties of Modern History 1648–1967* (New York: Chelsea House with McGraw Hill, 1967), Vol. 4, pp. 2615 ff. (Finland 1947); 2709 ff. (Austria 1955). The latter does, however, prohibit Austria from any reunification with Germany. See also Fred Singleton, 'The Myth of Finlandisation', *International Affairs* 57 (Spring 1981), 2: 270–85.
46. The Asia and World Forum, *Forum on ASEAN* (Taipei: The Asia and World Forum, 1980), p. 43; Bowett, *International Institutions*, p. 235.
47. Walter C. Clemens, Jr, 'Ideology in Soviet Disarmament Policy', *Journal of Conflict Resolution* 8 (1964), 1: 7–22.
48. Connell-Smith, pp. 190–6; Francis A. Beer, *Alliances: Latent War Communities in the Contemporary World* (New York: Holt Rinehart & Winston, 1970).
49. Bowett, *International Institutions*, pp. 234–5.
50. Robert Endicott Osgood, *NATO: The Entangling Alliance* (Chicago, Ill.: University of Chicago Press, 1962).
51. Bowett, *International Institutions*, p. 219.
52. L.L. Farrar, 'The Limits of Choice: July 1914 Reconsidered', *Journal of Conflict Resolution* 16 (1972), 1: 1–23.

53. Cf. Beer, *Alliances*.
54. J. David Singer and Melvin Small, 'Alliance Aggregation and the Onset of War, 1815–1945', in Beer, *Alliances*, pp. 12–67.
55. United Kingdom Parliament, House of Commons. *Official Report*, 6th series, Commons, 45, 1982–83, col. 759 (12 July 1983). See also *ibid.*, 35, 1982–83, col. 168 (18 January 1983).
56. For text see Henry Steele Commager (ed.), *Documents of American History*, 6th edn (New York. Appleton-Century-Crofts, 1958), pp. 169–75.
57. Dwight David Eisenhower, *The White House Years: Waging Peace 1956–1961* (Garden City, NY, Doubleday, 1964), p. 616.
58. The Sunday Times Insight Team, *The Falklands War: The full story* (London, Sphere Books, 1982), pp. 223–30, 237–8.

3. THE DOMESTIC ENVIRONMENT

1. Calvert, *Politics, Power and Revolution*, p. 7.
2. Convergence theory, which holds that the USSR and the US will tend to become more like one another, has not been accepted, but its refutation implies the refutation of both the earlier views; see Zbigniew K. Brzezinski and Samuel Huntington, *Political Power, USA/USSR* (London: Chatto & Windus, 1963).
3. Leonard Schapiro, *The Government and Politics of the Soviet Union* (London: Hutchinson, 1970), pp. 28 ff., 56, 57 ff.
4. Cf. Ali A. Mazrui, *Africa's International Relations: The Diplomacy of Dependency and Change* (London: Heinemann, 1977), pp. 234–45.
5. Calvert, *Politics, Power and Revolution*, pp. 70–3.
6. Satow, pp. 142 ff.
7. Calvert, *Revolution and International Politics*, p. 154.
8. Keith Robbins, 'James Ramsey Macdonald', in Herbert van Thal, (ed.), *The Prime Ministers* (London: Allen & Unwin, 1975), II, pp. 273 ff., esp. pp. 279–80, 283.
9. Frank Stacey, *The Government of Modern Britain* (Oxford: Clarendon Press, 1968), pp. 256–7.
10. Plischke, p. 176.
11. Eldon Kenworthy, 'Coalitions in the Political Development of Latin America', in Sven Groennings, E.W. Kelley and Michael Leiserson, (eds.), *The Study of Coalition Behavior* (New York: Holt Rinehart & Winston, 1970).
12. Giovanni Sartori, *Parties and Party Systems: A Framework for Analysis* (Cambridge: Cambridge University Press, 1976), pp. 3–13.
13. Classification of interest groups here follows Almond & Coleman, pp. 33 ff.; see also Calvert, *Politics, Power and Revolution*, pp. 87–90.
14. Cf. Samuel E Finer, *Comparative Government* (London: Allen Lane, 1972), pp. 152–4.
15. Michael Edwardes, *Nehru: A Political Biography* (Harmondsworth:

Penguin, 1971), p. 264; Jean Chesneaux, *China: The People's Republic, 1949–1976* (Hassocks, Sussex: Harvester Press, 1979), p. 91; Ross Terrill (ed.), *The China Difference: A Portrait of Life Today inside the Country of One Billion* (New York: Harper & Row, 1979), p. 41.

16. Peter Calvert, 'Demilitarisation in Latin America', *Third World Quarterly* 7 (Jan. 1985), 1: 31–43; see also Michael Howard, (ed.), *Soldiers and Governments: Nine Studies in Civil–Military Relations* (London: Eyre and Spottiswoode, 1957); Samuel P. Huntington, *The Soldier and the State; The theory and Practice of Civil–Military Relations* (Cambridge, Mass.: Harvard University Press, 1957); Morris Janowitz, *The Military in the Political Development of New Nations* (Chicago, III.: University of Chicago Press, 1964); Martin C. Needler, 'Military Motivations and the Siezure of Power', *Latin American Research Review* 10 (Fall 1975), 3: 63–79; Edwin Lieuwen, *Arms and Politics in Latin America* (New York: Praeger, 1961), pp. 125–32, and *Generals versus Presidents: Neomilitarism in Latin America* (London: Pall Mall Press, 1964); cf. John J. Johnson, *The Military and Society in Latin America* (Stanford: Stanford University Press, 1964), pp. 102–5.

17. Altaf Gauhar, 'Pakistan: Ayub Khan's Abdication', *Third World Quarterly* 7 (Jan. 1985), 1: 102–31; Ulf Sundhausen, *The Road to Power: Indonesian Military Politics, 1945–1967* (Kuala Lumpur: Oxford University Press, 1982).

18. Samuel Decalo, *Coups and Army Rule in Africa: Studies in Military Style* (New Haven: Yale University Press, 1976).

19. John Duncan Powell, 'Military Assistance and Militarism in Latin America', *Western Political Quarterly* 18 (June 1965), 2, Pt 1: pp. 382–392; see also R.D. McKinlay and A. Mughan, *Aid and Arms to the Third World: An Analysis of the Distribution and Impact of US Official Transfers* (London: Frances Pinter, 1984).

20. Needler.

21. Wight, *Power Politics*, p. 167, speaks of their influence on public opinion in the larger states, but direct influence on the military establishment seems in many ways to be more important. On the size of the US military establishment in Central America, see Don L. Etchison, *The United States and Militarism in Central America* (New York: Praeger, 1975), pp. 101–11. On Soviet military relations with the Third World states see Mark N. Katz, *The Third World in Soviet Military Thought* (London: Croom Helm, 1982).

22. On the Suriname coup, see *The Annual Register, 1980*, pp. 96–7. Alfred Stepan, *The Military in Politics: Changing Patterns in Brazil* (Princeton, NJ: Princeton University Press, 1971) reminds us that in the early 1960s the leading expert on the African military, William Gutteridge, in his *Military Institutions and Power in the New States* (New York: Praeger, 1965), pp. 143–4, rated the chances of a military coup in either Nigeria or Ghana low on account of the relatively small size of their forces. He notes that the first military coup in sub-Saharan Africa occurred in Togo, which then had an army of only 200 men. It should be said, however, that the events of 13 January 1963 can be, and were then

generally, interpreted as a political assassination of President Olympio for largely personal motives.

23. Compare Alexandre de S.C. Barros, 'The Formulation and Implementation of Brazilian Foreign Policy: Itamaraty and the New Actors', with Manfred Wilhelmy, 'Politics, Bureaucracy and Foreign Policy in Chile', both in Heraldo Muñoz and Joseph S. Tulchin (eds.), *Latin America Nations in World Politics* (Boulder, Col.: Westview Press, 1984), pp. 30–44, 45–62.

24. 'Diplomacy', in *Encyclopaedia Britannica*, 14th edn (1973), vol. 7, p. 472C.

25. Ian Roxborough, Phil O'Brien and Jackie Roddick, *Chile: The State and Revolution* (London: Macmillan, 1977), p. 188; cf. Paul Sigmund, *The Overthrow of Allende and the Politics of Chile, 1964–1976* (Englewood Cliffs, NJ: Prentice-Hall, 1977), pp. 258–60.

26. Tulchin, 'Authoritarian Regimes and Foreign Policy', p. 196.

27. Etchison, *The United States and Militarism*, *passim*.

28. McLaurin, Peretz and Snider, *Middle East Foreign Policy*, p. 45.

29. *Ibid.*, pp. 92, 248–9, 306.

30. Calvert, *The Falklands Crisis*, pp. 28–30; 34 lists members.

31. Alexander M. Haig, Jr, *Caveat: Realism, Reagan and Foreign Policy* (London: Weidenfeld & Nicolson, 1984), p. 289.

32. Helan Jaworski C., 'Peru: The Military Government's Foreign Policy in Its Two Phases (1968–1980)', in Muñoz and Tulchin, *Latin American Nations*, pp. 204–5.

33. Gérard Chaliand, *Revolution in the Third World: Myths and Prospects* (Hassocks, Sussex: Harvester Press, 1977), p. 91; Jeanne S. Mintz, *Mohammed, Marx and Marhaen: The Roots of Indonesian Socialism* (London: Pall Mall Press, 1965), p. 129 ff.; Donald E. Weatherbee, *Ideology in Indonesia: Sukarno's Indonesian Revolution* (New Haven, Conn.: Yale University Southeast Asia Studies, 1966), pp. 16–17.

34. Ivan Vallier, 'The Roman Catholic Church: A Transnational Actor', in Keohane and Nye (eds.), *Transnational Relations*, pp. 129–52.

35. Walter Ullmann, *A History of Political Thought: The Middle Ages* (Harmondsworth: Penguin, 1965).

36. Wight, *Systems of States*, p. 143.

37. Erwin I.J. Rosenthal, *Political Thought in Mediaeval Islam: An Introductory Outline* (Cambridge: Cambridge University Press, 1962).

38. Gauhar, 'Pakistan'; Saleem Qureshi, 'Military in the Polity of Islam: Religion as a Basis for Civil–Military Interaction', *International Political Science Review* 2 (1981), 2: 271–82; cf. Hisham B. Sharabi, *Nationalism and Revolution in the Arab World* (Princeton, NJ: D. van Nostrand, 1966), pp. 5–6, where Islamic fundamentalism is still regarded as being in retreat.

39. Alexandra David-Neel, *Buddhism: Its Doctrines and Its Methods* (London: The Bodley Head, 1977), pp. 21, 47, 132, 162.

40. Calvert, *Image-Making*.

41. Frankel, *The Making of Foreign Policy*, pp. 70–81.

42. Peter Donaldson, *Economics of the Real World* (London: British

Broadcasting Corporation and Penguin Books, 1977), p. 51; J.L. Hanson, *Monetary Theory and Practice* (London: Macdonald and Evans, 1974), pp. 3–5, 12–15.

43. Adam Smith, *The Wealth of Nations* (London: J.M. Dent, 1910), vol. II, pp. 180–1.

44. Anell and Nygren, *The Developing Countries*, pp. 119 ff.

4. HOW FOREIGN POLICY IS MADE

1. Harold Nicolson, *Diplomacy*, 3rd edn (London: Oxford University Press, 1963); Fred Charles Iklé, *How Nations Negotiate* (New York: Harper & Row, 1964); John Ensor Harr, *The Professional Diplomat* (Princeton, NJ: Princeton University Press, 1969); Ivone Kirkpatrick, *The Inner Circle: Memoirs of . . .* (London, Macmillan, 1959).

2. *The Annual Register, 1984*, pp. 39–41.

3. Frederick W. Ilchman, *Professional Diplomacy in the United States, 1779–1939: A Study in Administrative History* (Chicago, Ill.: University of Chicago Press, 1961); Alexander DeConde, *The American Secretary of State: An Interpretation* (London: Pall Mall Press, 1962). By contrast, Jorge I. Dominguez and Juan Lindau, 'The Primacy of Politics: Comparing the Foreign Policies of Cuba and Mexico', *International Political Science Review* 5 (1984), 1: 75–101, say that the foreign policy establishments of those two countries only became capable of projecting power outside national boundaries in the period 1950–70.

4. In 1982, Luis Arce Gómez, formerly General Garcia Meza's minister of the interior, was 'hastily transferred to the Bolivian Embassy in Buenos Aires before Dr Siles Zuazo was sworn in'—*The Guardian*, 12 October 1982. See also Harold Eugene Davis (ed.), *Government and Politics in Latin America* (New York, Ronald Press, 1958), pp. 431–2.

5. Sir Ernest Satow, *A Guide to Diplomatic Practice*, 4th edn, corrected (London: Longman, 1966), pp. 220–23.

6. *Ibid.*, pp. 99–100; see also p. 4.

7. Bull, pp. 179–80.

8. L.F.L. Oppenheim, *International Law: A Treatise,* 7th edn, ed. H. Lauterpracht (London: Longman, 1952, 7th edn.).

9. On UK, see Lord Strang, *The Foreign Office* (London: Allen & Unwin, 1965), pp. 146 ff.; Geoffrey McDermott, *The New Diplomacy and Its Apparatus* (London: Plume with Ward Lock, 1973); on the United States, Elmer Plischke, *Conduct of American Diplomacy*, 3rd edn (Princeton, NJ: D. van Nostrand, 1967), pp. 164 ff.; W. Wendell Blancké, *The Foreign Service of the United States* (New York: Praeger, 1969).

10. Peru's records were destroyed during Chilean occupation following the War of the Pacific (1879) when they were burnt to keep the Chilean forces warm; see Frederick B. Pike, *The Modern History of Peru* (London: Weidenfeld & Nicolson, 1967), p. 147.

11. Roberta Wohlstetter, *Pearl Harbor: Warning and Decision* (Stanford, Cal.: Stanford University Press, 1962), p. 206–27.

28. See Tulchin.
29. In Brazil, for example, Simonsen was transferred from Finance to Planning in 1979. His successor, Rischbieter, was in turn replaced in January 1980 by Galveas, also a former president of the Central Bank, while negotiations on debt resettlement were handled by the minister of planning, Professor Antonio Delfim Netto, and the new president of the Central Bank, Sr Carlos Langoni.
30. McLaurin, *et al.*, pp. 31–7.
31. Brian May, *The Indonesian Tragedy* (Singapore: Graham Brash, 1978), pp. 92–4.
32. Alfred Stepan, *The State and Society: Peru in Comparative Perspective* (Princeton, NJ: Princeton University Press, 1978), pp. 299–301.

5. CAPABILITIES

1. Implied by Max Weber, *The Theory of Social and Economic Organization*, ed. Talcott Parsons (New York: The Free Press, 1964), pp. 424–9.
2. Carlo Cipolla, *The Economic History of World Population*, 7th edn (Harmondsworth: Penguin, 1978); Hugh Tinker, 'Indira Gandhi', *Yearbook of World Affairs, 1979*.
3. Joseph Frankel, *International Relations in a Changing World* (Oxford: Oxford University Press, 1979), p. 31, accurately speaks of China as 'the most likely runner-up to the superpower status'. A. Doak Barnett, *The Making of Foreign Policy in China: Structure and Process* (London: Tauris for Johns Hopkins University Foreign Policy Institute, 1985), is the most recent analysis of its foreign policy.
4. Stepan, *The Military and Politics*, pp. 3–6.
5. John Keegan, *World Armies*, 2nd edn (London: Macmillan, 1983), pp. 65–79, 606–13; International Institute for Strategic Studies, *The Strategic Balance, 1984–1985* (London: International Institute for Strategic Studies, 1985).
6. Keegan, p. 366, notes that Libya has over 3,000 tanks, and ranks tenth in the world, despite being faced with no 'recognisable' military threat. See also First, *Libya*, pp. 59–86, on the role of foreign bases in Libya's independence.
7. Keegan, pp. 430–1; see also Richard A. Gabriel (ed.), *Fighting Armies: Nonaligned, Third World, and Other Ground Armies: A Combat Assessment* (Westport, Conn.: Greenwood Press, 1983), preface by editor; Wayas, *Nigeria's Leadership Role*, p. 26.
8. *Whitaker's Almanack, 1983*.
9. Morison and Commager, *The Growth of the American Republic*, pp. 566, 601–2. The US, however, lost some 5,000 square miles in Maine—*ibid.*, p. 567. See also George Elian, *The Principle of Sovereignty over Natural Resources* (Alphen aan den Rijn: Sijthoff & Noordhoff, 1979).
10. Keegan, p. 402. See also I.W. Zartman, 'The Politics of Boundaries in North and West Africa', *Journal of Modern African Studies*, April 1965.
11. Calvert, *Boundary Disputes in Latin America*, pp. 9–12.

12. Seton-Watson, pp. 85, 131, notes importance of military settlements on frontier of each.
13. R.D. McLaurin, Don Peretz, and Lewis W. Snider, *Middle East Foreign Policy: Issues and Processes* (New York: Praeger, 1982), p. 261. Interestingly, this strategic objective is not mentioned in Walter Laqueur's substantive treatment of the causes of the Six-day War, *The Road to War 1967: The Origins of the Arab–Israeli Conflict* (London: Weidenfeld & Nicolson, 1968).
14. Calvert, *Boundary Disputes*, p. 5.
15. Bryce Wood, *The United States and Latin American Wars, 1932–1942* (New York: Columbia University Press, 1966), pp. 150–66, 169–70.
16. Wight, *Power Politics*, p. 148.
17. Keegan, p. 447.
18. *The Times*, 14 August 1975.
19. Doudou Thiam, *The Foreign Policy of African States: Ideological Bases, Present Realities, Future Prospects* (London: Phoenix House, 1965), pp. 44–5; see also I. William Zartman, *International Relations in the New Africa* (Englewood Cliffs, NJ: Prentice-Hall, 1966).
20. Mitchell Bainwoll, 'Cuba', in Gabriel, *Fighting Armies*, pp. 225–45; Edwina Moreton, 'The East Europeans and the Cubans in the Middle East: Surrogates or Allies?' and for diplomatic background of conflict see Robert Patman, 'Ideology, Soviet Policy and Realignment in the Horn', in Adeed Dawisha and Karen Dawisha (eds.), *The Soviet Union in the Middle East: Policies and Perspectives* (London: Heinemann for the Royal Institute of International Affairs, (1982), pp. 62–84, 45–61, and James Mayall, 'The Battle of the Horn: Somali Irredentism and International Diplomacy', *The World Today*, September 1978.
21. D.G.E. Hall, *A History of South-East Asia*, 3rd edn (New York: St Martin's Press, 1968), pp. 507–10, 648–9.
22. John D. Hargreaves, *West Africa Partitioned, Volume I: The Loaded Pause, 1885–1889* (London: Macmillan, 1974); Seton-Watson, pp. 339–40.
23. Georges-André Fiechter, *Brazil since 1964: Modernisation under a Military Régime* (London: Macmillan, 1975), p. 209, describes plans.
24. See, *inter alia*, Robert Keith Middlemas, *The Master Builders* (London: Hutchinson, 1963); Desmond Young, *Member for Mexico: A Biography of Weetman Pearson, First Viscount Cowdray* (London: Cassell, 1966); Watt Stewart, *Keith and Costa Rica: A Biographical Study of Minor Cooper Keith* (Albuquerque, NM: University of New Mexico Press, 1964).
25. *Encyclopaedia Britannica*, 15th edn, 1974, vol. 15, p. 481. In Colombia, the Atlantic Railway, linking the departmental lines in the Magdalena Valley, was opened only in July 1961; for its impact, see Pat M. Holt, *Colombia Today—and Tomorrow* (London: Pall Mall Press, 1964), pp. 149–50.
26. Basil Davidson, *Black Star* (New York: Praeger, 1973), pp. 200–2.
27. R.J. Rummel, 'Some Empirical Findings on Nations and Their Behavior', *World Politics* 18 (Jan. 1966), 2: 236–82.
28. *The Times*, 27 October 1982; see also *ibid.*, 15 May 1981. See also R.A.

Nickson, 'The Itaipú Hydro-Electric Project: The Paraguayan Perspective', *Bulletin of Latin American Research* 2 (Oct. 1982), 1:1.

29. In 1763 at the Treaty of Paris, the French exchanged Guadaloupe and Martinique for the whole of Canada, and both the French negotiators and Voltaire thought that they had got the best of the bargain.

30. Central Office of Information, *The Falklands Islands and Dependencies* (London: HMSO, 1973).

31. Helmut Bley, *South-West Africa under German Rule, 1894–1914* (London: Heinemann, 1971), pp. 3, 193–6, 202; the discovery of diamonds in 1908 benefited the German Treasury but not the colonists nor the colonized (pp. 196 ff.)

32. Marshall R. Singer, *Weak States in a World of Powers: The Dynamics of International Relationships* (New York: The Free Press), p. 67; Bruce M. Russett (ed.), *World Handbook of Political and Social Indicators* (New Haven, Conn.: Yale University Press, 1964); on Nyerere's self-help policies see John Hatch, *Two African Statement: Kaunda of Zambia and Nyerere of Tanzania* (London: Secker & Warburg, 1976).

33. L.G. Espejo, 'Neutral but not Indifferent: Colombian Foreign Policy since 1900', unpublished PhD dissertation, University of Southampton, 1981; Holt, pp. 101–31.

34. James Dunkerley, *The Long War: Dictatorship and Revolution in El Salvador* (London: Junction Books, 1982), pp. 59–71.

35. Stacy May and Galo Plaza, *The United Fruit Company in Latin America* (Washington, DC: The National Planning Association, 1958).

36. David Rock, *Politics in Argentina, 1890–1930: The Rise and Fall of Radicalism* (Cambridge: Cambridge University Press, 1975), p. 9.

37. Ronald M. Chilcote and Joel Edelstein (eds.), *Latin America: The Struggle with Dependency and Beyond* (New York: John Wiley, 1974), introduction; Hélio Jaguaribe, *Problemas do desenvolvimiento Latino-Americano* (Rio de Janeiro: Ed. Civilizacao Brasiliera, 1967); Samir Amin, *Imperialism and Unequal Development* (Brighton: Harvester Press, 1977); Fernando Enrique Cardoso and Enzo Faletto, *Dependency and Development in Latin America* (Berkeley, Cal., University of California Press; 1979); Theotonio dos Santos, 'The Structure of Dependence', *American Economic Review* 60 (May 1970), pp. 231–6; André Gunder Frank, *Dependent Accumulation and Underdevelopment* (London: Macmillan, 1978) and *Latin America: Underdevelopment or Revolution* (New York: Monthly Review Press, 1969); Ivar Oxaal, Tony Barnet and David Booth (eds.), *Beyond the Sociology of Development: Economy and Society in Latin America and Africa* (London: Routledge, 1975); Ian Roxborough, *Theories of Underdevelopment* (London: Macmillan, 1979); Dudley Seers (ed.), *Dependency Theory: A Critical Reassessment* (London: Frances Pinter, 1981).

38. Robert J. Alexander, *The Bolivian National Revolution* (New Brunswick, NJ: Rutgers University Press, 1958); Richard W. Patch, 'Bolivia: US Assistance in a Revolutionary Setting', in Richard N. Adams (ed.), *Social Change in Latin America Today* (New York: Harper & Row for Council on Foreign Relations, 1960), p. 108.

39. Peter Calvert, *Guatemala: A Nation in Turmoil* (Boulder, Col.: Westview Press, 1985), pp. 79–80.
40. Paul Baran, *The Political Economy of Growth* (Harmondsworth: Penguin, 1957); cf. Cardoso and Faletto, pp. 76–80.
41. See e.g. Aldo Ferrer, *Living within our Means: An Examination of the Argentine Economic Crisis* (Boulder, Col.: Westview Press for Third World Foundation, 1985), p. 70.
42. Louis T. Wells, 'The Multinational Business Enterprise: What Kind of International Organization?', in Robert E. Keohane and Joseph S. Nye, Jr, *Transnational Relations and World Politics* (Cambridge, Mass.: Harvard University Press, 1973), pp. 97, 107, 111.
43. Gary W. Wynia, *The Politics of Latin American Development* (Cambridge: Cambridge University Press, 1980), pp. 16, 75 ff. and *passim*.
44. Lars Anell and Birgitta Nygren, *The Developing Countries and the World Economic Order* (London: Methuen, 1980), p. 146; R.H. Green, 'Things Fall Apart: The World Economy in the 1980s', *Third World Quarterly* 5 (Jan. 1983), 1.
45. Charles Curtis Cumberland, *Mexico, the Struggle for Modernity* (New York: Oxford University Press, 1968), p. 14.
46. Anell and Nygren, pp. 71, 144.
47. The term 'positional goods' was coined by Fred Hirsch, *The Social Limits to Growth* (London: Routledge, 1977).
48. Jorge I. Domínguez and Juan Lindau, 'The Primary of Politics: Comparing the Foreign Policies of Cuba and Mexico', *International Political Science Review* 5 (1984), 1: 75–101.
49. Calvert, *Guatemala*, p. 151; *Financial Times*, 27 May 1971; *New York Times*, 16 March 1974.
50. Amartya Sen, *Poverty and Famines* (Oxford: Clarendon Press, 1982); Teresa Hayter, *The Creation of World Poverty* (London: Pluto Press, 1981); C. Stevens, *Food Aid and the Developing Countries* (London: Overseas Development Institute and Croom Helm, 1979).
51. André Gunder Frank, 'The Development of Underdevelopment', *Monthly Review* 18 (Sept. 1966), 4: 17–31.
52. Anell and Nygren, *op. cit.*; Jorge I. Domínguez, *Economic Issues and Political Conflict: US-Latin American Relations* (London: Butterworths, 1982); John C. Griffin and William Rouse, 'Counter-trade as a Third World strategy of development', *Third World Quarterly* 8 (1986), 1, 177–204; Inter-American Development Bank, *Economic and Social Progress in Latin America: External Debt: Crisis and Adjustment* (Washington, DC: Inter-American Development Bank, 1985); Jaime Lozoya and Jaime Estevez, eds., *Latin America and the New International Economic Order* (Oxford: Pergamon Press, 1980); James F. Petras, ed., *Class, State, and Power in the Third World, with Case Studies on Class Conflict in Latin America* (London: Zed Press, 1981); Thomas, *op. cit.*

6. LIMITATIONS

1. Joseph Frankel, *International Relations in a Changing World* (Oxford: Oxford University Press, 1979), p. 30.
2. Ambursley and Dunkerley, p. 34; *The Annual Register, 1977*, p. 273.
3. David Vital, *The Inequality of States: A Study of the Small Power in International Relations* (Oxford: Clarendon Press, 1967), pp. 61, 121; see also Jonathan Alford, 'Security Dilemmas of Small States', *The World Today* 40 (Aug.–Sept. 1984), 8–9: 363–9.
4. Vital, p. 125; Anthony D. Smith, 'States and Homelands: The Social and Geopolitical Implications of National Territory', *Millennium* 10/3.
6. Andrew Boyd, *United Nations: Piety Myth and Truth* (Harmondsworth: Penguin, 1962), pp. 123 ff.
7. See, *inter alia*, John J. Stremlau, *The International Politics of the Nigerian Civil War 1967–1970* (Princeton, NJ: Princeton University Press, 1977), pp. 55–9 and map, p. 57; S.K. Panter-Brick (ed.), *Nigerian Politics and Military Rule: Prelude to Civil War* (London: Athlone Press, for Institute of Commonwealth Studies, 1970).
8. In Jamaica Crown Colony status was requested by the planters in 1865 to avoid democratization—see Emanuel de Kadt (ed.), *Patterns of Foreign Influence in the Caribbean* (London: Oxford University Press, for Royal Institute of International Affairs, 1972), p. 34.
9. N.S. Carey Jones, *The Anatomy of Uhuru: An essay on Kenya's Independence* (Manchester: Manchester University Press, 1966).
10. Sunday Times Insight Team, *Insight on Portugal: The Year of the Captains* (London: André Deutsche, 1975), pp. 13–30.
11. *The Times*, 21 December 1979; cf. *The Sunday Times*, 6 January 1980.
12. Thomas M. Franck, *Nation against Nation* (New York: Oxford University Press, 1985).
13. For the effects, see Sue Branford and Oriel Glock, *The Last Frontier: Fighting for Land in the Amazon* (London: Zed Press, 1985).
14. Peter Calvert, 'On Attaining Sovereignty', in Anthony Smith (ed.), *Nationalist Movements* (London: Macmillan, 1976), pp. 134 ff.
15. Henry Valen, 'National Conflict Structure and Foreign Politics: The Impact of the EEC Issue on Perceived Cleavages in Norwegian Politics', *European Journal of Political Research* 4 (March 1976), 1: 47–82.
16. See, *inter alia*, Norman Miller and Roderick Aya (eds.), *National Liberation: Revolution in the Third World* (New York: The Free Press, 1971); J. Bowyer Bell, *On Revolt: Strategies of National Liberation* (Cambridge, Mass.: Harvard University Press, 1976).
17. James Manor, 'Sri Lanka's Crisis', *The World Today* 41 (July 1985), 7: 121–2.
18. Marshall Singer, *Weak States*, pp. 90–1, points out that modern Cameroun was formerly united under German rule. On the complex background of Somalia, see John Drysdale, *The Somali Dispute* (London: Pall Mall Press, 1964), and see also A.C. McEwen, *International Boundaries of East Africa* (Oxford: Clarendon Press, 1971).
19. Kevin Boyle and Tom Hadden, *Ireland: A Positive Proposal*

(Harmondsworth: Penguin, 1985), pp. 68–9 emphasise the causes; see also Adrian Guelke, 'International Legitimacy, Self-determination and Northern Ireland', *Review of International Studies*, 11, No. 1, January 1985, pp. 37–52. On Anglo-Irish relations, see Paul Arthur, 'Anglo-Irish Relations since 1968: A "Fever Chart" Interpretation', *Government and Opposition* 18 2: 157–74.

20. Peter Calvert, *Boundary disputes in Latin America* (London: Institute for the Study of Conflict, 1983; Conflict Studies No. 146).

21. M.W. Williams, *Anglo-American Isthmian Diplomacy, 1815–1915* (Washington, DC: American Historical Association, 1915); Dana Gardner Munro, *Intervention and Dollar Diplomacy in the Caribbean 1900–1921* (Princeton, NJ: Princeton University Press, 1964).

22. Cecil Eprile, *War and Peace in the Sudan, 1955–1972* (Newton Abbot, Devon, David & Charles, 1974).

23. Karl Marx and Frederick Engels, 'Manifesto of the Communist Party', in Marx and Engels, *Selected Works* (Moscow: Foreign Languages Publishing House, 1962), vol. I, p. 38.

24. David Lane, *The End of Inequality? Stratification under State Socialism* (Harmondsworth: Penguin, 1971), p. 39.

25. Merrilee S. Grindle, *Bureaucrats, Politicians and Peasants in Mexico* (Berkeley, Cal.: University of California Press, 1977); Richard R. Fagen and William S. Tuohy, 'Aspects of the Mexican Political System', *Studies in Comparative International Development* 7 (Fall 1973), 208–20.

26. Mehmet Beqiraj, *Peasantry in Revolution* (Ithaca, NY: Cornell University Center for International Studies, 1966); for case studies see Eric Wolf, *Peasant Wars of the Twentieth Century* (New York: Harper & Row, 1970).

27. Insight, pp. 155–58.

28. For the official Comintern view of these, see 'A Neuberg', *Armed Insurrection* (London: NLB, 1970).

29. Thomas P. Anderson, *Matanza: El Salvador's Communist Revolt of 1932* (Lincoln, Neb.: University of Nebraska Press, 1971).

30. Werner Baer, Richard Newfarmer and Thomas Treber, 'On State Capitalism in Brazil: Some New Issues and Questions', *Inter-American Economic Affairs* 30 (Winter 1976), 63–93.

31. See, for example, Claude Ake, *Revolutionary Pressures in Africa* (London: Zed Press, 1978), p. 40.

33. Calvert, *Revolution and International Politics*, pp. 54–5; see also Kwame Nkrumah, *Neocolonialism: The Last State of Imperialism* (New York: International Publishers, 1965).

34. Paul C. Rosenblatt, 'Origins and Effects of Group Ethnocentrism and Nationalism', *Journal of Conflict Resolution* 8 (1964), 2: 131–46; see also Kenneth Minogue, *Nationalism* (London: Methuen, 1969).

35. George McTurnan Kahin (ed.), *Governments and Politics of Southeast Asia* (Ithaca, NY, Cornell University Press, 1964), pp. 421–2, 569–70.

36. McLaurin *et al.*, p. 279 ff.

37. *The Annual Register, 1974*, p. 194.

38. Frank L. Klingberg, 'Historical Periods, Trends and Cycles in

International Relations', *Journal of Conflict Resolution* 14 (1970), 4: 505–11, discusses the periodicity of conflict. On Antarctica see, *inter alia*, Peter Beck, 'Britain's Antarctic Dimension', *International Affairs* 59 (Summer 1983), 3: 429–44; F.M. Auburn, *Antarctic Law and Politics* (London: Hurst, 1982).

39. Paul Kennedy, *The Realities behind Diplomacy: Background Influences on British External Policy 1865–1980* (London: Fontana, 1981), pp. 372–4.
40. Haig, *Caveat*.
41. Henry A. Kissinger, *Nuclear Weapons and Foreign Policy* (New York: Harper & Row, 1957); cf. his 'Limited War: Conventional or Nuclear', in Donald G. Brennan (ed.), *Arms Control, Disarmament and National Security* (New York: George Braziller, 1961), pp. 138–52; Carl Sagan, 'Frozen in the Heat of Battle', *The Guardian*, 9 August 1984; Hans J. Morgenthau, 'The Four Paradoxes of Nuclear Strategy', *American Political Science Review* 58 (1964), 123–35; Arthur Herzog, *The War–Peace Establishment* (New York: Harper and Row, 1963); J. David Singer, *Deterrence, Arms Control and Disarmament* (Columbus, Ohio: Ohio State University Press, 1962); Thomas C. Schelling, *The Strategy of Conflict* (Cambridge, Mass.: Harvard University Press, 1960); Glenn H. Snyder, *Deterrence and Defense: Towards a Theory of National Security* (Princeton, NJ: Princeton University Press, 1961); Herman Kahn, *On Thermonuclear War* (Princeton, NJ: Princeton University Press, 1960).
42. John Simpson, *Ploughshares into Swords? The International Nuclear Non-Proliferation Network and the 1985 NPT Review Conference* (London: The Council for Arms Control, Faraday Discussion Paper No. 4, 1985), pp. 9, 16.
43. Quincy Wright, *A Study of War*, abridged edn (Chicago, Ill.: University of Chicago Press, 1970), pp. 163–4.
44. Steve Chan, 'Mirror, Mirror on the Wall'; see also, R.J. Rummel, 'Libertarianism and International Violence', *Journal of Conflict Resolution* 27 (March 1983), 1: 27–7; *Keesing's Contemporary Archives*, 1984, 33220A.
45. Jonathan Randal, *The Tragedy of Lebanon: Christian Warlords, Israeli Adventurers and American Bunglers* (London: Chatto & Windus, 1983), pp. 243 ff.
46. Michael Haas, 'Societal Approaches to the Study of War', *Journal of Peace Research* 4 (1965), 307–23.
47. Vincent Cable, 'The "Football War" and the Central American Common Market', *International Affairs* 45 (Oct. 1969), 4: 658–71.
48. Wood, *The United States and Latin American Wars*.
49. L.L. Farrar, 'The Limits of Choice'; see also Paul Kennedy (ed.), *The War Plans of the Great Powers, 1880–1914*, Foreword by Fritz Fischer (London: Allen & Unwin, 1971).
50. Gordon Connell-Smith, *The Inter-American System* (London: Oxford University Press for Royal Institute of International Affairs, 1966).
51. See, for example, Basil Collier, *A Short History of the Second World War* (London: Collins, 1967), pp. 68–72.
52. John Child, 'Geopolitical Thinking in Latin America', *Latin American*

Research Review 14 (1979), 2: 89–111.

53. Sprout and Sprout, pp. 318–26; see also A.T. Mahan, *the Influence of Sea Power upon History* (London: Sampson Low, 1892).

54. Sprout and Sprout, pp. 326–39; A.F.K. Organski, *World Politics* (New York: Alfred A. Knopf, 1959), p. 118.

55. On the strategic value of territory, see, for example, E.S. May, *An Introduction to Military Geography* (London: Hugh Rees, 1909) pp. 107–48.

56. J. Alvarez Díaz *et al.*, *Cuba: Geopolítica y Pensamiento Económico* (Miami, Fla.: Colegio de Economistas de Cuba en Exilio, 1964).

57. Lewis A. Tambs, 'Geopolitical Factors in Latin America', in Norman A Bailey (ed.), *Latin America, Politics, Economics, and Hemispheric Security* (New York: Praeger and the Center for Strategic Studies, 1965) p. 31.

58. Peter Calvert, 'Recent Political and Diplomatic Changes in South America', in Peter Jones (ed.), *The International Yearbook of Foreign Policy Analysis*, I, 1973 (London: Croom Helm, 1974), pp. 117–31.

59. Sprout and Sprout, pp. 597 following George Modelski.

60. Theodore C. Sorenson, *Kennedy* (London: Hodder & Stoughton, 1965) pp. 695–6, 714; see also Robert Francis Kennedy, *13 Days: The Cuban Missile Crisis, October 1962* (London: Macmillan, 1969).

61. Domínguez & Lindau, 'The Primary of Politics'; Esperanza Durán, 'The Contadora Approach to Peace in Central America', *The World Today*, 40 (Aug.–Sept. 1984), 8–9: 347–54.

62. Keegan, *World Armies*, discusses the position of Sweden pp. 548 ff. and Switzerland pp. 554 ff.

63. Basil Chubb, *The Government and Politics of Ireland* (London: Oxford University Press, 1971), pp. 314–16; Herbert L. Matthews, *The Yoke and the Arrows: A Report on Spain* (London: Heinemann, 1958), pp. 43–8.

64. Luard, *History of the United Nations*, pp. 229–74.

65. Richard W. Nelson, 'Multinational Peacekeeping in the Middle east and the United Nations Models', *International Affairs* 61 (Winter 1984–85), 1: 67–89.

66. On the validity of intervention in the Dominican Republic, see Akehurst, *International Law*, p. 267, but cf. Piero Gleijeses, *The Dominican Crisis. The 1965 Constitutionalist Revolt and American Intervention* (Baltimore. Md.: Johns Hopkins University Press, 1978), pp. 295–96.

67. See Selig S. Harrison, 'Dateline Afghanistan: Exit through Finland?', *Foreign Policy* 41 (Winter 1980–81), 163–87. For background, see also David Chaffetz, 'Afghanistan in Turmoil', *International Affairs* 56 (Jan. 1980), 1: 15–36.

68. James N. Rosenau, 'Intervention as a Scientific Concept', *Journal of Conflict Resolution* 13 (1969), 2: 149–71, gives a good critique of the varied meanings of the term. Richard Little, *Intervention: External Involvement in Civil Wars* (London: Martin Robertson, 1975) speaks of a 'bifurcated actor'. On the background to intervention in the Americas, see, *inter alia*, Decter perkins, *A History of the Monroe Doctrine* (London: Longman, 1960); Donald M. Dozer, *Are We Good Neighbors? Three*

Decides of Inter-American Relations, 1930–1960 (Gainesville, Fla.: (University of Florida Press, 1959); Jenny Pearce, *Under the Eagle: US Intervention in Central America* (London: Latin American Bureau, 1981).
69. Gary MacEoin, *Chile: The Struggle for Dignity* (London: Coventure, 19757.

7. PLAYING THE GAME

1. Cf. Lieuwen, *Generals versus Presidents*, p. 45.
2. DeLesseps S. Morrison, *Latin American Mission, An Advantage in Hemispheric Diplomacy*, ed. and intro. Gerold Frank (New York, Simon & Schuster, 1965), pp.
3. Cable.
4. *The Times*, 17 September 1957; reply 19 September.
5. Henry Pachter, *Collision Course: The Cuban Missile Crisis and Coexistence* (London: Pall Mall Press, 1963), p. 14.
6. Kenneth W. Grundy, *Confrontation and Accomodation in Southern Africa: The Limits of Independence* (Berkeley, Cal.: University of California Press, 1973).
7. Nora Beloff, *The General Says No: Britain's Exclusion from Europe* (Harmondsworth: Penguin, 1963). See also Richard E. Neustadt, *Alliance Politics* (New York: Columbia University Press, 1970).
8. Terence Robertson, *Crisis: The Inside Story of the Suez Conspiracy* (London: Hutchinson, 1965), p. 48.
9. Panayotis J. Vatikiotis, *Nasser and His Generation* (London: Croom Helm, 1978), pp. 255–7.
10. Jonathan Randal, *The Tragedy of Lebanon: Christian Warlords, Israeli Adventurers and American Bunglers* (London: Chatto & Windus, 1983), p. 243 ff. See also Daniel Pipes, 'The Real Problem', *Foreign Policy* 51 (Summer 1983), pp. 139–59.
11. Randal, *The Tragedy of Lebanon*, pp. 253–4.
12. Arnold Wolfers, *Discord and Collaboration: Essays on International Politics* (Baltimore, Md.: The Johns Hopkins Press, 1965), p. 83; cf. Organski, *World Politics*, pp. 325–33.
13. Milan Hauner, 'Siezing the Third Parallel: Geopolitics and the Soviet Advance into Central Asia', *Orbis* 29 (Spring 1985), 1: 5–31.
14. Irving L. Janis, *Victims of Groupthink: A Psychological Study of Foreign Policy Decisions and Fiascos* (Boston, Mass.: Houghton Mifflin, 1972).
15. Sunday Times, *The Falklands War*, p. 51, and personal communications.
16. *Daily Telegraph*, 8 and 18 February 1979, 16 March 1979. Estimate of casualties, *ibid.*, 8 May 1979.
17. Azahary, *The Iran–Iraq War*, p. 2.
18. Represented by Sukarno by the acronym NEFO; see Weatherbee, *Ideology in Indonesia*, p. 59.
19. Donell H. Meadows, Dennis L. Meadows, Jorgen Randers and William

W. Behrens III, *The Limits to Growth: A Report for the Club of Rome's Project on the Predicament of Mankind* (London: Pan Books, 1974); Jack Anderson, *Oil* (London: Sidgwick & Jackson, 1984).

20. Richard E. Feinberg, *The Intemperate Zone: The Third World Challenge to US Foreign Policy* (New York: W.W. Norton, 1983).

Bibliography

Adams, Richard N., ed., *Social Change in Latin America Today*, New York: Harper & Row for Council on Foreign Relations, 1960

Ake, Claude, *Revolutionary Pressures in Africa*, London: Zed Press, 1978

Alexander, Robert J., *The Bolivian National Revolution*, New Brunswick, NJ: Rutgers University Press, 1958

Alford, Jonathan, 'Security dilemmas of small states', *The World Today*, 40, Nos. 8–9, August–September 1984

Allison, Graham T., *Essence of Decision: Explaining the Cuban Missile Crisis*, Boston: Little–Brown, 1971

Almond, Gabriel A., and Coleman, James H., *The Politics of the Developing Areas*, Pinceton, NJ: Princeton University Press, 1959

Alvarez Díaz, J., Arredondo, A., Shelton, R.M., and Vizcaino, J. *Cuba: Geopolítica y Pensamiento Económico*, Miami,: Colegio de Economistas de Cuba en Exilio, 1964

Akehurst, Michael, *A Modern Introduction to International Law* London: Allen & Unwin, 1984 4th edn.

Ambursley, Fitzroy, and Dunkerley, James, *Grenada—Whose Freedom?*, London: Latin American Bureau, 1984

Amin, Samir, *Imperialism and Unequal Development*, Brighton: Harvester Press, 1977

Amnesty International, *Torture*, London: Amnesty International, 1973

Andersen, Jack, *Oil*, London: Sidgwick & Jackson, 1984

Anderson, Thomas P., *Matanza: El Salvador's Communist Revolt of 1932*, Lincoln, Neb.: University of Nebraska Press, 1971

Anell, Lars, and Nygren, Birgitta, *The Developing Countries and the World Economic Order*, London: Methuen, 1980

Ansprenger, Franz, 'Namibia and apartheid: what type of conflict? what kind of United Nations action?', in Rüdiger Jütte and Annemarie Grosse-Jütte, eds., *The Future of International Organisation*, London: Frances Pinter, 1981, pp. 181–200

Archer, Clive, *International Organisations*, London: Allen & Unwin, 1983

Aron, Raymond, *Main Currents in Sociological Thought 1*, Harmondsworth,: Penguin Books, 1972

Asia and World Forum, The, *Forum on ASEAN*, Taipei: The Asia and World Forum, 1980

Auburn, F.M., *Antarctic Law and Politics*, London: Hurst, 1982

Baran, Paul, *The Political Economy of Growth*, Harmondsworth: Penguin Books, 1957

Baer, Werner, Newfarmer, Richard, and Trebar, Thomas, 'On state capitalism in Brazil: some new issues and questions', *Inter American Economic Affairs*, 30, Winter 1976, pp. 63–93

Bainwoll, Mitchell, 'Cuba', Richard A. Gabriel, ed., *Fighting Armies: Nonaligned, Third World, and Other Ground Armies: a Combat Assessment*, Westport, Conn.: Greenwood Press, 1983, pp. 225–45

Barker, Elizabeth, *Britain in a Divided Europe 1945–1970*, London: Weidenfeld & Nicolson, 1972

Barnett, A., Doak, *The Making of Foreign Policy in China: Structure and Process*, London: Tauris for Johns Hopkins University Foreign Policy Institute, 1985

Barros, Alexandre de S.C., 'The formulation and implementation of Brazilian foreign policy: Itamaraty and the new actors', in Heraldo Muñoz and Joseph S. Tulchin, eds., *Latin American Nations in World Politics*, Boulder, Col.: Westview Press, 1984, pp. 30–44

Beck, Peter J.,'Britain's Antarctic dimension', *International Affairs*, 59, No. 3, Summer 1983, pp. 429–44

Beer, Francis A., *Alliances: Latent War Communities in the Contemporary World*, New York: Holt Rinehart & Winston, 1970

Bell, J. Bowyer, *On Revolt: Strategies of National Liberation*, Cambridge, Mass.: Harvard University Press, 1976

Beloff, Nora, *The General Says No: Britain's Exclusion from Europe*, Harmondsworth: Penguin Books, 1963

Beqiraj, Mehmet, *Peasantry in Revolution*, Ithaca, NY: Cornell University Center for International Studies, 1966

Blancké, W. Wendell, *The Foreign Service of the United States*, New York: Praeger, 1969

Bley, Helmut, *South-West Africa under German Rule, 1894–1914*, London: Heinemann, 1971

Bolland, O. Nigel, *The Formation of a Colonial Society*, Baltimore: Johns Hopkins University Press, 1977

Bowett, D.W., *The Law of International Institutions*, London: Stevens & Sons., 4th edn., 1982

Boyle, Kevin, and Hadden, Tom, *Ireland A Positive Proposal*, Harmondsworth: Penguin Books, 1985

Branford, Sue, and Glock, Oriel, *The Last Frontier: Fighting for Land in the Amazon*, London: Zed Press, 1985

Brecher, Michael, *Crisis Decision-Making: Israel 1967 and 1973*, Berkeley, Cal.: University of California Press, 1980

——, *Decisions in Israel's Foreign Policy*, London: Oxford University Press, 1974

——, *The Foreign Policy System in Israel*, London: Oxford University Press, 1972

Brecher, Michael, Steinberg, B. and Stein, J., 'A Framework for research on foreign policy behaviour', *Journal of Conflict Resolution*, 13, March 1969, pp. 75–102

Brennen, Donald G., ed., *Arms Control, Disarmament and National Security*, New York: George Braziller, 1961

Boyd, Andrew, *United Nations: Piety Myth and Truth*, Harmondsworth: Penguin Books, 1962

Brogan, D.W., and Verney, D.V., *Politics in the Modern World*, London: Hamish Hamilton, 1963

Brzezinski, Zbigniew K., and Huntington, Samuel, *Political Power U.S.A./U.S.S.R.*, London: Chatto & Windus, 1963

Bull, Hedley, *The Anarchical Society*, London: Macmillan, 1977

——, 'International theory: the case for a classical approach', *World Politics*, 18, 1966, pp. 361–77

Burch, Martin, and Wood, Bruce, *Public Policy in Britain*, Oxford, Martin Robertson, 1983

Cable, Vincent, 'The "Football War" and the Central American Common Market', *International Affairs*, 45, No. 4, October 1969, pp. 658–71

Cady, John F., *The United States and Burma*, Cambridge, Mass.: Harvard University Press, 1976

Calvert, Peter, *Boundary Disputes in Latin America*, London: Institute for the Study of Conflict, 1983—Conflict Studies No. 146

——, 'Demilitarization in Latin America', *Third World Quarterly*, 7, No. 1, January 1985, pp. 31–38

——, *The Falklands Crisis, the Rights and the Wrongs*, London: Frances Pinter, 1982

——, *Guatemala, a Nation in Turmoil*, Boulder, Col: Westview Press, 1985

——, *The Mexican Revolution, 1910–1914: the Diplomacy of Anglo-American Conflict* Cambridge: Cambridge University Press, 1968

——, 'On attaining sovereignty', Anthony Smith, ed., *Nationalist Movements*, London: Macmillan, 1976, pp. 134–49

——, *Politics, Power and Revolution: an Introduction to Comparative Politics*, Brighton: Harvester, 1983

——, 'Recent political and diplomatic changes in South America',

Peter Jones, ed., *The International Yearbook of Foreign Policy Analysis*, I, 1973, London: Croom Helm, 1974, pp. 117–31

——, *Revolution and International Politics*, London: Frances Pinter, 1984

Calvocoressi, Peter, *World Order and New States*, London: Chatto & Windus for the Institute for Strategic Studies, 1962

Cardozo, Fernando Enrique, and Faletto, Enzo, *Dependency and Development in Latin America*, Berkeley, Cal.: University of California Press, 1979

Central Office of Information, *The Falkland Islands and Dependencies*, London: HMSO, 1973

Chaliand, Gérard, *Revolution in the Third World: Myths and Prospects*, Hassocks, Sussex,: Harvester, 1977

Chan, Steve 'Mirror, mirror on the wall—are the freer countries more pacific?', *Journal of Conflict Resolution*, 28, No. 4, December 1984, pp. 617–48.

Chesnaux, Jean, *China: The People's Republic, 1949–1976,* Hassocks, Sussex: Harvester Press, 1979

Chilcote, Ronald M. and Edelstein, Joel, eds., *Latin America: The S Struggle with Dependency and Beyond*, New York: Wiley, 1974.

Child, John, 'Geopolitical thinking in Latin America', *Latin American Research Review*, 14, No. 2, 1979, pp. 89–11

Chorley, Katherine C., *Armies and the the Art of Revolution*, London: Faber & Faber, 1943

Chubb, Basil, *The Government and Politics of Ireland*, London: Oxford University Press, 1971

Cipolla, Carlo M., *The Economic History of World Population*, Harmondsworth: Penguin Books, 7th edn., 1978

Clemens, Walter C., Jr., 'Ideology in Soviet disarmament policy', *Journal of Conflict Resolution*, 8, No. 1, 1964, pp. 7–22

Cohen, Raymond, *International Politics: The Rules of the Game*, London: Longman, 1981

Collier, Basil, *A Short History of the Second World War*, London: Collins, 1967

Collis, Maurice, *Siamese White,* Harmondsworth: Penguin Books, 1941

Commager, Henry Steele, ed., *Documents of American History*, New York: Appleton–Century–Crofts, 6th edn., 1958

Conil Paz, Alberto A., and Ferrari, Gustavo E., *Argentina's Foreign Policy 1930–1962*, Notre Dame, Ind.: Notre Dame University Press, 1966

Connell-Smith, Gordon, *The Inter-American System,* London: Oxford University Press for Royal Institute of International Affairs, 1966

Cox, Robert W., ed., *International Organization: World Politics*, London: Macmillan, 1969

Cumberland, Charles Curtis, *Mexico, the Struggle for Modernity*, New York: Oxford University Press, 1968

Daily Telegraph, the

David-Neel, Alexandra, *Buddhism, Its Doctrines and its Methods*, London: The Bodley Head, 1977

Davidson, Basil, *Black Star*, New York: Praeger, 1973

Davis, Harold Eugene, ed., *Government and Politics in Latin America*, New York, Ronald Press, 1958

Dawisha, Adeed and Dawisha, Karen, eds., *The Soviet Union in the Middle East: Policies and Perspectives*, London: Heinemann for the Royal Institute of International Affairs, 1982

De Kadt, Emanuel, ed., *Patterns of Foreign Influence in the Caribbean*, London: Oxford University Press for Royal Institute of International Affairs, 1972

DeConde, Alexander, *The American Secretary of State, an interpretation*, London: Pall Mall Press, 1962

Decalo, Samuel, *Coups and Army Rule in Africa: Studies in Military Style*, New Haven, Conn.: Yale University Press, 1976

Deutsch, Karl, 'The crisis of the state', *Government & Opposition*, 16, No. 3, 1981, pp. 331–43

Diedrich, Bernard, *Somoza and the Legacy of US Involvement in Central America*, London: Junction Books, 1982

Dogan, Mattei, and Pelassy, Dominique, *How to Compare Nations: Strategies in Comparative Politics*, Chatham, NJ: Chatham House Publishers Inc., 1984

Domínguez, Jorge I., ed., *Economic Issues and Political Conflict: US-Latin American Relations*, London: Butterworths, 1982

Domínguez, Jorge I., and Lindau, Juan, 'The primary of politics: comparing the foreign policies of Cuba and Mexico', *International Political Science Review*, 5, No. 1, 1984, pp. 75–101

Donaldson, Peter, *Economics of the Real World*, London: British Broadcasting Corporation and Penguin Books, 1977

Donovan, Robert J., *Eisenhower, the Inside Story*, New York: Harper, 1956

Dos Santos, Theotonio, 'The structure of dependence', *American Economic Review*, 60, May 1970, pp. 231–6

Dozer, Donald M., *Are We Good Neighbours? Three Decades of Inter-American Relations, 1930–1960*, Gainsville, Fla: University of Florida Press, 1959

Dunkerley, James, *The Long War: Dictatorship and Revolution in El Salvador*, London: Junction Books, 1982

Durán, Esperanza, 'The Contadora approach to peace in Central

America', *The World Today*, 40, Nos. 8–9, August–September 1984, pp. 347–54

Edwardes, Michael, *Nehru, A Political Biography*, Harmondsworth: Penguin Books, 1971

Eisenhower, Dwight David, *The White House Years: Waging Peace 1956–1961*, Garden City, NY: Doubleday, 1964

El Azhary, M.S., ed., *The Iran–Iraq War: An Historical, Economic and Political Analysis*, London: Croom Helm and Centre for Arab Gulf Studies, University of Exeter and Basra, 1984

Elian, George, *The Principle of Soveriegnty over Natural Resources,* Alphen aan den Rijn: Sijthoff & Noordhoff, 1979

Encyclopaedia Britannica, Chicago, Ill., 14 edn., 1973

Encyclopaedia Britannica, Chicago, Ill., 15 edn., 1974

Eprile, Cecil, *War and Peace in the Sudan, 1955–1972,* Newton Abbot, Devon: David & Charles, 1974

Espejo, L.G., 'Neutral but not indifferent; Colombian foreign policy since 1990', Unpublished PhD dissertation, University of Southampton, 1981

Etchison, Don L., *The United States and Militarism in Central America*, New York: Praeger, 1975

Etzioni, Amitai, *Political Unification, a comparative study of leaders and forces*, New York: Holt Rinehart and Winston, 1965

Fagen, Richard R., and Tuohy, William S., 'Aspects of the Mexican political system', *Studies in Comparative International Development*, 7, Fall 1973, pp. 208–20

Farar, Tom J., *The Future of the Inter-American System,* New York: Praeger, 1979

Farrar, L.L., 'The limits of choice: July 1914 reconsidered', *Journal of Conflict Resolution*, 16, No. 1, 1972, pp. 1–23

Feinberg, Richard E., *The Intemperate Zone: The Third World Challenge to U.S. Foreign Policy*, New York: W.W. Norton, 1983

Ferrer, Aldo, *Living within our Means: an Examination of the Argentine Economic Crisis*, Boulder, Col.: Westview Press for Third World Foundation, 1985

Fiechter, Georges-André, *Brazil since 1964: Modernization under a Military Régime*, London: Macmillan, 1975

Finer, Samuel E., *Comparative Government*, London: Allen Lane, 1972

First, Ruth, *Libya: The Elusive Revolution*, Harmondsworth: Penguin Books, 1974

Franck, Thomas M., *Nation against Nation: What Happened to the U.N. Dream and what the U.S. can do about it*, New York: Oxford University Press, 1985

Frank, André Gunder, *Dependent Accumulation and Underdevelop-*

ment, London: Macmillan, 1978

Frank, André Gunder, 'The development of underdevelopment', *Monthly Review*, 18, No. 4, September 1966, pp. 17–31

Frank, André Gunder, *Latin America, Underdevelopment or Revolution*, New York: Monthly Review Press, 1969

Frankel, Joseph, *International Relations in a Changing World*, Oxford: Oxford University Press, 1979

Frankel, Joseph, *The Making of Foreign Policy: An Analysis of Decision Making*, London: Oxford University Press, 1963

Frankel, Joseph, *The State and the Realm of Values*, Southampton: University of Southampton, 1965

Gabriel, Richard A., ed., *Fighting Armies: Nonaligned, Third World, and Other Ground Armies: a Combat Assessment*, Westport, Conn.: Greenwood Press, 1983

Galbraith, John Kenneth, *A Life in our Times: Memoirs*, London: André Deutsch, 1981

Gleijeses, Piero, *The Dominican Crisis: the 1965 Constitutionalist Revolt and American Intervention*, Baltimore: Johns Hopkins University Press, 1978

Goldblat, Josef, ed., *Non-Proliferation: the Why and the Wherefore*, London: Taylor & France, 1985

Goldenberg, Boris, *The Cuban Revolution and Latin America*, London: Allen & Unwin, 1965

Goodspeed, D.J., *The Conspirators, a Study of the Coup d'Etat*, London: Macmillan, 1962

Goulbourne, Harry, ed., *Politics and State in the Third World*, London: Macmillan, 1980

Grant, C.H., *The Making of Modern Belize,* Cambridge: Cambridge University Press, 1976

Green, R.H., 'Things fall apart: the world economy in the 1980s', *Third World Quarterly*, 5, No. 1, January 1983

Griffin, John C., and Rouse, William, 'Counter-trade as a Third World strategy of development', *Third World Quarterly*, 8, No. 1, January 1986, pp. 177–204

Grindle, Merrilee S., *Bureaucrats, Politicians and Peasants in Mexico*, Berkeley, Cal.: University of California Press, 1977

Groennings, Sven, Kelley, E.V. and Leiserson, Michael, eds., *The Study of Coalition Behavior*, New York: Holt Rinehart & Winston, 1970

Gross, Feliks, *The Seizure of Political Power in a Century of Revolutions*, New York: Philosophical Library, 1958

Grundy, Kenneth W., *Confrontation and Accommodation in Southern Africa: The Limits of Independence*, Berkeley, Cal.: University of California Press, 1973.

Englewood Cliffs, NJ: Prentice–Hall, 1967

Holt, Pat M., *Colombia Today—And Tomorrow*, London: Pall Mall Press, 1964

Homan, Roger, 'The origins of the Iranian revolution', *International Affairs*, 56, Autumn 1980, pp. 673–7

Howard, Michael, ed., *Soldiers and Governments: Nine Studies in Civil-military Relations*, London: Eyre & Spottiswoode, 1957

Humphreys, R.A., *The Diplomatic History of British Honduras, 1638–1901*, London: Oxford University Press for Royal Institute of International Affairs, 1961

Huntington, Samuel P., *The Soldier and the State: The Theory and Politics of Civil-military Relations*, Cambridge, Mass.: Harvard University Press, 1957

Iklé, Fred Charles, *How Nations Negotiate*, New York: Harper & Row for Center for International Affairs, Harvard University, 1964

Ilchman, Frederick Warren, *Professional Diplomacy in the United States, 1779–1939: a Study in Administrative History*, Chicago: University of Chicago Press, 1961

Inter-American Development Bank, *Economic and Social Progress in Latin America: External Debt: Crisis and Adjustment*, Washington, DC: Inter-American Development Bank, 1985

International Institute of Strategic Studies, *The Strategic Balance, 1984–1985*, London: International Institute for Strategic Studies, 1985

Israel, Fred L., ed., *Major Peace Treaties of Modern History 1648–1967*, New York: Chelsea House with McGraw Hill, 1967, 4 vols

Jacobson, Harold Karan, 'New states and functional international organisations: a preliminary report', in Robert W. Cox, ed., *International Organization: World Politics*, London: Macmillan, 1969, pp. 74–97

Jaguaribe, Hélio, *Problemas do desenvolvimiento Latino–Americano*, Rio de Janeiro: Ed. Civilização Brasiliera, 1967

Janis, Irving L., *Victims of Groupthink: a Psychological Study of Foreign Policy Decisions and Fiascos,* Boston, Mass.: Houghton Mifflin, 1972

Janowitz, Morris, *The Military in the Political Development of New Nations*, Chicago: University of Chicago Press, 1964

Jaworski C., Helen, "Peru: The Military Government's Foreign Policy in its Two Phases", in Heraldo Muñoz and Joseph S. Tulchin, *Latin American Nations in World Politics*, Boulder, Col.: Westview Press, pp. 200–15

Johnson, John J., *The Military and Society in Latin America*,

Stanford, Cal.: Stanford University Press, 1964

Jordan, Hamilton, Jr., *Crisis: The Last Year of the Carter Presidency*, New York: Putnam, 1982

Jütte, Rüdiger, and Grosse-Jütte, Annemarie, *The Future of International Organization*, London: Frances Pinter, 1981

Kahin, George McTurnan, ed., *Governments and Politics of Southeast Asia*, Ithaca, NY: Cornell University Press, 1964

Kahn, Hermann, *On Thermonuclear War*, Princeton, NJ: Princeton University Press, 1960

Kaplan, Morton A., ed., *The Revolution in World Politics*, New York, John Wiley, 1962

Kaplan, Morton A., *System and Process in International Politics*, New York: John Wiley, 1957

Katz, Mark N., *The Third World in Soviet Military Thought*, London: Croom Helm, 1982

Keegan, John, *World Armies*, London: Macmillan, 2nd edn., 1983

Kennedy, Paul, *The Realities Behind Diplomacy: Background Influences on British External Policy, 1865–1980*, London: Fontana, 1981

Kennedy, Paul, ed., *The War Plans of the Great Powers, 1880–1914*, fwd. Fritz Fischer, London: Allen & Unwin, 1971

Kennedy, Robert Francis, *13 Days: the Cuban Missile Crisis, October 1962*, London: Macmillan, 1969

Kenworthy, Eldon, "Coalitions in the political development of Latin America", in Sven Groennings, E.W. Kelley and Michael Leiserson, eds., *The Study of Coalition Behavior*, New York: Holt Rinehart & Winston, 1970

Keohane, Robert O. and Nye, Joseph S., Jr., *Transnational Relations and World Politics*, Cambridge, Mass.: Harvard University Press, 1973

Kirkpatrick, Ivone, *The Inner Circle: memoirs of . . .* , London: Macmillan, 1959

Kirkpatrick, Jeane, 'The Hobbes problem: order, authority, and legitimacy in Central America', *Across the Board*, 18, September 1981, pp. 22–31

Kissinger, Henry A., 'Limited war: conventional or nuclear?', in Donald G. Brennan, ed., *Arms Control, Disarmament, and National Security*, New York: George Braziller, 1961, pp. 138–52

Kissinger, Henry A., *Nuclear Weapons and Foreign Policy*, New York: Harper & Row, 1957

Klingberg, Frank L., 'Historical periods, trands and cycles in international relations', *Journal of Conflict Resolution*, 14, No. 4, 1970, pp. 505–11

Knorr, Klaus, and Rosenau, James N., eds., *Contending Approaches to International Politics*, Princeton, NJ: Princeton University Press, 1969

Knorr, Klaus, and Verba, Sidney, eds., *The International System: Theoretical Essays*, Princeton, NJ: Princeton University Press, 1961

Korany, Bahgat, 'Foreign policy in the Third World: an introduction', *International Political Science Review*, 5, No. 1, 1984, pp. 7–20

LaFeber, Walter, *Inevitable Revolutions: The United States in Central America*, New York: W.W. Norton & Co., expanded edition 1984

Langhorne, Richard, *The Collapse of the Concert of Europe: International Politics 1890–1914*, London: Macmillan, 1981

Laqueur, Walter, *The Road to War 1967: The Origins of the Arab-Israeli Conflict*, London: Weidenfeld & Nicolson, 1968

Li Chien-nung, *The Political History of China 1840–1928*, trans. & ed. Ssu-yu Teng and Jeremy Ingalls, Princeton, NJ: D. van Nostrand, 1956

Lieuwen, Edwin, *Arms and Politics in Latin America,* New York: Praeger, 1961

Lieuwen, Edwin, *Generals versus Presidents: Neomilitarism in Latin America*, London, Pall Mall, 1964

Lins, Alvaro, *Rio-Branco (O Barão do Rio-Branco),* São Paulo: Companhia Editorial Nacional, 1965

Little, Richard, *Intervention: External Involvement in Civil Wars*, London: Martin Robertson, 1975

Lozoya, Jorge, and Estevez, Jaime, eds., *Latin America and the New International Economic Order*, Oxford: Pergamon Press, 1980

Luard, Evan, *A History of the United Nations: Volume I: The Years of Western Domination, 1945–1955*, London: Macmillan, 1984

Luard, Evan, *The United Nations*, London: Macmillan, 1979

Lyon, Peter, *Neutralism*, Leicester: Leicester University Press, 1963

McCann, Frank D., Jr., *The Brazilian–American Alliance 1937–1945*, Princeton, NJ: Princeton University Press, 1974

McDermott, Geoffrey, *The New Diplomacy and its Approaches*, London: Plume with Ward Lock, 1973

MacEoin, Gary, *Chile, the Struggle for Dignity*, London: Coventure, 1975

McKinlay, R.D., and Mughan, A., *Aid and Arms to the Third World: An Analysis of the Distribution and Impact of US Official Transfers*, London: Frances Pinter, 1984

McLaren, Robert I., 'Mitranian functionalism: possible or impossible?', *Review of International Studies*, 11, No. 2, April 1985, pp. 139–52

McLaurin, R.D., Peretz, Don, and Snider, Lewis W., *Middle East*

Foreign Policy: Issues and Processes, New York: Praeger, 1982

McMaster, Carolyn, *Malawi—Foreign Policy and Development*, Devizes, Wilts.: Davison, 1974

MacPherson, C.B., 'Do we need a theory of the state?', *Archives Européennes de Sociologie*, 18, No. 2, 1977, pp. 223–44

Mahan, Alfred Thayer, *The Influence of Sea Power upon History*, London: Sampson Low, 1892

Manor, James, 'Sri Lanka's crisis', *The World Today*, 41, No. 7, July 1985, pp. 121–2

March, Janes, and Simon, Herbert, *Organizations*, New York: Wiley, 1958

Marx, Karl, and Engels, Frederick, *Selected Works*, Moscow: Foreign Languages Publishing House, 1962, 2 vols

Matthews, Herbert L., *The Yoke and the Arrows: a report on Spain*, London: Heinemann, 1958

May, Brian, *The Indonesian Tragedy*, Singapore: Graham Brash (Pte) Ltd., 1978

May, E.S., *An Introduction to Military Geography*, London: Hugh Rees, 1909

May, Stacy, and Plaza, Galo, *The United Fruit Company in Latin America*, Washington, DC: The National Planning Association, 1958

Mayall, James, 'The Battle for the Horn, Somali Irredentism and International Diplomacy', *The World Today*, 34, No. 9, September 1978, pp. 336–45

Mazrui, Ali, *Africa's International Relations, The Diplomacy of Dependency and Change*, London: Methuen, 1977

Meadows, Donell H., Meadows, Dennis L., Randers, Jorgen, and Behrens, William W., III, *The Limits to Growth: A report for The Club of Rome's Project on the Predicament of Mankind*, London: Pan Books, 1974

Middlemas, Keith, *The Master Builders*, London: Hutchinson, 1963

Milenky, Edward S., *Argentina's Foreign Policies*, Boulder, Col.: Westview Press, 1978

Miller, Norman, and Aya, Roderick, eds., *National Liberation: Revolution in the Third World*, New York: The Free Press, 1971

Minogue, Kenneth, *Nationalism*, London: Methuen, 1969

Mintz, Jeanne S., *Mohammed, Marx and Marhean: the roots of Indonesian socialism*, London: Pall Mall Press, 1965

Mitrany, David, *The Functional Theory of Politics*, London: London School of Economics and Martin Robertson, 1975

Moneta, Carlos J., 'The Malvinas conflicts: analysing the Argentine military regime's decision-making process', in Heraldo Muñoz and Joseph Tulchin, eds., *Latin American Nations in World Politics*,

Boulder, Colo.: Westview Press, 1984, pp. 119–32

Moreton, Edwina, 'The East Europeans and the Cubans in the Middle East: surrogates or allies?', in Adeed Dawisha and Karen Dawisha, eds., *The Soviet Union in the Middle East: Policies and Perspectives*, London: Heinemann for the Royal Institute of International Affairs, 1982, pp. 62–84

Morgenthau, Hans J., 'The four paradoxes of nuclear strategy', *American Political Science Review*, 58, 1964, pp. 123–35

Morison, Samuel Eliot, and Commager, Henry Steele, *The Growth of the American Republic*, New York: Oxford University Press, 4th edn., 1950, 2 vols.

Morrison, DeLesseps S., *Latin American Mission, An Adventure in Hemispheric Diplomacy*, ed. and intro. Gerold Frank. New York: Simon & Schuster, 1965

Muñoz, Heraldo, and Tulchin, Joseph, eds., *Latin American Nations in World Politics*, Boulder, Col.: Westview Press, 1984

Munro, Dana Gardner, *Intervention and Dollar Diplomacy in the Caribbean, 1900–1921*, Princeton, NJ: Princeton University Press, 1964

Needler, Martin C., 'Military motivations and the siezure of power', *Latin American Research Review*, 10, No. 3, Fall 1975, pp. 63–79

Nelson, Richard W., 'Multinational peacekeeping in the Middle East and the United Nations model', *International Affairs*, 61, No. 1, Winter 1984–5, pp. 67–89

"Neuberg, A.", *Armed Insurrection*, London: NLB, 1970

Neustadt, Richard E., *Alliance Politics*, New York: Columbia University Press, 1970.

Nickson, R.A., 'The Itaipú hydro-electric project; the Pataguayan perspective', *Bulletin of Latin American Research*, 2, No. 1, October 1982, p. 1

Nicolson, Harold, *Diplomacy*, London: Oxford University Press, 3rd edn., 1963

Nkrumah, Kwame, *Neocolonialism, the Last Stage of Imperialism*, New York: International Publishers Ltd., 1965

Northedge, F.S., ed., *The Foreign Policies of the Powers*, London: Faber & Faber, 1968

Oppenheim, Lassa Francis Lawrence, *International Law: a Treatise*, London: Longmans, 7th edn., 1952

Osgood, Robert Endicott, *NATO, the Entangling Alliance*, Chicago: University of Chicago Press, 1962

O'Shaughnessy, Hugh, *Grenada: Revolution, Invasion and Aftermath*, London: Sphere Books with The Observer, 1984

Organski, A.F.K., *World Politics*, New York: Alfred A. Knopf, 1959

Oxaal, Ivar, Barnett, Tony, and Booth, David, eds., *Beyond the*

Sociology of Development: Economy and Society in Latin America and Africa, London: Routledge, 1975

Panter-Brick, S.K., ed., *Nigerian Politics and Military Rule: Prelude to Civil War,* London: Athlone Press for Institute of Commonwealth Studies, 1970

Patch, Richard W., 'Bolivia: U.S. assistance in a revolutionary setting', in Richard N. Adams, Ed., *Social Change in Latin America Today,* New York: Harper & Row for Council on Foreign Relations, 1960, pp. 108–76

Patman, Robert, 'Ideology, Soviet policy and realignment in the horn', in Adeed Dawisha and Karen Dawisha, eds., *The Soviet Union in the Middle East: Policies and Perspectives,* London: Heinemann for the Royal Institute of International Affairs, 1982, pp. 45–61.

Payne, Anthony, and Sutton, Paul, eds., *Dependency under Challenge: the Political Economy of the Commonwealth Caribbean,* Manchester: Manchester University Press, 1984

Pearce, Jenny, *Under the Eagle: U.S. Intervention in Central America,* London: Latin American Bureau, 1981

Perkins, Dexter, *A History of the Monroe Doctrine,* London: Longmans, 1960

Perry, Roland, *The Programming of the President,* London: Aurum Press, 1984

Petras, James F., ed., *Class, State, and Power in the Third World, with Case Studies on Class Conflict in Latin America,* London: Zed Press, 1981

Petras, James F. and Morley, Morris H., *How Allende Fell: a study in U.S.–Chilean relations,* London: Spokesman Books, 1974

Pike, Frederick B., *The Modern History of Peru,* London: Weidenfeld & Nicolson, 1967

Plischke, Elmer, *Conduct of American Diplomacy,* Princeton, NJ: D. Van Nostrand, 3rd edn., 1967

Poggi, Gianfranco, *The Development of the Modern State: A Sociological Introduction,* London: Hutchinson, 1978

Pollitt, Christopher, Lewis, Lew, Negro, Josephine, and Patten, Jim, *Public Policy in Theory and Practice,* Sevenoaks, Kent: Hodder & Stoughton with the Open University Press, 1979

Powell, John Duncan, 'Military assistance and militarism in Latin America', *Western Political Quarterly,* 18, No. 2, Pt. 1, June 1965, pp. 382–92

Qureshi, Saleem, 'Military in the polity of Islam: religion as a basis for civil-military interaction', *International Political Science Review,* 2, No. 3, 1981, pp. 271–82

Randal, Jonathan, *The Tragedy of Lebanon: Christian Warlords,*

Israeli Adventurers and American Bunglers, London: Chatto & Windus, 1983

Reuter, Paul, *International Institutions*, London: Allen & Unwin, 1968

Riggs, Fred W., *Thailand: the Modernization of a Bureaucratic Polity*, Honolulu, Hawaii: The East-West Center Press, 1966

Robbins, Keith, 'James Ramsay Macdonald', in Herbert van Thal, ed., *The Prime Ministers*, London: Allen & Unwin, 1975, II, pp. 273ff.

Rock, David, *Politics in Argentina, 1890–1930: the rise and fall of Radicalism*, Cambridge: Cambridge University Press, 1975

Robertson, Terence, *Crisis: The Inside Story of the Suez Conspiracy*, London: Hutchinson, 1965

Rodway, James, *Guiana, British Dutch and French*, London: T. Fisher Unwin, 1902

Rosenblatt, Paul C., 'Origins and effects of group ethnocentrism and nationalism', *Journal of Conflict Resolution*, 8, No. 2, 1964, pp. 131–46

Rosenau, James, *International Politics and Foreign Policy*, Gelncoe, Ill.: The Free Press, 1961

Rosenau, James N., 'Intervention as a scientific concept', *Journal of Conflict Resolution*, 13, No. 2, 1969, pp. 149–71

Rosenau, James H., ed., *Linkage Politics: Essays on the Convergence of National and International Systems*, New York: The Free Press, 1969

Rosenau, James N., 'The premises and promises of decision-making analysis', in J. Charlesworth, ed., *Contemporary Political Analysis*, New York: The Free Press, 1967, pp. 189–211

Rosenthal, Erwin I.J., *Political Thought in Mediaeval Islam, an Introductory Outline*, Cambridge: Cambridge University Press, 1962

Rossiter, Clinton, *The American Presidency*, New York: Time Magazine, 2nd edn., 1960

Roxborough, Ian, O'Brien, Phil, and Roddick, Jackie, *Chile: the State and Revolution*, London: Macmillan, 1977

Roxborough, Ian, *Theories of Underdevelopment*, London: Macmillan, 1979

Rummel, R.J., 'Libertarianism and International Violence', *Journal of Conflict Resolution*, 27, No. 1, March 1983, pp. 27–71

Russett, Bruce M., ed., *World Handbook of Political and Social Indicators*, New Haven, Conn.: Yale University Press, 1964

Sagan, Carl, 'Frozen in the heat of battle', *The Guardian*, 9 August 1984

Sartori, Giovanni, *Parties and Party Systems, A Framework for*

Analysis, Cambridge: Cambridge University Press

Satow, Sir Ernest, *A Guide to Diplomatic Practice*, London: Longmans, 1957

Schapiro, Leonard, *The Government and Politics of the Soviet Union*, London: Hutchinson, 1970

Schelling, Thomas, C., *The Strategy of Conflict*, Cambridge, Mass,: Harvard University Press, 1960

Scott, George, *The Rise and Fall of the League of Nations*, London: Hutchinson, 1973

Seers, Dudley, *Dependency Theory: A Critical Reassessment*, London: Frances Pinter, 1981

Sen, Amartya, *Poverty and Famines*, Oxford: Clarendon Press, 1982

Seton-Watson, Hugh, *Nations and States: an Inquiry into the Origins of Nations and the Politics of Nationalism*, London: Methuen, 1977

Sharabi, Hisham B., *Nationalism and Revolution in the Arab World*, Princeton, N.J.: D. Van Nostrand, 1966

Shearman, Peter, 'The Soviet Union and Grenada under the New Jewel Movement', *International Affairs*, 61, No. 4, Autumn 1985, pp. 661–73

Sigmund, Paul, *The Overthrow of Allende and the Politics of Chile, 1964–1976*, Englewood Cliffs, NJ: Prentice-Hall, 1977

Simpson, John, *Ploughshares into Swords? The International Nuclear Non-Proliferation Network and the 1985 NPT Review Conference*, London: The Council for Arms Control, Faraday Discussion Paper No. 4, 1985

Singer, J. David, *Deterrence, Arms Control and Disarmament*, Columbus, Ohio: Ohio State University Press, 1962

Singer, Marshall R., *Weak States in a World of Powers: the dynamics of international relationships*, New York: The Free Press, 1972

Singleton, Fred., 'The Myth of Finlandisation', *International Affairs*, 57, No. 2, Spring 1981, pp. 270–85

Smith, Adam, *The Wealth of Nations*, London: J.M. Dent, 1910, 2 vols.

Smith, Anthony D., ed., *Nationalist Movements*, London: Macmillan, 1976

Smith, Anthony D., 'States and homelands: the social and geopolitical implication of national territory', *Millinnium*, 10, No. 3, 1981

Snyder, Glenn H., *Deterrence and Defense: Toward a Theory of National Security*, Princeton, NJ: Princeton University Press, 1961

Snyder, Richard, Bruck, H.W., and Sapin, Burton, eds., *Foreign-Policy Decision Making: An Approach to the Study of Inter-*

national Politics, New York: Free Press of Glencoe, 1962

Sorensen, Theodore C., *Kennedy,* London: Hodder & Stoughton, 1965

Spanier, John, *Games Nations Play: Analysing International Politics,* New York: Holt Rinehart & Winston/Praeger, 3rd edn., 1978

Sparrow, Gerald, *Land of the Moon Flower,* London: Elek Books, 1955

Spear, Joseph, *President and the Press: the Nixon Legacy,* Cambridge, Mass.: MIT Press, 1984.

Spero, J., *The Politics of International Economic Relations,* London: Allen & Unwin, 2nd edn., 1982.

Sprout, Harold, and Sprout, Margaret, *Foundations of International Politics,* Princeton, NJ: D. Van Nostrand, 1962.

Stepan, Alfred, *The Military in Politics: Changing Patterns in Brazil,* Princeton, NJ: Princeton University Press, 1971.

Stepan, Alfred, *The State and Society: Peru in Comparative Perspective,* Princeton, NJ: Princeton University Press, 1978.

Stewart, Watt, *Keith and Costa Rica: A Biographical Study of Minor Cooper Keith,* Albuquerque, NM: University of New Mexico Press, 1964.

Stevens, C., *Food Aid and the Developing Countries,* London, Croom Helm for Overseas Development Institute, 1979

Strang, Lord, *The Foreign Office,* London, Allen & Unwin, 1955.

Strange, Susan, 'The study of transnational relations', *International Affairs,* 52, No. 3, July 1976, pp. 333–45

Stremlau, John J., *The International Politics of the Nigerian Civil War 1967–1970,* Princeton, NJ: Princeton University Press, 1977

Sunday Times Insight Team, *The Falklands War: the Full Story,* London: Sphere Books, 1982

Sunday Times Insight Team, *Insight on Portugal: the Year of the Captains.* London: Andre Deutsch, 1975

Sundhausen, Ulf, *The Road to Power: Indonesian Military Politics, 1945–1967,* Kuala Lumpur: Oxford University Press, 1982

Tambs, Lewis A., 'Geopolitical factors in Latin America', in Norman A. Bailey ed., *Latin America: Politics, Economics, and Hemispheric Security,* New York: Praeger and the Center for Strategic Studies, 1965, p. 31

Terrill, Ross, ed., *The China Difference: a portrait of life today inside the country of one million,* New York: Harper & Row, 1979

Thiam, Doudou, *The Foreign Policy of African States: Ideological Bases, Present Realities, Future Prospects,* London: Phoenix House, 1965

Thomas, Alan, *Third World: Images, Definitions, Connotations,* Milton Keynes: Open University Press, 1983

Thomas, Caroline, *New States, Sovereignty and Intervention*, London: Gower, 1985

Thompson, Mark, *The Secretaries of State, 1681–1782*, Oxford: Clarendon Press, 1932

Times, The

Tulchin, Joseph S., 'Authoritarian regimes and foreign policy: the case of Argentina', in Heraldo Muñoz and Joseph S. Tulchin, eds., *Latin American Nations in World Politics*, Boulder, Col:. Westview Press, 1984, pp. 186–99

Ullmann, Walter, *A History of Political Thought, The Middle Ages*, Harmondsworth: Penguin Books, 1965

United States. Departments of State and Defense, *Grenada Documents: an Overview and Selection*, Washington, DC: Departments of State and Defense, 1984

Valen, Henry, 'National conflict structure and foreign politics: the impact of the EEC issue on perceived cleavages in Norwegian politics', *European Journal of Political Research*, 4, No. 1, March 1976, pp. 47–82

Vallier, Ivan, 'The Roman Catholic church: a transnational actor", in Robert O. Keohane and Joseph S. Nye, eds., *Transnational Relations and World Politics*, Cambridge, Mass: Harvard University Press, 1973, pp. 129–52

van Thal, Herbert, ed., *The Prime Ministers*, London: Allen & Unwin, 1975, 2 vols

Vatikiotis, Panayotis J., *Nasser and His Generation*, London: Croom Helm, 1978

Vital, David, *The Inequality of States: A Study of the Small Power in International Relations*, Oxford: Clarendon Press, 1967

Waddell, D.A.G., *British Honduras: a Historical and Contemporary Summary*, London: Oxford University Press for Royal Institute of International Affairs, 1961

Wayas, Joseph, *Nigeria's Leadership Role in Africa*, London: Macmillan, 1979

Weatherbee, Donald E., *Ideology in Indonesia: Sukarno's Indonesian Revolution*, New Haven, Conn.: Yale University Southeast Asia Studies, 1966

Weber, Max, *The Theory of Social and Economic Organization*, ed. Talcott Parsons, New York: The Free Press, 1964

Wedgwood, C.V., *The Thirty Years War*, London: Jonathan Cape, 1938

Whitaker's Almanack, 1983, London: J. Whitaker & Sons, 1982

Wight, Martin, *Power Politics*, Leicester: Leicester University Press for Royal Institute of International Affairs, 2nd edn., 1978, ed.

Hedley Bull and Carsten Holbraad
Wight, Martin, *Systems of States*, Leicester: Leicester University Press with London School of Economics and Political Science, 1977
Wilhelmy, Manfred, 'Politics, bureaucracy, and foreign policy in Chile', in Heraldo Muñoz and Joseph S. Tulchin, eds., *Latin American Nations in World Politics*, Boulder, Col.: Westview Press, 1984, pp. 45–62
Wilkie, James W., and Wilkie, Edna Monzón de, *The Mexican Revolution: Federal Expenditure and Social Change since 1910*, Berkeley, Cal.: University of California Press, 1970
Wilkinson, Paul, *Political Terrorism*, London: Macmillan, 1974
—— *Terrorism and the Liberal State*, London: Macmillan, 1978
Willetts, Peter, *The Non-Aligned Movement: The Origins of a Third World Alliance*, London: Frances Pinter, 1978
Williams, M.W., *Anglo-American Isthmian Diplomacy, 1815–1915*, Washington, DC: American Historical Association, 1915
Wolf, Eric, *Peasant Wars of the Twentieth Century*, New York: Harper & Row, 1970
Wolfers, Arnold, 'The actors in international politics', in William Fox, ed., *Theoretical Aspects of International Relations*, Notre Dame, Ind.: University of Notre Dame Press, 1959
Wolfers, Arnold, *Discord and Collaboration: Essays on International Politics*, Baltimore: Johns Hopkins University Press, 1962
Wohlstetter, Roberta, *Pearl Harbor: Warning and Decision*, Stanford, Cal.: Stanford University Press, 1962
Wolf-Philips, Leslie, 'Why Third World?', *Third World Quarterly*, 1, No. 1, January 1979, pp. 105–16
Wood, Bryce, *The United States and Latin American Wars*, New York, Columbia University Press, 1966
Worsley, Peter, 'How many worlds?', *Third World Quarterly*, 1, No. 2, April 1979, pp. 100–8
Wright, Quincy, *A Study of War*, Chicago: University of Chicago Press, abridged edition, 1970
Wynia, Gary W., *The Politics of Latin American Development*, Cambridge: Cambridge University Press, 1980
Young, Desmond, *Member for Mexico: A Biography of Weetman Pearson, First Viscount Cowdray*, London: Cassell, 1966
Zartman, I. William, *International Relations in the New Africa*, Englewood Cliffs, NJ: Prenctice-Hall, 1966
Zartman, I. William, 'The politics of boundaries in north and west Africa', *Journal of Modern African Studies*, 3, April 1965, p. 156

Index

212